BRIGHT IDEAS

Inspirations for ENVIRONMENTAL EDUCATION

Published by Scholastic
Publications Ltd,
Villiers House,
Clarendon Avenue,
Leamington Spa,
Warwickshire CV32 5PR

© 1994 Scholastic Publications Ltd
Text © 1994 Winnie Wade and
Colin Hughes

Written by Winnie Wade and
Colin Hughes
Edited by Jane Wright and
Christine Lee
Sub-edited by Sophie Jowett
Designed by Tracey Ramsey
Series designed by Juanita Puddifoot
Illustrated by Gary Wing
Cover design and artwork by
Linda Murray

Designed using Aldus Pagemaker
Processed by Pages Bureau,
Leamington Spa
Artwork by Steve Williams &
Associates, Leicester
Printed in Great Britain by
Ebenezer Baylis & Son, Worcester

British Library Cataloguing in Publication Data
A catalogue record for this book is available from the British Library.

ISBN 0-590-53142-5

The right of Winnie Wade and Colin Hughes to be identified as the Authors of this Work has been asserted by them in accordance with the Copyright, Designs and Patent Act 1988.

All rights reserved. This book is sold subject to the condition that it shall not, by way of trade or otherwise, be lent, hired out or otherwise circulated without the publisher's prior consent in any form of binding or cover other than that in which it is published and without a similar condition, including this condition, being imposed upon the subsequent purchaser.

No part of this publication may be reproduced, stored in a retrieval system, or transmitted, in any form or by any means, electronic, mechanical, photocopying, recording or otherwise, without the prior permission of the publisher, except where photocopying for educational purposes within a school or other educational establishment is expressly permitted in the text.

CONTENTS

Introduction		5
Chapter 1	*Environmental issues*	11
Chapter 2	*Sampling, collecting and other environmental techniques*	27
Chapter 3	*Organising environmental activities*	45
Chapter 4	*Planning a trail through the local environment*	51
Chapter 5	*Shops and shopping*	57
Chapter 6	*Streets and transport*	69
Chapter 7	*Farms*	83
Chapter 8	*The garden*	95
Chapter 9	*Woodlands*	107
Chapter 10	*School and home environment*	125
Chapter 11	*Leisure*	137
Chapter 12	*The churchyard*	147
Chapter 13	*Resources*	157
Photocopiable pages		163

INTRODUCTION

Environmental education

Concern about the environment grows daily. Environmental issues are discussed regularly in the media, and children are becoming increasingly aware of environmental global problems, such as depletion of the ozone layer and the damaging effects of acid rain. It is, however, only through environmental education that children will come to a proper understanding of these problems and will be able to make informed decisions and judgements about them. We are all facing the environmental challenge and in order to make sensible decisions about positive action, children need to be able to consider environmental issues from a variety of perspectives. A broad, balanced approach to environmental education will enable children to explore their own ideas and values and develop a respect for the views of others. We have a responsibility to create in children an awareness and understanding of the environment, coupled with a sense of trusteeship.

BACKGROUND

The Council of Ministers of the European Community (now the European Union) in 1988 stated that the objective of environment education is to 'lay the foundations for a fully informed and active participation of the individual in the protection of the environment and the prudent and rational use of natural resources'.

In order to fully inform our children about the care of the environment, environmental education should start at an early age in the primary school.

A useful starting point is the definition of environmental education as stated by the National Association for Environmental Education: 'Environmental Education is the process of recognising values and clarifying concepts in order to develop skills and attitudes necessary to understand the inter-relatedness among people, their culture and biophysical surroundings. It also entails practice in decision-making and self-formulation of a code of behaviour about issues concerning environmental quality.'

Environmental education has been identified as one of the cross-curricular themes in the National Curriculum (NCC Circular 6: The National Curriculum and Whole Curriculum Planning – November 1989). It is closely linked with the other cross-curricular themes such as Education for Citizenship and Education for Economic and Industrial Understanding. Environmental education is not a statutory subject but is every child's entitlement and should permeate subject areas. The *Education Reform Act of 1988* requires schools to give children 'a broad and balanced curriculum' and addressing the cross-curricular themes helps teachers to deliver this broad curriculum as a number of subjects are linked within the curriculum.

The National Curriculum Council document Curriculum Guidance 7: Environmental Education (1990) identified three main aims of environmental education:
Environmental education aims to:
• provide opportunities to acquire the knowledge, values, attitudes, commitment and skills needed to protect and improve the environment;
• encourage pupils to examine and interpret the environment from a variety of perspectives – physical, geographical, biological, sociological, economic, political, technological, historical, aesthetic, ethical and spiritual;
• arouse pupils' awareness and curiosity about the environment and encourage active participation in resolving environmental problems.

The National Curriculum also sets out a range of objectives which are necessary to develop an environmental curriculum. These are expressed in terms of knowledge, skills and attitudes.

Objectives

Knowledge

As a basis for making informed judgements about the environment pupils should develop knowledge and understanding of:
- the natural processes which take place in the environment;
- the impact of human activities on the environment;
- different environments, both past and present;
- environmental issues such as the greenhouse effect, acid rain, air pollution;
- local, national and international legislative controls which protect and manage the environment; how policies and decisions are made about the environment;
- the environmental interdependence of individuals, groups, communities and nations – how, for example, power station emissions in Britain can affect Scandinavia;
- how human lives and livelihoods are dependent on the environment;
- the conflicts which can arise about environmental issues;
- how the environment has been affected by past decisions and actions;
- the importance of planning, design and aesthetic considerations;
- the importance of effective action to protect and manage the environment.

Skills

Six cross-curricular skills are identified which can be developed through environmental education.

Communication skills
- expressing views and ideas about the environment through different media – oral, written, dramatic or artistic;
- arguing clearly and concisely about an environmental issue.

Numeracy skills
- collecting, classifying and analysing data, for example, carrying out an ecological survey;
- interpreting statistics, for example, about weather.

Study skills
- retrieving, analysing, interpreting and evaluating information about the environment from a variety of sources;
- organising and planning a project, for example, on the improvement of part of the school's environment.

Problem-solving skills
- identifying causes and consequences of environmental problems;
- forming reasoned opinions and developing balanced judgements about environmental issues.

Personal and social skills
- working co-operatively with others, particularly in group activities for the environment;
- taking individual and group responsibility for the environment, for example for disposal of litter.

Information technology skills
- collecting information and entering it into a database;
- simulating an investigation using information technology.

Attitudes

The development of positive attitudes is essential if children are to develop a concern for the care of the environment. These attitudes are:
• appreciation of, and care and concern for the environment and for other living things;
• independence of thought on environmental issues;
• a respect for the beliefs and opinions of others;
• a respect for evidence and rational argument;
• tolerance and open-mindedness.

There are three linked components of environmental education:
• education about the environment – knowledge;
• education for the environment – developing values, attitudes, and taking positive action;
• education in and through the environment – using the environment as a resource.

Education about the environment
Curriculum Guidance 7 identifies seven topics which cover the knowledge and understanding about the environment:
• climate
• soils, rocks and minerals
• water
• materials and resources, including energy
• plants and animals
• people and their communities
• buildings, industrialisation and waste

Education for the environment
This is concerned with finding ways of ensuring caring use of the environment now and in the future, finding solutions to environmental problems and informing the choices which have to be made.

Education in and through the environment
The emphasis is on enquiry and first-hand investigation, drawing on the environment as a stimulus to learning.

Teaching and learning

Children should experience a wide range of teaching and learning approaches in their environmental work. Each child is an individual and learning experiences should be adapted to the needs of the individual in order to develop all his/her capabilities. This approach calls for flexibility and creativity by the teacher. Diverse learning experience should be provided for the children to encourage them to become more involved in and to take a greater responsibility for their own learning. Children should be encouraged to work in groups and to develop a positive, co-operative approach. They should be provided with opportunities for discussion and should be encouraged to listen to the views of others. First-hand enquiry and exploration are important aspects to develop. It is also essential that children understand how to behave in different environments and learn to respect the environment through developing appropriate codes of behaviour and learning from existing codes such as the Country Code. Organisational skills and self-reliance should be encouraged and opportunities for problem-solving should be provided.

Activities both within and outside the classroom should be undertaken. Environmental investigations could be undertaken in the school grounds or other locations outside the immediate environment. Debates, role-plays and group and individual research should be an integral part of environmental education. Critical thinking and questioning of ideas should be encouraged, and opportunities should be provided for evaluation of work carried out. The investigation of real-life problems will encourage the children to develop their own attitudes and a personal approach to the environment.

Teaching approach

Environmental education can be taught in a variety of ways. A topic-based approach could be adopted where the teacher plans the work through an environmental topic such as those identified in Curriculum Guidance 7, for example, Plants and animals, Water, or Energy. A more general topic could be chosen such as some of those identified in this book, for example, Leisure, Farms, or The school and home environment. Links with the subject areas of the National Curriculum can be identified, and investigative skills should be developed through the topic. A good way of ensuring that environmental education is embedded in the primary school curriculum is to develop a whole school policy for this cross-curricular theme.

Global and local connections

Through developing an understanding of local environmental issues in their everyday surroundings, children relate more easily to global environmental issues and environmental problems of other countries.

'The local area provides excellent starting points through which understanding can grow to encompass other places and other times' (The Scottish Office Education Department – Environmental Studies 5–14, 1993).

Younger children, for example, carrying out a litter survey of their school grounds, can then broaden their understanding to such strategies as waste disposal, recycling, and later widen their knowledge to pollution and use of the Earth's resources.

It is important to begin with the individual and the impact he/she can have on the local environment through being aware of issues such as amount of packaging on products and disposal of litter for recycling. Key questions can be raised in reaching an understanding of local environmental problems and these can be asked in a wider context. With regard to packaging and litter, questions could be raised such as why do we need so much packaging? What is the purpose of the packaging? Who decides how much packaging goes on to products? Who benefits? What is the environmental impact of disposal of the packaging? Similar questions could be asked about wider environmental issues such as deforestation. Why do we need to remove trees from the rainforest? Who makes decisions? Who benefits? What is the environmental impact of such decisions? How can the loss of rainforests be slowed down or prevented?

Through making local-global connections, children will come to make sense of their world and develop informed caring attitudes towards the environment.

What is in this book for you?

This book aims to increase the confidence and competence of primary teachers to help children to develop an understanding of the world they live in and to develop caring and responsible attitudes towards the environment. Children will come to understand that people and the environment are interdependent and will develop an understanding of environmental issues through first-hand enquiry and investigation. As a result of this knowledge, understanding and skills development, children will be better informed to make decisions about the environment and be able to consider the role they have to play in caring for the environment in the future.

This knowledge, skills and attitude development will come from carrying out the activities in this book.

Chapter 1 gives detailed background information on a whole range of environmental issues which children will need to understand. Four main themes are identified here and apply to all the activity chapters: Pollution; Environmental changes; Conservation; and Plants, animals and their habitats. These themes are closely connected with each other and topics within the themes frequently cross boundaries. Major issues are explored in this chapter which offers a comprehensive framework for this book on environmental education. A number of activities are also presented here which relate to the identified themes.

Chapter 2 discusses the development of the skills used

in environmental education investigations. Practical ideas are offered for sampling and collection techniques for plants and animals, weather recording, soil analysis, mapping skills, and interview and questionnaire design and use. Information is given about essential equipment required for such investigative work.

Chapter 3 gives advice on organising environmental activities, including the various stages which need to be considered when taking children outside the classroom. This will include the need for thorough preparation and safety aspects to be taken into consideration. These activities are thoughtful with clearly defined objectives and relevant, motivating follow-up activities. Chapter 4 goes on to offer teachers assistance in planning a trail through the local environment.

Chapters 5–12 provide a comprehensive range of activities which focus on a particular topic frequently taught in infant, junior and primary schools.

A table is provided at the beginning of each chapter which relates the content of the activities to the appropriate Key Stage (whether KS1 [P1–3], KS2 [P4–7] or both) and the relevant environmental theme. A whole investigation is included at the end of each chapter which offers a strategic approach into a number of topic-related activities. Practical skills can be developed through the whole investigation and ideas are given for recording. Each activity suggests the age range for which it is best suited and lines of progression for each of the four identified environmental themes are provided in a table at the beginning of each chapter. Activities are related to National Curriculum and Scottish 5–14 Guidelines subject areas. Many of the activities include ideas for further study and advice on safety.

Chapter 13 provides a large number of useful addresses of environmental groups and resource materials which will be helpful for the activities within this book.

Finally, there is a useful set of photocopiable sheets which relate directly to particular activities and will save time in the busy primary classroom.

This book will help teachers offer their children a greater understanding and a more informed view of the complex nature of environmental issues.

'The transition to a society that has respect for the other 30 million on the planet and provides for the reasonable needs of all humans will not be easy, but it will be easier than not doing it.'
(The Royal Forest and Bird Protection Society of New Zealand)

CHAPTER 1

Environmental issues

The environment is very dynamic and is subject to a variety of changes, such as loss of habitat due to human activity (for example, the construction of an industrial site), or the raising of global temperature due to the Greenhouse Effect. There are a number of aspects associated with the environment which children need to learn about, and which underpin the activities in this book. These aspects are all inter-related, for example the pollutant gases CFCs released from air coolant systems are known to damage the ozone layer, leading to global warming.

This book identifies four main themes: Pollution; Environmental change; Conservation; Plants, animals and their habitats. However, these themes are not mutually exclusive and areas of overlap exist, as indicated in the diagram on the following page.

BACKGROUND

POLLUTION
CONSERVATION
Energy
Recycling
Biodiversity
Endangered species
Rain forest destruction
CFCs
ENVIRONMENTAL PLANNING
Global warming
ENVIRONMENTAL CHANGE
PLANTS, ANIMALS AND THEIR HABITATS

WILDLIFE TRAIL
TURN OFF LIGHTS
TURN OFF TAP

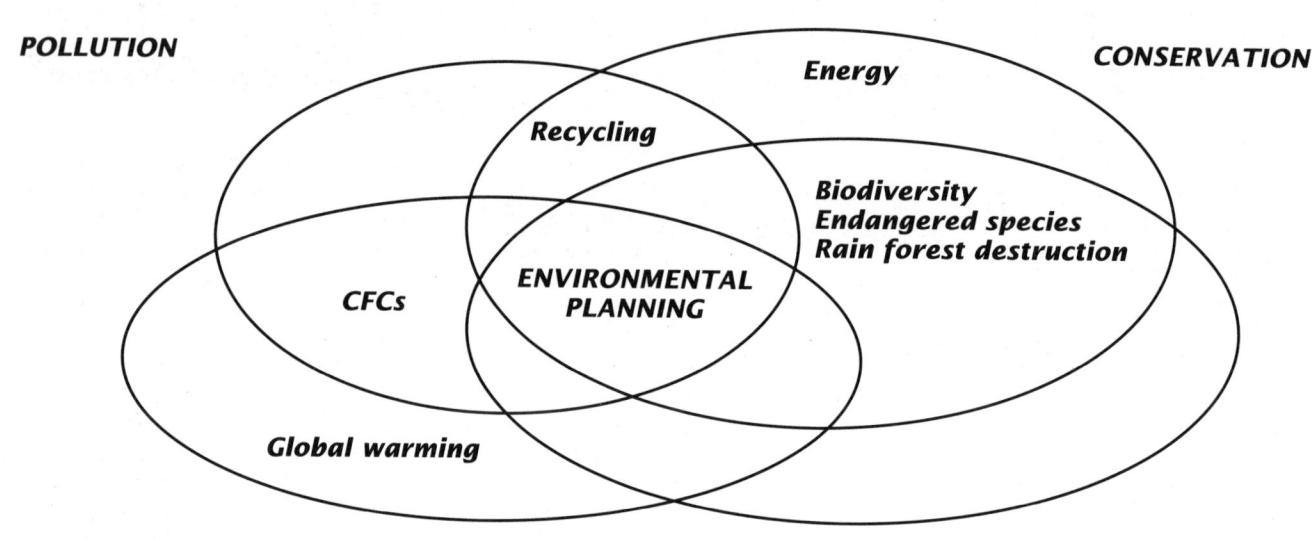

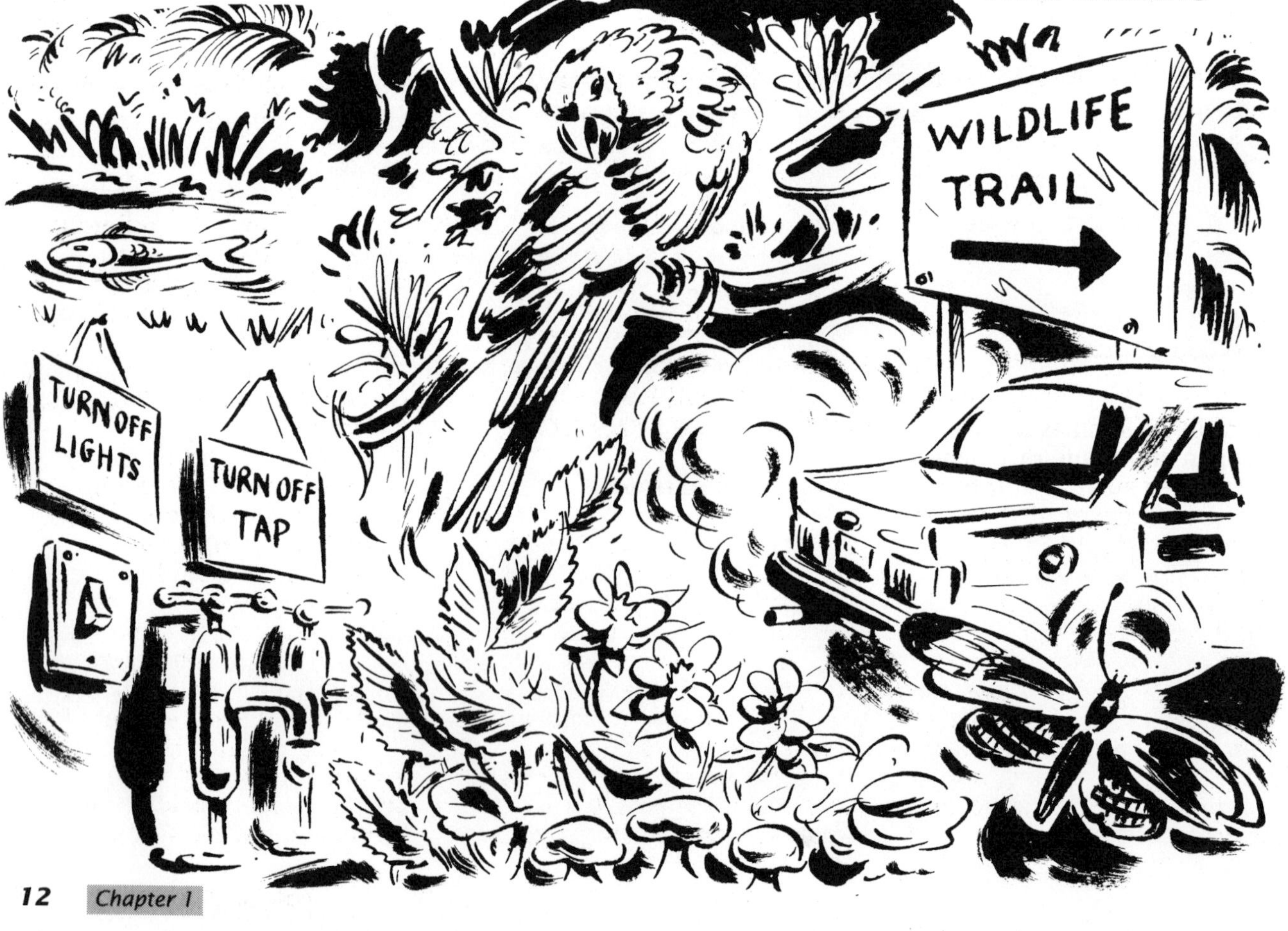

ACTIVITIES

Pollution

Pollution is an undesirable change in the physical, chemical or biological characteristics of the natural environment, usually brought about by human activity. The Earth's air, land and water are made 'dirty' by substances present in the environment.

There are various types of pollution in the environment and these include air pollution, noise pollution, water pollution and land pollution.

1. Air pollution

Apart from the gases naturally found in air such as oxygen, nitrogen and some rare gases, other gases such as sulphur dioxide, oxides of nitrogen and carbon monoxide can be present. These gases and particles can cause air pollution and build up in some cases to form smog. Harmful gases come from the burning of coal, gas and oil, as well as from car exhaust fumes. When fossil fuels are burned, smoke and dust are also emitted into the atmosphere.

Acid rain

Sulphur dioxide, carbon monoxide and oxides of nitrogen produced from the burning of fossil fuels (see *Energy* page 20), dissolve in rain water to make dilute acid solutions which damage trees and other plants. Soils and water become more acidic. Some aquatic organisms are killed by acid rain, and buildings are damaged as the acids in the rain react chemically with the materials of the building. Corrosion of metals can also be speeded up by acid rain. Iron railings in city areas are damaged. Measures can be taken to reduce sulphur dioxide emissions such as using a lower sulphur content fuel, or removing the sulphur dioxide with a chemical absorbent. This is known as scrubbing.

Vehicle emissions

Lead in certain types of petrol is released into the air by millions of cars on our roads every day. This is a cumulative poison. In other words it can build up to dangerous levels in the bodies of animals including humans. Exhaust fumes from cars contain harmful substances such as unburned hydrocarbons, carbon monoxide and oxides of nitrogen. Strong sunlight acting on these gases can cause the build up of smog such as the well-known smogs of Los Angeles, California. All new cars are now being fitted with three-way catalytic converters which reduce the pollutants, converting them into relatively harmless gases. Exhaust gases enter the catalytic converter (which is inserted into the car exhaust pipe). Inside the converter a ceramic honeycomb coated with precious metals such as platinum and rhodium causes oxygen to change the harmful gases to carbon dioxide, water and nitrogen.

Smoke

Smoke can be given off when fossil fuels are incompletely burnt. It blackens buildings and increases the risk of respiratory diseases such as bronchitis.

Chlorofluorocarbons (CFCs)

Chemicals called chlorofluorocarbons (CFCs) can break down the ozone layer (see *Environmental change* page 16). These chemicals are found in some aerosols, air conditioning systems, packaging materials, refrigerators and freezers. At present, attempts are being made to reduce the level of CFCs in the atmosphere, for example, by using pump action aerosols as alternatives to those requiring CFCs.

2. Land pollution

Soils can be contaminated by a range of pollutants. Examples are chemicals used by farmers such as pesticides and herbicides, and waste chemicals from industry. Farmers use a wide range of chemicals to control pests and diseases of plants. These chemicals can also be harmful to other animals and plants. In the past waste chemicals have been disposed of in such a way that the land has become polluted. Crops cannot be grown on polluted land as in extreme cases there is a danger to human health.

3. Water pollution

Discharges from industry and sewage works flow into many of our rivers and streams as well as the sea. Some of these cause pollution. Excess fertilisers put in the soil by farmers can be washed into the water from the land. Some chemicals, such as nitrates and phosphates, cause an increase in the growth of green algae in the water. When the algae die, they are broken down by bacteria which respire and we use up the oxygen in the water. The fish and other organisms in the water die as a result of not having enough oxygen.

4. Noise pollution

This is caused by sounds which are too loud or unpleasant to the ear. The increasing world population with advancing technologies have brought problems of noise pollution. Children will be aware of the obtrusive nature of some sounds in the environment.

What can be done?

- Use smokeless fuels.
- Use unleaded petrol.
- Use bicycles or walk instead of going by car.
- Find out about catalytic converters which are being fitted to cars to eliminate dangerous exhaust gases.
- Find out about organic farming.
- Farmers could use pesticides that are specific to the pest and are not harmful to other organisms.
- Farmers could only add as much fertiliser as the plants can use.
- Use biodegradable products.
- Recycle as many materials as possible.

1. Is it polluted – how can I tell?

Age range
Five to seven.

Group size
Pairs or small groups.

What you need
Two pictures of the same scene, one showing different kinds of pollution and the other a pollution-free scene, photocopiable page 164.

What to do
Look at photocopiable page 164 with the children. Which picture shows aspects of pollution in the environment? How do they know? Ask them to name any ways in which the environment is being polluted. What differences can they see in the pictures? What type of pollution is it – air, water, noise, land?

Content
Various types of pollution are shown in one of the pictures. These can be compared with a picture of an unpolluted environment.

Subject links
NC science and geography
Scottish 5–14 science and social subjects

2. Pollutants – what are their effects?

Age range
Seven to eleven.

Group size
Pairs or small groups.

What you need
Seeds, plant pots or containers such as margarine tubs or large yoghurt pots, labels for plant pots, ruler or tape measure.

What to do
Talk to the children about the harmful effects of pollutants on plants. An extensive discussion should take place in order to identify the various types of pollution (water or air for example). Ask the children to investigate the effect of adding certain substances such as detergent or oil to growing seedlings. They could think of other pollutants they could add to the plants.

Ask them to think about the variables involved such as the amount of pollutant added to the soil, the time of adding the pollutant and so on. They should remember to grow a 'control' plant – that is, one which has had no pollutant added to it. The growth of the seeds could be monitored over a period of time and close observations of the plants should be made, such as colour of leaves and height of seedlings.

Ask each group to record their results on a chart or in a table and present it to the rest of the class.

Content
Harmful chemicals are often present in the soil which can restrict or alter the natural growth of plants, by inhibiting the enzyme activity which is required for growth processes.

Further activity
The children could compare growth of plants which have had pollutants added to the soil with those which have had liquid fertiliser (such as Baby Bio) added to the soil.

Subject links
NC science
Scottish 5–14 science

Environmental change

Few environments remain static for very long, with fluctuations taking place on a seasonal if not daily basis. These environmental changes and others such as the long-term changes in global climate are natural. Human activity also brings about environmental change, some of which is unplanned, for example, global warming, and others planned, for example, the siting and construction of a supermarket.

The Greenhouse Effect and global warming

This is the trapping of heat in the earth's atmosphere and is caused by three main factors:
1. The build-up of carbon dioxide and other gases in the atmosphere;
2. The destruction of the ozone layer;
3. The destruction of tropical rainforests.

Carbon dioxide is a colourless, odourless gas produced naturally by animals in respiration, and is given off also when carbon-containing materials (for example, fossil fuels) are burnt in a plentiful supply of air. Carbon dioxide released from fossil fuels such as wood, coal and oil, lingers above the earth's surface, traps heat and causes the earth's temperature to rise. Loss of the ozone layer causes harmful ultra-violet rays to penetrate into the earth's atmosphere and add to the global warming. Trees take in carbon dioxide from the air and convert it to oxygen. If vast areas of rainforest are destroyed the balance of carbon dioxide is upset and levels of carbon dioxide build up in the atmosphere, raising the temperature.

One consequence of global warming could be that the sea level will rise due partly to the water in the oceans expanding slightly as they warm, partly to the melting of glaciers and partly to the melting of some of the ice covering Antarctica and Greenland. Weather patterns may change and flooding or droughts may occur. The warming of the oceans and seas may increase the rate of growth of microscopic plants in the water, and water quality could be affected.

Ozone layer

Ozone is a form of oxygen which is formed when ultra-violet radiation from the sun causes oxygen in the atmosphere to change its structure. Ozone is an unstable gas which lies in a layer about 15km above the Earth's surface, in the stratosphere. It protects the Earth from the sun's invisible, harmful, ultra-violet radiation. Ozone is destroyed by some chemicals which contain chlorine. These chemicals are called chlorofluorocarbons (CFCs). Chemicals called halons also destroy the ozone layer. Once the chlorine-containing chemicals are released into the atmosphere they are split up into different parts by the intense ultra-violet rays, and these different parts attack the ozone, forming oxygen. These often take place in the form of chain reactions, so just a small amount of CFCs can destroy large amounts of ozone. CFCs are used as cooling agents in refrigerators and freezers. They are also used in some air conditioning systems, some packaging materials and in some aerosols.

In the 1980s a hole was discovered in the ozone layer over the Antarctic. Large amounts of ultra-violet radiation can get through to the Earth as a result of this thinning of the ozone layer. This can result in harmful effects on health, such as increased risk of skin cancer and eye disorders.

Environmental planning

In order to manage our natural resources widely we have developed a system in planning. This includes strategies for conserving waste (see *Recycling* page 20) and the planning process associated with decision-making for building and siting constructions.

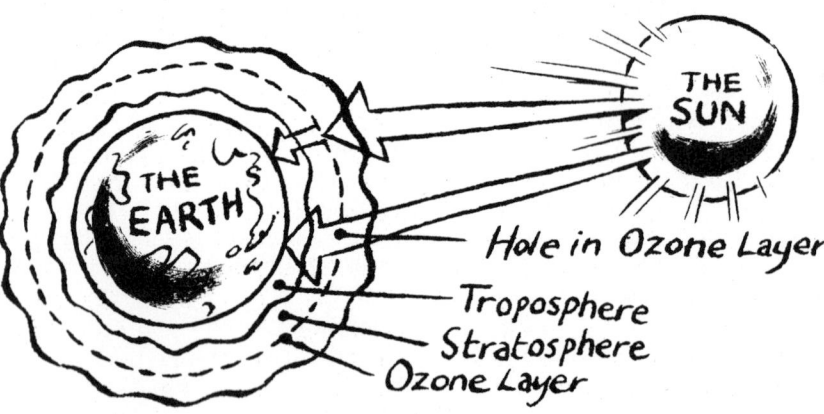

All-in-one at Walkham – to build or not to build?

Age range
Nine to eleven.

Group size
Whole class.

What you need
Photocopiable page 165 (map of the town showing the proposed site for the new supermarket), photocopiable page 166, role cards and issues to be cut out and given to those children assuming the various roles.

What to do
The purpose of this activity is to raise the children's awareness of the environmental, economic and social effects of building a supermarket in a town. The children will debate the advantages and disadvantages to various interested individuals and groups of the proposed plan. It is proposed to build the supermarket – All-In-One – on the outskirts of the town of Walkham which already has other supermarkets in its locality. Conflicts arising from the proposal have resulted in the setting up of a public enquiry where experts, interested individuals and groups will give evidence as to the suitability of the proposal.

Using the information contained on the map and role cards, the children will take on the various roles and present a case for or against the proposal. Roles should be chosen or assigned to the children and relevant issues and questions for each role are identified on each role card. The children should debate these issues and the inspector who presides over the public enquiry should make the final decision as to whether the supermarket will gain planning permission.

After the simulation, discuss with the whole class the fact that costs and benefits to the environment must be weighed up in any new development proposal to decide whether it can proceed.

Content
There are benefits and costs in the building of a new supermarket. These may be environmental, economic and social. Large supermarkets will be built on extensive sites which provide ample car parking space but there could be habitat destruction or incursions into the Green Belt. The buildings may be visually obtrusive. Traffic congestion may be eased if the town centre traffic is deflected to the edge of town sites but there may be an increased risk of traffic accidents on the edge of town. Out of town shops may only be accessible to car-owners and may be more difficult to reach for older people or people without cars. Wider aisles and checkout tills make access easier for people in wheelchairs. Local shops may have to close because of reduced trade. Large numbers of jobs are created when a new supermarket opens but local shopkeepers may lose their livelihoods.

Subject links
NC science, geography, English and history
Scottish 5–14 science and social subjects

Conservation

Conservation is concerned with the sensible use of the earth's natural resources in order to avoid destruction of species and habitats. It involves the maintenance and preservation of natural habitats and the operation of new ones such as national parks or nature reserves. The term conservation also implies an awareness of the dangers of pollution.

Conservation can take place at a number of levels – international, national and local. There are a number of large organisations which are concerned with conservation. You could write to these to find out about the work that they do. Some of these are listed below. Full details are included in Chapter 13 – *Resources*.

International – Greenpeace, Friends of the Earth, World Wide Fund for Nature
National – RSPB, English Heritage, National Trust, Royal Society for Nature Conservation, English Nature
Local – Local conservation group

Habitats are continually being destroyed by people changing the land to suit their own needs, for example, to build roads, houses, hotels, industrial estates and other developments. Increased pressure is put on wildlife by this habitat destruction. In order to conserve habitats, officially protected areas are being designated as National Parks so that animals and plants are protected but people can still enjoy the natural beauty of the countryside.

Many species of animals have been hunted to the edge of extinction. Every day the abundance and distribution of thousands of plant and animal species at local and global levels are being affected by human activity. Living things are dependent upon each other for their survival. By destroying habitats and removing species, others are inevitably affected. Some species are also in serious danger because of illegal trading, for example, in rhinoceros horn. When people hunt animals it is often for their skins or a particular (usually valuable) part of their bodies. National conservation groups can provide information on threatened species and there are a number of campaigns to help endangered species such as the World Wide Fund for Nature's campaign to save the tiger.

Practical conservation

Much can be done at a local level to protect habitats and conserve species. There are many local conservation volunteer groups now in existence which carry out practical conservation work such as wildflower and tree planting, ditch clearing, hedgelaying and dry stone walling, creation of habitats and management of nature reserves. The local library can put the children in touch with the conservation groups in their areas. They could join a local group and help them in their free time. There may be an endangered habitat in the local area which the conservation group is trying to save.

Form a class or school conservation group

Age range
Seven to eleven.

Group size
Groups, class, other children in the school.

What you need
Garden tools, paper, pencils, pens.

What to do
The aim of this activity is to establish a class or school conservation group to improve or conserve a small area in the school grounds. This is a long-term activity which may take place over a year or more and could become part of an extra-curricular activity or the work of a school club.

There are a number of stages in establishing a group. Discuss these stages with the children. An initial meeting should be arranged and a group leader chosen. Records of the meeting should be kept by an elected secretary. Roles should be identified for other group members such as taking responsibility for publicity or finding out information about local groups which may be able to help or come into school to offer advice or give a talk.

Encourage the children to identify a school conservation project(s) that they could become involved in. This may be an existing project which a local conservation group is already tackling or it may be a new project which has been identified by the class, for example, keeping the school grounds free from litter or making a wildflower garden.

The group may need access to garden tools and other resources such as gardening gloves, dustbin bags and so on. Inform the headteacher of the existence of the group and of its plans to see if the school and parents could offer support for the venture, and help to raise money for necessary resources by organising a fund-raising event. Help the group to identify what action they are going to take. They should make an action plan which includes a time scale of activities.

A photographic record of the activities should be made over the duration of the project. At the end of the project the children could invite a conservation volunteer or a local expert to assess their work and give them tips on how to improve their conservation strategy.

Subject links
NC science, geography
Scottish 5–14 science, social subjects

Energy

Energy keeps us warm, enables us to switch on lights, watch television and cook our food. Most of our energy comes from the sun. Plants and animals use its light and heat. Other sources of energy are nuclear energy and energy generated from hydro-electric power. Plants use light energy to make sugar for growth. Animals eat plants or other animals and energy is passed along a food chain. Fuels are used to produce energy. The fuels we use, like coal, petrol, gas and oil, were formed millions of years ago from plant and animal remains. They are called fossil fuels. We are rapidly using up these fuels. The amounts of fossil fuels in the earth are limited and will eventually be used up. These fossil fuels are therefore non-renewable sources of energy. This source of energy is non-sustainable.

It makes more sense to use renewable sources of energy such as solar power, water, wind, tidal power and vegetation and to use existing sources of energy with care. Some buildings now are designed with solar panels which trap the sun's heat. In Brazil, sugar cane is grown to produce a chemical called ethanol which is used like petrol to run motor vehicles. Wind power and tidal power are being harnessed to produce electricity.

We should try to use energy more efficiently and not waste it. There are many ways of doing that. Here are a few:
- Save electricity by turning off lights when rooms are not being used.
- Have a shower instead of having a bath – you use less hot water this way.
- Turn down the central heating thermostat by one or two degrees – wear woolly jumpers.
- Use energy efficient light bulbs. They will last longer and use less energy than ordinary light bulbs.
- Turn off your television, computer or radio when you're not using them.
- Find out how your home is insulated. Are your doors and windows draught proofed?
- Use rechargeable batteries in your battery-operated games.

Recycling

The term recycling refers to the collection and re-using of waste products. Increased use of the world's resources has resulted in a concern for the future supply of these resources. Re-using waste materials is generally a more efficient use of energy. Recycling makes materials cheaper as well as making resources last longer. Energy needed to extract metals from their ores, for example, can be very expensive and the extraction process only occurs once. Recycling waste materials uses only a small amount of energy needed for extraction. It is important to realise, however, that other costs are involved in recycling, such as transport of the waste materials from their collection points and also the separation, cleaning and re-processing costs.

Household waste accounts for approximately 5% of all solid waste created in the UK. Industry and agriculture produce far more waste.

Many types of materials are potentially recyclable. These include paper, glass, certain types of plastics, metals, and textiles. A range of paper products are made from recycled materials. Many supermarket and Local Authority car parks now have bottle banks, paper banks, can banks and textile banks where it is possible to deposit recyclable items. It is not possible yet to recycle all plastics as there are so many different sorts. Many soft drinks come in bottles made from a plastic called PET (polyethylene terepthalate) which can be recycled. Plastic recycling schemes are now being established in some areas but these are not very common at present.

Nearly all food cans and half of drinks cans are made of steel with a very fine coating of tin. Of all the steel cans we use, 12.5% are now recycled. They are extracted by magnetic attraction from domestic waste. Some local authorities operate the Save-a-Can scheme where people can take their cans for collection. Aluminium is widely used in drinks cans. Extraction is very costly because large amounts of energy are used. Aluminium can collection points are common now. You can find out if a can is made of aluminium by testing with a magnet. The aluminium can is not attracted to the magnet.

Glass makes up about 8% of domestic waste. Glass can be recycled, thus saving energy and the raw materials used to make it which are sand, limestone and soda-ash. Other materials are added in small amounts for colour and to add strength to the glass. Some glass containers like milk and beer bottles can be re-used. Waste glass (called cullet) is worth more if it is separated by colour so bottle banks for clear, green or brown glass are often provided.

A bottle bank code has been developed which says:
• do not put returnable bottles in bottle banks;
• do not leave litter at the site – this is unsightly and costs money to clean up;
• never put crockery or anything other than glass jars or bottles in the bottle bank;
• do not use bottle banks at night when you might disturb residents;
• try to combine the disposal of bottles with shopping or other journeys to conserve fuel;
• rinse bottles before taking them in to the bottle bank;
• remove caps from bottles and jars (these contaminate the glass and can cause extensive damage to glass furnaces);
• dispose of bottles and jars in the correct space for each colour.

Some textile collection points are available in car parks and shopping centres. The textiles are re-made into other furnishings and paper.

Recycling paper means that energy is saved and fewer trees are cut down. Most paper and card can be recycled and now paper collection points are common.

Environmental issues

Action points
1. Save drinks cans. If you have a can crusher reduce their bulk by crushing them. Sort cans into those made of aluminium (magnets will not stick to aluminium so sort them by testing them with a magnet) and those made of other non-magnetic metals such as tin or alloys.
2. Buy products made of recyclable material such as writing paper, envelopes, kitchen rolls and toilet rolls.
3. Re-use plastic carrier bags and cardboard boxes when you visit the supermarket.
4. Return empty milk bottles (washed) to the dairy (via your milk delivery service if you have one).
5. Use paper, bottle and can banks – you will find these collection points in supermarket or local authority car parks and in some residential areas.
6. Re-use plastic containers (such as margarine and ice cream containers) as storage containers. Use yoghurt pots to grow seedlings.
7. Start a compost heap in the garden.

What can we recycle?

Age range
Five to seven.

Group size
Whole class.

What you need
Photocopiable page 167 which identifies items of household waste.

What to do
Start a discussion with the children about the amount of rubbish they throw away in one day. What sort of rubbish is it? They will identify items such as empty crisp packets, sweet and chocolate wrappers, drinks cans and cartons and so on. Talk to them about the rubbish thrown away at home. This will include other items such as vegetable peelings, plastic bottles, egg cartons, glass bottles. Many of the children will have seen the bottle and paper banks at the local supermarket car park and will be aware of the fact that it is possible to recycle certain items. What does the family do with their rubbish? Is it all put into the dustbin or do they separate out items such as paper and glass and take them to collection points such as bottle banks?

Ask the children to look at photocopiable page 167. The picture shows a number of items of rubbish that are to be thrown away. Discuss each item with the children – talk about the material from which each item is composed and ask them to identify whether or not the items could be recycled. How would they recycle them? Ask questions

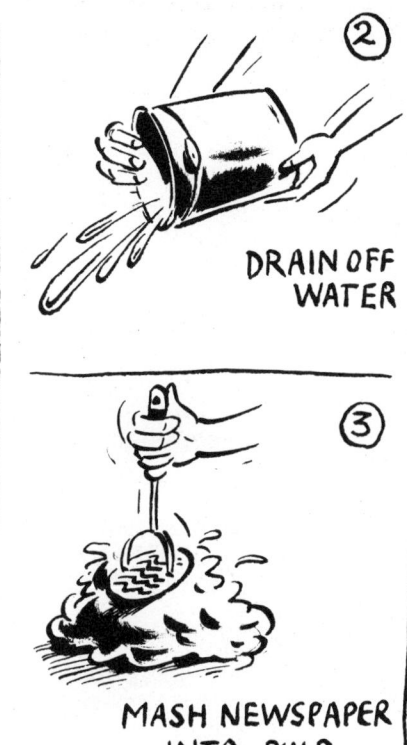

SOAK PIECES OF NEWSPAPER IN WATER OVERNIGHT

DRAIN OFF WATER

MASH NEWSPAPER INTO PULP

PLACE MESH BETWEEN FRAMES

SPREAD PULP OVER MESH

DRAIN AND TIP OUT THEN ROLL OUT AND DRY

such as, 'Would you take the item to a bottle bank, paper bank, put it in the compost heap or return it to be refilled?'

Once they have identified a destination for each item, they could colour in the pictures – green for items which can be recycled and red for those items which cannot be recycled.

Subject links
NC science
Scottish 5–14 science

Make your own recycled paper

Age range
Five to eleven.

Group size
Whole class or large groups.

What you need
A piece of rectangular wire or nylon mesh, two wooden frames, old newspaper, a large bowl, a bucket, water, an old rolling pin, a wooden spoon or potato masher.

What to do
Ask the children to tear up the newspaper into small pieces and soak these pieces in a bucket of water overnight. The next day, drain off the water and mash up the newspaper into a pulp. Pour some more water over the newspaper pulp and mash it again. The children should put the wire or nylon mesh on one of the wooden frames and secure it with staples or nails (they may need help or supervision here). They should then attach the second wooden frame so that the mesh lies between the two frames.

The pulp should then be spread out evenly over the mesh. Excess water will drain off. The pulp should be tipped carefully onto a clean surface and rolled out with a rolling pin and left to dry.

The paper can be coloured if required by using natural dyes made by boiling then straining off liquid from fruits such as blackberries and blackcurrants. These coloured dyes should be added to the newspaper pulp before pouring it on to the mesh.

Further activity
The children can research how paper is made from wood. They can also find out about the commercial recycling of paper. Reference books can be used to find out how paper was made in ancient times, e.g. papyrus in Ancient Egypt.

Subject links
NC science and geography
Scottish 5–14 science and social subjects

Tropical rainforest and deforestation

Almost one third of the Earth's land area is covered by areas of forest. The world's tropical rainforests lie in a hot, wet band across the Equator, but they are being destroyed at an alarming rate to provide land for farming, to produce timber, and for mining minerals. The process of removing forests is called deforestation. Tropical rainforests help to maintain the heat balance in the atmosphere (see *Greenhouse Effect* page 16). Rainforests also prevent soil erosion and flooding. However, forest conservation often takes second place to the short-term need for more farmland.

Removal of rainforests in hilly areas results in large amounts of water running off the land so soil is washed away and flooding occurs. The burning of rainforests results in the release of carbon dioxide which adds to the Greenhouse Effect. Farming on land cleared in the rainforest can cause long-term damage as the soil has no tree roots to hold it together. The soil starts to break up and blows away as dust. This process is called desertification.

Rainforests are home to between 50 and 70% of all plant and animal species. As well as timber, many other products such as fruits, nuts, oils and raw materials for medicines come from the rainforests. These forests are also home to many native peoples.

Hardwoods like mahogany, sapele, iroko, teak and melanti come from the rainforest. Timber could be managed sustainably so that it could be taken from plantation forests where land has been cleared and trees especially planted to provide a raw material. If timber is taken from virgin rainforest, the amount removed should be carefully controlled to enable other trees to grow up to replace those cut down.

Friends of the Earth issue a publication called The Good Wood Guide which lists companies that have agreed to sell tropical timbers only if they have been obtained from sustainably managed sources, that is, where other hardwood trees have been planted to replace those cut down.

Rainforests all have a similar structure, consisting of five main layers, each with its own plant and animal species. Sometimes the layers merge together. The top layer is the *emergent layer* made up of the tallest trees, up to 50m in height. The next layer is called the *canopy* where the top branches of trees, up to 30m above the ground, form a continuous layer. This layer absorbs 70% of the light and intercepts 80% of the rainfall. The soil is thus protected from erosion. Smaller trees (up to 20m in height) grow below the main canopy and form a lower layer, the *sub-canopy*. Next is the *shrub layer*, and finally, some plants like ferns grow on the *forest floor*. Plants called lianas climb the trunks of trees and grow from the forest floor to the canopy. Continuous leaf fall in the forest gives a thick litter layer.

Plants, animals and their habitats

A habitat is the place in which an organism is found naturally and where it is provided with its needs for survival. The habitat of some wild plants might be a stream or river bank, and the habitat of a woodlouse might be a rotting log or the underside of a stone. Habitats are being destroyed through human activity because of population growth and the need for more land and the increased use of chemicals. A large percentage of chalk and limestone grasslands, ancient woodlands, lowland heaths, lowland fens and marshes have been lost in recent years. Hedgerow loss has been accelerated, and many public footpaths are being ploughed up or obstructed.

As a result of this habitat loss, biological diversity (or biodiversity as it is termed today) has decreased. Biodiversity means the diversity of living things: a resource which needs to be managed wisely. For instance, the functioning of a food chain depends on a variety of plant and animal species which exist in a delicately balanced relationship. The loss of a species from the food chain can disrupt the ecology, thus causing instability. Some of the species in the food chain may be directly important to humans such as insects for pollinating crops. A decrease in the number of pollinators might affect crop yields. In the tropical rainforest the US National Cancer Institute has identified 3000 plants which may help to develop a cancer cure. Disruption to the rainforest system could result in the extinction of some of these species.

The organisation English Nature has a Species Recovery Programme which aims to achieve long-term self-sustained survival in the wild of the species of plants and animals currently under threat of extinction. The programme involves a combination of detailed survey work and ecological studies leading to an understanding of habitat requirements so that site management can be carefully targeted. Animal species included in this programme are the common dormouse, the natterjack toad, the red squirrel, the field cricket and the large blue butterfly. Wild plant species include the rough marsh-mallow, starfruit and strapwort.

A full list of species in this programme can be obtained from English Nature (address listed in Chapter 13 – *Resources*) as can a list of species specially protected under the *Wildlife and Countryside Act, 1981* (amended by the *Environmental Protection Act, 1990*).

Investigating habitats

Age range
Five to seven.

Group size
Individuals or pairs.

What you need
Photocopiable page 168, pencils or coloured pens.

What to do
Discuss with the children the meaning of the word habitat. Talk about the type of habitat that a human being needs to survive. The children can then think about the survival needs of a plant or animal. Identify with the children the habitats of common plants and animals. Give an example, such as a tadpole's habitat is a pond. Show the children the photocopiable sheet which shows pictures of some common plants and animals and pictures their habitats. Ask them to link the habitat with the appropriate animal or plant (there may be some animals or plants that occupy the same habitat).

Endangered species

These are plants and animals with population numbers so low that there is a danger of their becoming extinct. The cause is often habitat destruction or over-exploitation for commercial profit.

There are international agreements to protect endangered species, but these agreements are often ignored. TRAFFIC Network is the world's largest wildlife trade monitoring programme. This, with The International Union for the Conservation of Nature and Natural Resources (IUCN), monitors trade in and utilisation of wild plants and animals.

The Convention on International Trade in Endangered Species (CITES) controls the movement of animals and animal products such as caged birds and rhino horn.

The World Wide Fund For Nature has many projects to protect wildlife and publishes the conservation yearbook which reports on its activities.

Animals are often put into a safe place to breed, such as a zoo. Animals that have been saved from complete extinction in this way include the Arabian Oryx and the Hawaiian Goose.

Animals in danger

Age range
Seven to eleven.

Group size
Individuals or pairs.

What you need
Photocopiable sheet 169, reference books on endangered species.

What to do
Discuss with the children the need to conserve endangered species of plants and animals and the reasons why these species are in danger. The children should use the reference books to identify the endangered species, and using the photocopiable map of the world they can colour or mark areas on the map where these species are found. They should try to find out why numbers of species have declined and what steps are being taken to protect the plants and animals from the danger of extinction. Using reference books the children could find out more information about the animals, their habitats, food preferences, behaviour and so on.

CHAPTER 2
Sampling, collecting and other environmental techniques

To gain concrete experiences of the environment through first-hand investigation, children must be able to carry out successfully a number of sampling and collecting techniques and be familiar with other environmental techniques. Having sampled and collected the plants and animals, the children will need to record their findings accurately and methodically. Once they have obtained results, they must then analyse them, interpret them and consider those interpretations in the light of their prior knowledge and experiences.

This chapter will consider a number of techniques for sampling and collecting plants and animals as well as techniques associated with the environment, for example, tree planting and devising food chains and webs. Particular techniques will be described and discussed in detail with appropriate references made to the advantages and disadvantages of the method, required apparatus and safety considerations.

These techniques will include:
• sampling vegetation (e.g., quadrats, transects);
• tree planting;
• estimating the age of a tree;
• estimating the height of a tree or structure;
• pressing plants;
• estimating the area of a leaf;
• using a sweep net;
• using a beating tray;
• pootering;
• using pitfall traps;
• analysing leaf litter;
• making plaster casts;
• sampling fresh water using kick samples;
• estimating water flow rate;
• devising food chains and webs;
• water pollution and analysis;
• air pollution and analysis;
• soil analysis (e.g., profile, composition, water content, pH, mineral composition);
• recording the weather (e.g., wind direction, wind speed, rainfall, temperature);
• survey and recording techniques (e.g., sketch maps, map enlargement, compass bearings);
• dating buildings;
• obtaining information from people (e.g., street questionnaires, written questionnaires, interviews).

An attempt has been made to arrange the techniques in a logical order as far as possible. However, use of the Thermostik, a device to measure the temperature of soil or water, could just as appropriately be covered with the techniques concerned with soil as with those concerned with fresh water or the weather. Likewise, pitfall trapping would be equally appropriate in the section on collecting animals or in the section on soil.

While some reference will be made to observing, recording results and interpreting results, readers are advised to consider more exhaustive discussion of these skills, for example in Chapters 2 to 7 of Inspirations for Investigations in Science.

Sampling, collecting and other environmental techniques

BACKGROUND

Equipment

To carry out work in the field, a relatively large amount of simple equipment is required. The setting up of a school 'field bag' including a list of contents might be one way of ensuring that the equipment is always available. This equipment should include:
- beating tray or white sheet;
- canes or rulers (to make quadrats);
- card strips (for animal track moulds);
- clipboards;
- compass;
- containers (for specimens);
- chisel;
- first aid kit;
- hand fork;
- hand lenses and magnifiers;
- labels;
- light and moisture meters;
- marker pens;
- metre rulers;
- minerals kit;
- nature viewers and mini-, midi-, magni-spectors;
- paper;
- pH kit;
- pH meter;
- plaster of Paris;
- polythene bags;
- pond nets;
- pooters;
- secateurs;
- sieves (small);
- specimen tubes (plastic);
- spoons (plastic);
- sweep net;
- tape measure or string marked at 10cm intervals;
- tape recorder;
- thermometers;
- Thermostik;
- tins (for mixing plaster of Paris);
- weather instruments
- white plastic trays;
- trowel;
- yoghurt pots (for pitfall traps).

A camera and a pair of binoculars would also be useful additions to the field bag.

Equipment for observing plants and animals

Magnifying glass
Low-magnification, plastic magnifiers are suitable for younger children as they are easy to hold, easy to use and are relatively inexpensive. It might be worthwhile paying a little more if a slightly higher magnification is available. While magnifiers are perfectly acceptable for older children, it would also be beneficial for them to have some experience of using hand lenses.

Nature viewers and mini-, midi-, magni-spectors
These are particularly useful because animals may be contained within them. They are made of plastic, are very robust, and are circular in shape with a lens lid. The midi-spectors and magni-spectors are more expensive due to their size, but they allow animals to be measured on the cm and mm grid printed on the base. It is always useful to have some of these in the 'science cupboard'.

Hand lenses (pocket magnifiers)
Older juniors would benefit from the added magnification given by a X5, X8 or X10 hand lens. The children will initially find them difficult to use, so clear instructions are important. Explain how they should hold the lens close to the eye, then move the specimen towards the lens or, alternatively move the lens and eye towards the specimen. The specimen can be brought into focus with the lens some distance from it, but the details will be more difficult to see in this case. Attach string to the 'cases' and insist that the children wear them around

Chapter 2

their necks to reduce losses. Count the lenses out and in to reduce disappearances!

Plants

Sampling vegetation

There are a number of techniques for sampling plants in the school grounds or elsewhere which are well within the capabilities of older junior children. By carrying out sampling at first hand, children will not only become more familiar with identifying common British plants, but will also begin to understand the reasons for the different distributions of these plants. Four techniques will be discussed here:
• assessing the presence or absence of a plant (frequency);
• using the DAFOR method to estimate how much of it is present (cover);
• making a plan of the area and mapping the plant cover;
• using a line to identify changes in vegetation (transect).

Frequency using quadrats

Ask the children to assess plant frequency by sampling a number of small squares of the area under investigation. This may be carried out by randomly dropping a standard school (30cm) ruler and then making it into a square (quadrat) with the addition of a further three rulers. The children record the presence or absence of plants from the quadrat as shown in Figure 1. The total number of occurrences is calculated and the percentage frequency calculated.

| | | | | | Quadrat | | | | | | | |
Plant	1	2	3	4	5	6	7	8	9	10	Total (%)	Frequency
Grass	+	+	+	+	+	+	+	+	+	+	10	100
Daisy	+	−	+	+	−	−	−	+	−	−	4	40
Dandelion	−	−	+	−	−	−	−	−	−	−	1	10
Plantain	−	−	−	−	+	−	+	−	−	+	3	30
Clover	+	+	+	−	−	−	−	−	−	−	3	30
Speedwell	−	−	−	−	−	−	−	+	−	−	1	10
Buttercup	−	−	−	−	−	+	−	−	−	−	1	10
Bare ground	−	+	−	+	+	+	+	+	+	+	8	80

Figure 1

Cover by estimation (DAFOR)

In this method, the area occupied by a plant is given a relative cover provided by the DAFOR scale. Quadrats are placed on the ground and an estimation of the plant's cover is determined as follows:

D – Dominant plant, with one species occupying over 50 per cent of the area;
A – Abundant plants, with one or two species occupying about half of the area;
F – Frequent plants, which are common but cover less than half the area;
O – Occasional plants which cover only small parts;
R – Rare plants which are very scarce.

A cover rating may then be given for each plant as in Figure 1.

Plant	Cover rating
Grass	D
Daisy	F
Dandelion	O
Plantain	O
Clover	O
Speedwell	R
Buttercup	R

Figure 1

Estimation by mapping

A metre quadrat should be placed on the ground at random. The plants within it are then identified and a plan of the quadrat is drawn (Figure 2), with each plant represented by a different symbol on the key. The area (cover) occupied by each plant may be added to the key. For more accurate results, the figures from five or more quadrats should be combined and averaged.

	Plant	%
|/	Grass	65%
❀	Daisy	10%
🌼	Dandelion	10%
	Plantain	7%
✿	Clover	5%
	Speedwell	2%
	Buttercup	1%

Figure 2

Using line transects

A line transect is used to investigate changes in vegetation over a relatively short area, particularly when there is a clear change, for example from hedgerow to grassland or from a land community to an aquatic one. A tape measure is placed on the ground and pre-set intervals are determined, for example every 10cm. Those plants which touch the selected point or are vertically above it are recorded, such that more than one plant type may be present at each sample point. The transect can then be represented by drawing the plants or by a map and key as before.

Planting a tree

While it is undoubtedly exciting for children to grow their own trees from seed, it takes a relatively long time for a reasonably-sized sapling to develop. It might be beneficial to suggest that the children grow some trees from seed to supplement others which will be purchased. Seed such as acorns (oak), beech nut, conkers (horse chestnut) and ash keys should be collected in the autumn and planted outside in pots. Many seeds will germinate the following spring following a period of cold but others, such as ash,

will not germinate for a further year.

The very young saplings should be planted in the ground once they have reached a height of 10 to 15cm, preferably in the late autumn or very early spring. Prepare a hole in the ground slightly deeper and larger than the pot in which the tree has been grown. Place some compost or fertiliser in the bottom of the hole, remove the sapling from the pot and carefully plant it at the same depth as before, ensuring that the soil is in contact with the root ball of the tree. Ensure that the sapling is firm in the ground, water it well and protect it with a small fence if necessary. Water the sapling well throughout its first spring.

Larger trees can be purchased from nurseries and garden centres or can be obtained from local authorities or conservation groups. If trees are being purchased, ensure that they have a straight stem, a balanced shape and strong root growth.

Thorough preparation is needed when planting larger saplings. A hole needs to be dug which is deep enough for the tree to rest in so that its collar (the area just above the point where the roots meet the stem – see below) is level with the surrounding soil and wide enough to take its roots as they are naturally positioned. The soil at the bottom of the hole should be loosened and compost added if necessary, then a stake should be driven firmly into the hole. Place the tree in the hole so that the stem is at an approximately 10cm from the stake. Water the roots well then carefully add soil, gently shaking the tree so that the soil particles are in contact with all parts of the roots. Firm the soil carefully with your foot, ensuring that no damage is caused to the roots. Add more soil and repeat the process several times, using more and more pressure until the soil around the tree is firm, but ensuring that the collar is still level with the top of the permanent soil level. The tree may now be attached to the stake with a rubber tie to prevent it from being dislodged by the wind. It could be further protected by erecting a small fence if appropriate.

Water the sapling well and continue to water it through dry periods in the spring and summer, and dry, windy periods during the rest of the year; school grounds are notorious for dead saplings and trees which have been planted during or just before a prolonged drought. Weed the area around the trunk, mulch it with fibrous material and be prepared to adjust the tie when necessary.

Estimating the age of a tree by measuring the diameter

Measure the diameter of the tree trunk in centimetres at a height of half a metre above the ground, by placing two rules parallel with each other on opposite sides of the tree. Measuring the distance between the two rules will give the diameter of the tree.

The approximate age of the tree can be estimated by multiplying the diameter of the trunk by two. Thus an ash tree with a trunk of 35cm diameter would be approximately 70 years old. Because oak trees grow more slowly, it is necessary to multiply the diameter by three.

Sampling, collecting and other environmental techniques

Estimating the age of a tree by counting the rings

It is possible to age a tree accurately by counting the number of rings visible in a carefully sawn section of the stem or trunk. Because of the distinct contrast in size and appearance of new small wood cells formed in the spring, annual growth appears in a cross-section of a stem or trunk as a series of concentric lines (see diagram). The width of each ring reflects the nature of the weather in that year; the greater the width the better the weather conditions which are reflected in the growth of the tree.

Estimating the height of a tree or structure

Many methods may be used to estimate the height of a tree or other structure. Three such methods are discussed below.

1. The ruler and rotate method

One of the children should stand at a distance from the tree holding her arm out straight with a ruler or stick in her hand. She should then move her hand until the top of the ruler appears to be at the top of the tree and the thumb is at the base (A) as in Figure 4. The child then rotates the stick through 90 degrees, ensuring that her thumb stays at the base of the tree. Another child should then stand at the new position of the end of the ruler (B), thus making a right angle between B, the tree and the ruler/stick. Measuring the distance from the base of the tree (A) to position B will give the height of the tree

This method may be used to measure the height of any structure such as a building or statue, as long as there is sufficient space to position B accurately.

2. The looking through the legs method

The children bend down and look backwards through their legs at the tree. They must move backwards or forwards with care until they can just see the top of the tree (Figure 5). The distance from them (C) to the tree (D) should be similar to the height of the tree.

3. The ruler and metre ruler method

One child should place a metre ruler at the base of the tree so that it stands against the trunk in a vertical position. Standing at some distance from the tree, another child should hold out a small ruler vertically and, with one eye closed, move it until the top of the ruler appears to be at the same level as the top of the metre rule (E). Keeping these together, she should move her thumb to the point on the ruler which corresponds to the base of the metre rule and hence the base of the tree (F). The children can then estimate the height of the tree by finding out how many times the section of the ruler EF (which is the equivalent of one metre) can be divided into the height of the tree. If the tree is tall it might be useful to mark it two metres above ground level to reduce the number of manipulations.

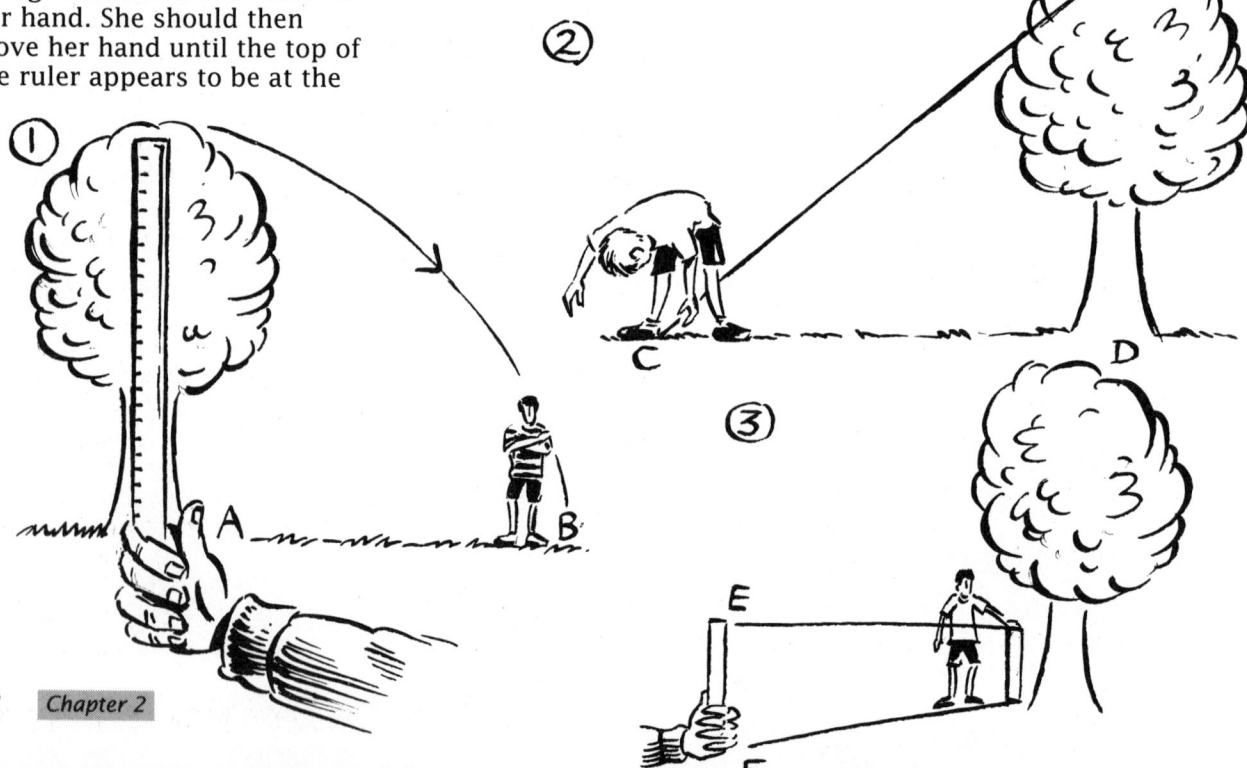

Estimating the area of a leaf

Place a leaf on cm squared paper and draw around it accurately. Colour in the leaf shape with a crayon. If the coloured area (the leaf) occupies more than half of any centimetre square, the square should be ticked or marked in some other way. Count up the ticks or marks to ascertain the area of the leaf. If each member of the class or group repeats this activity, using a different leaf from the same tree, the average area of a leaf of a particular tree type may be calculated.

Pressing plants

Some may consider the pressing of plants incompatible with the ethos of an environmental issues book. Clearly, it should be emphasised to children that any collection should be minimal and occasional and should only involve plants which are known to be common. However, pressing plants may help children increase their interest in, and knowledge of, different kinds of plants and their various parts.

While plant presses may be purchased (see Resources chapter), it is possible to preserve plants by pressing them under heavy objects such as books. Place the plant material between sheets of blotting paper on a flat surface, ensuring that all parts of the plant are displayed to advantage. Press the plants with heavy books, changing the blotting paper if it becomes damp. Leave it for two weeks when most plant material should be thoroughly dry and may be removed from the blotting paper.

The plant may then be carefully transferred to a piece of white paper where it may be attached to the page using clear tape or a suitable alternative. The plant may then be labelled, named and references to its collection point and date may be added.

Land animals

Catching insects in flight

For catching insects, short-handled nets may be manipulated with much greater ease and accuracy than their long-handled counterparts. A specialised butterfly net may be used, but a light, somewhat flexible frame with net curtaining or mosquito-netting is more than adequate. Ensure that the net is at least twice as long as the diameter of the frame to prevent the escape of rapid flying insects.

Use the net with a fast sweeping movement, using a twist of the wrist to seal the mouth of the net. Place the mouth of the bag on the ground or on a piece of paper or card and raise the net to enable larger insects to fly upwards, to be seen or to be introduced temporarily into a collecting vessel. Ensure that the insect is not damaged during any of these stages.

Using a sweep net

Grasshoppers, shield bugs, caterpillars, aphids, spiders and other animals (mainly insects) living in long grass may be collected using a sweep net. As the name suggests, the net is used by sweeping it from side to side mouth first in the long grass. The sweep net therefore needs to have a fairly strong frame and a bag of relatively tough material. A butterfly net should not be used as an alternative for a sweep net as it will soon get damaged on woody plants.

As the vegetation is swept, animals are dislodged and fall into the bag. Collect the animals every five to ten sweeps and record the findings. Observe them with a hand lens or magnifier.

Sweep nets and net frames or sweep trays are available from Philip Harris Education or from other scientific and environmental education suppliers (see *Resources* page 162).

Using a beating tray

A simple way of collecting the animals on a tree is to use a beating tray, a white sheet or a large piece of paper. Place the beating tray under the branch of a tree and then beat the main part of the branch with a stick. Non-flying insects will be dislodged and can then be collected from the sheet using a pooter or plastic spoon.

Pootering

Perry's pooters may be used for safely collecting small arthropods, particularly insects, for later examination. The pooter is made up of two flexible plastic tubes which lead into a strong, clear plastic container (see Figure 7).

The device is simple to use as long as the children have relatively good co-ordination and eyesight! Place the short tube (A) in the mouth and track an animal with the other (B) end, making sure that you do not damage it and that you do not squeeze the tubes. When the animal is close to the end of tube B, gently suck through tube A, drawing the animal into the container. A plastic safety valve in tube A prevents children swallowing any specimens. The animal can then be observed with a hand lens or magnifier.

Some of the small animals which may be collected with the pooter include:
- springtails;
- earwigs;
- beetles;
- gnats;
- ants;
- sandflies;
- mayflies;
- blackfly;
- mites;
- greenfly;
- centipedes;
- whitefly;
- spiders (small);
- silverfish;
- woodlice (small).

This simple and relatively cheap device has the advantage that the children do not have to touch the animal and therefore cannot harm it. Similarly, there is less need for the children to be squeamish abut the animals they collect. However, the pooter cannot be used to collect larger animals or larger specimens of the animals listed above as these may get stuck in the entrance to tube B. It is advisable not to collect moist animals, such as slugs and small worms, using this method, as they may stick to the sides of the tube. Try to encourage the children to suck with the minimum of force to reduce the speed with which the animal shoots up the tube and into the container.

Perry's pooters are available from Berol Limited and other educational suppliers (see *Resources* page 162).

Pitfall trapping

Carefully dig a small hole in the ground and sink a jam jar or plastic container into it, making sure that the rim of the container is absolutely level with the surface. This will allow the animals in the leaf litter and on the surface of the soil to drop easily into the container. Put a small amount of leaf litter in the bottom of the container to act as shelter for the animals. Prevent rain from entering the pitfall trap by covering the entrance to the container with a piece of wood raised above ground level by stones (Figure 1).

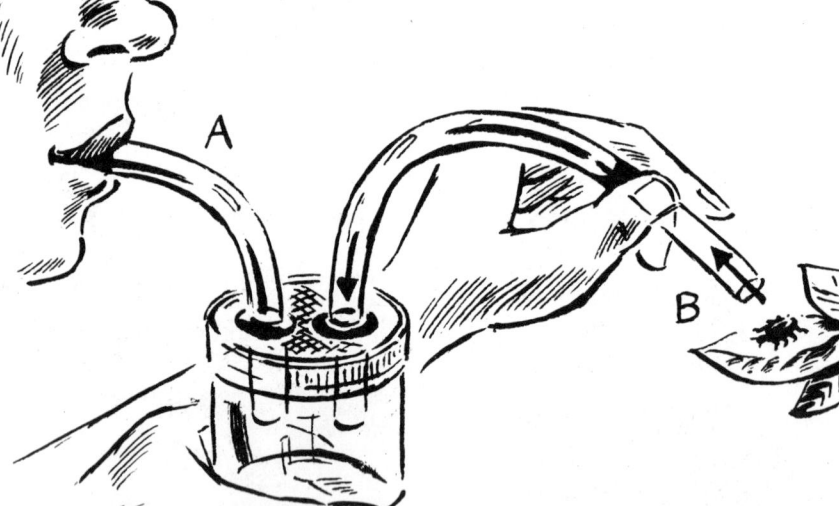

Empty the trap every morning and inspect and count the various animals. Place pitfall traps in different parts of the school grounds and see if the diversity of animals varies. Compare the diversity of animals in mown grass or flower beds with that in the school's nature area. This will demonstrate the importance of maintaining lightly managed areas.

Figure 1

Analysing leaf litter

Dig up a sample of leaf litter containing leaves and the remains of decayed leaves which are beginning to look like soil. Place the sample in a polythene bag and keep it moist until it is to be used. Place some wide mesh gauze inside a funnel or the cut top of a drinks bottle, then place the funnel over a jar containing some vegetation. Sprinkle some of the leaf litter over the gauze then leave the apparatus under a lamp overnight. The safety aspects of leaving the light on would need to be discussed with the caretaker.

Because the animals like moist, dark conditions they will tend to move away from the heat and the light, through the mesh and drop into the bottom container. The animals can then be observed using magnifiers and hand lenses.

Some of the animals may die during this procedure due to the heat, but also because with predator and prey in close proximity the natural processes of food chains may occur.

Making plaster casts

If the children find a clear footprint of a larger animal and want to make a record of it, surround it with a strip of card or stiff paper 4cm wide, making sure that the card is pushed firmly into the mud. Hold the card in place with a paper clip. Mix plaster of Paris with water (approximately sufficient to fill the card mould) in an old container until it is relatively thick but is still able to be poured. Pour the plaster over the footprint to a depth of 3cm, then leave it to dry for 20 minutes or until it is completely set. Remove the plaster of Paris and brush or wash off the soil. This should reveal an accurate cast of the animal's footprint.

Footprints of animals such as dinosaurs have been preserved as casts after mud sediments were deposited on their footprints. These were gradually compressed and eventually dried producing perfect casts.

Sampling fresh water

Sturdy net frames, nets and handles for pond dipping are expensive but are nevertheless extremely valuable, as will be witnessed by the catch hauled in by the children. A 20cm or greater D-shaped or circular net frame with a metre-long handle is ideal for the task. Cheaper and smaller alternatives are available (see Resources chapter), but most children normally have difficulty either in reaching the water or in collecting the animals. It is advisable to attach a long loose length of string to the handles of the nets in case the children drop them into the water.

While younger children will want to explore in their own way, older children should be shown how to sample the water more systematically, particularly if comparisons are being made between the animals on the surface of the water, in the open water, among the vegetation and at the bottom of the water. The rigours of a fair test should be emphasised if comparisons between different areas are being made.

Encourage the children to sample by moving the net in a figure-of-eight motion, being careful not to drop the net handle as they turn their wrists. Explain that if they 'dig' their net in too deeply, they will catch a large amount of stones and mud which will be extremely difficult to raise out of the water and may damage the net. The 'catch' should be transferred to a white tray of water by turning the net inside out. Animals may then be transferred to specimen tubes or midi-spectors using plastic spoons.

Kick samples

This is a useful technique to use in shallow streams and small rivers as long as the children are wearing Wellingtons and the teacher does not mind getting wet!

Use a net with a D-shaped frame, and hold the frame flat against the bottom of the stream with the pole in a vertical position, downstream from yourself. Shuffle your feet on the bottom of the stream, moving the stones and gravel and thus displacing any animals in the area. As you do so, walk towards the net which hopefully will catch the results of the kick sample.

Carefully turn the net inside out over a white tray containing water, emptying out the contents. The children can then observe and identify the animals.

Kick samples disturb the floor of the stream, therefore it is important to restrict their use to a minimum.

Estimating water flow rate (intellectual Pooh sticks)

The flow rate of a stretch of river or stream may be calculated using a modified version of the well-known game 'Pooh sticks'. As the river flows, any object carried in its waters is carried at the same rate as the water itself.

Place a tape measure parallel to the bank of the stream or alternatively measure a distance of 10 or 20 metres along the bank. Throw a stick into the middle of the river or stream, upstream from the marked area and time how long the stick takes to cover the prescribed distance. Ask the children to describe the flow rate simply as, for example, 20 metres in 10 seconds. Alternatively, the speed of the flow of the water may be calculated as 2 metres per second.

Another method is to use a lighter object such as a table tennis ball attached to a long thread or thin piece of string. This encourages the use of a fair test as the same piece of apparatus is used each time, which is unlikely to be the case when using sticks unless the water is shallow and the stick may be retrieved and used again.

Food chains and webs

Food chains and food webs help to introduce children to the difficult concept of food relationships and the interdependence of living organisms. The children should already have a basic understanding of the concept of one animal eating another from their observations of wildlife areas or water habitats. This can be fairly rapidly illustrated if a great diving beetle larva is left in a container of water with tadpoles or damselfly nymphs, mayfly nymphs or small fish.

Help the children to work out a few simple food chains and get them to construct a food web showing the interrelationships. Examples of food chains and a food web associated with a rural environment are shown in Figure 1.

Food web of a garden containing rose bushes and hazel trees

Sun → Rose → Greenfly → Blue tit → Sparrowhawk

Sun → Rose → Greenfly → Ladybirds

Sun → Rose → Aphids → Lacewings → Hedge sparrow (eggs) → Grey squirrel

Sun → Hazel → Greenfly → Blue tit → Sparrowhawk

Sun → Hazel (nuts) → Grey squirrel

Sun → Hazel → Aphids → Lacewings → Hedge sparrow (eggs) → Grey squirrel

Sun → Hazel → Aphids → Ladybirds

Sun → Hazel (nuts) → Bank vole → Sparrowhawk

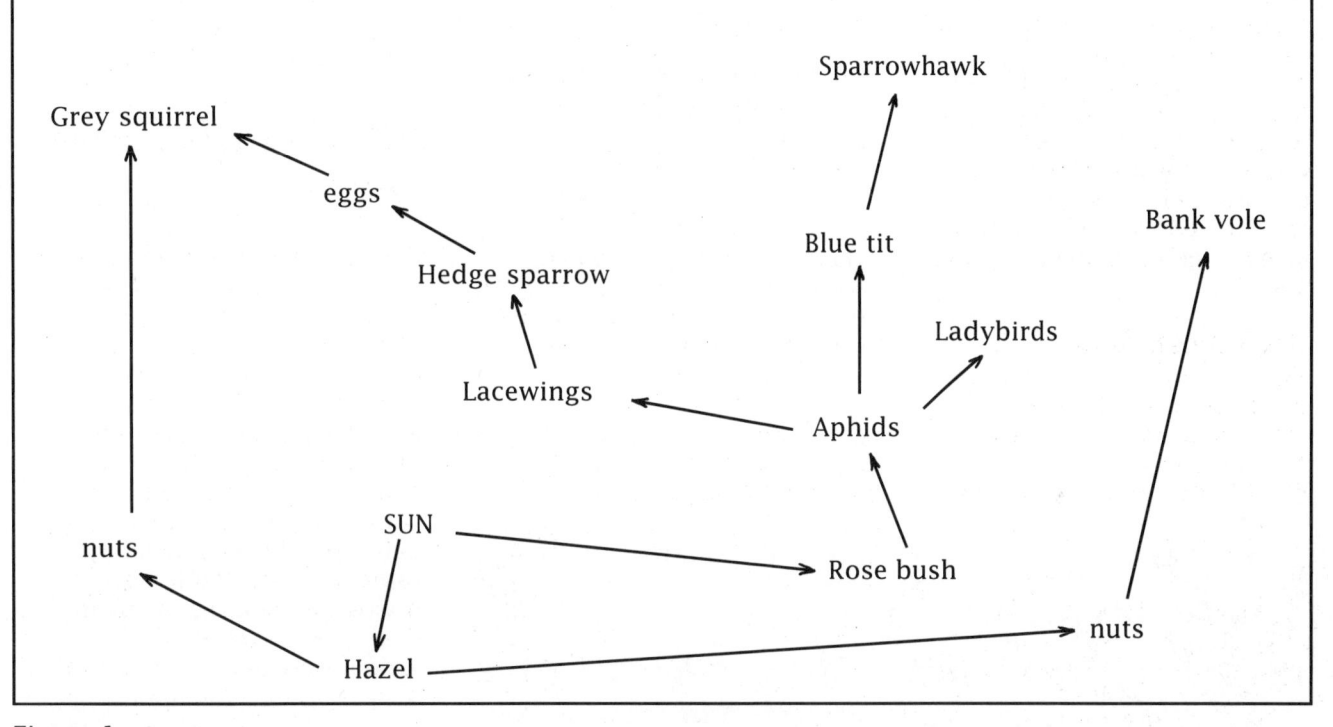

Figure 1

A great barrier to children's understanding of food chains is the direction in which the arrow is drawn. For example, Figure 1 might lead children to think that the blue tit eats the sparrowhawk and not vice versa. The children need to understand that the arrow means *eaten by* (or in some cases, *produced by,* or in the case of the Sun, *helped by*). Writing this on the arrows can help reinforce this concept.

Give each child a copy of photocopiable page 171 and ask them to consider the food chains which are associated with fresh water. Then ask the children to construct a food web using the animals and

Sampling, collecting and other environmental techniques **37**

plants shown on photocopiable page 170, putting the plants at the bottom and the larger animals at the top. The children must understand that all references (arrows) to the heron must be directed to the one picture. It is advisable that the children have their food web checked by the teacher before sticking it on to paper. Tell them to draw a pond outline and some vegetation around their food web.

Pollution level	Animals present	
Very high	Sludgeworm	Rat-tailed maggot
High	Bloodworm	Water louse
Low	Caddisfly larva	Freshwater shrimp
Clean	Mayfly nymph	Stonefly nymph

Figure 1

Water pollution and analysis

Few water sources in Great Britain are totally free from some form of pollution, whether it be in the form of dissolved chemicals or suspended solids. Chemical analysis requires complex equipment, and while data may be obtained from the National Rivers Authority or from your local water board, it may be difficult for children to interpret and understand.

A relatively simple way to estimate the level of pollution in water is to identify the animals present. Animals that are present exist there because they can tolerate the environmental conditions and those that are not, it has to be assumed, are absent because the conditions are not conducive to their survival. Thus a biological index of pollution may be drawn up using key specimens as in Figure 1 above.

Take samples from the surface of the water, the open water, around the water plants and from the bottom of the water source. Identify and list the specimens found. Figure 1 shows some of the key organisms associated with different levels of water pollution.

Ask the children to determine the pollution level of the water body they are investigating. Look at different locations along the same stretch of water. Is the level of pollution the same everywhere? For example, if sample A taken from the stream above the town contained caddisfly larvae and freshwater shrimps, while sample B taken from the stream below the town contained water lice, sludgeworms and rat-tailed maggots, what would be the level of pollution of the two locations? What possible reasons could there be for the change?

Air pollution and analysis

Air pollution is mainly caused by domestic and industrial emissions of gases and solids. Some of these gases dissolve in rain-water to form weak acids (so called 'acid rain'). Rain-water could be collected and its acidity found using universal pH paper, universal indicator solution or using a soil water pH kit. This would be particularly interesting if the school was in a heavily industrial area and the acidity of the rainfall was compared when the wind was blowing from different directions.

Further studies of air pollution might involve investigating the solid emissions which escape from industrial and domestic chimneys. One or more of the following activities might be selected.
• Clean a window sill and observe it over a period of time.
• Attach a piece of paper to a surface outside and observe it over a period of time.
• Place some two-sided tape outside for a period of time. Observe it closely with a hand lens or under a microscope. What shape are the particles? Are they similar sizes?
• Collect some leaves and look at the surface with a hand lens. Ask the children to devise a method to remove

and collect the dirt. (This may be achieved by firmly attaching sticky tape to the leaf and then peeling it off.) The tape may be mounted on white paper or observed under the microscope.
• Take the children on a lichen hunt. The presence or absence of particular types of lichens gives a measure of the amount of air pollution as shown below.

No lichens	Very bad air pollution
Only crusty lichens	Fairly polluted air
Leafy lichens	Slightly polluted air
Shrubby lichens	No air pollution

Soil analysis

As the soil is so vital to the growth and development of both plants and animals, it is important that children are familiar with its structure and characteristics. While it is possible to carry out some work on soils in the field, there are a number of aspects which the children can investigate in the classroom.

Soil profile

Dig a hole in the ground so that the children can see the soil profile. They should be able to see the darker topsoil, perhaps with a layer of humus on the surface, a lighter subsoil which might include a number of stones and, depending on the area from which the soil is taken, larger stones.

What is soil made of?

Place some soil in a tall, clear plastic container and add some water. Place the lid or stopper on the container and shake it up for a few seconds. Allow the soil to settle for a day or more until the water is clear (this time period will depend on the nature of the soil). Ask the children to draw and describe what they see. Why are the larger particles near the bottom? What are the bits floating on the top? The children could compare the composition of different soils such as clay, sand and loam. Ensure that the children do not shake their containers as they prepare to observe them.

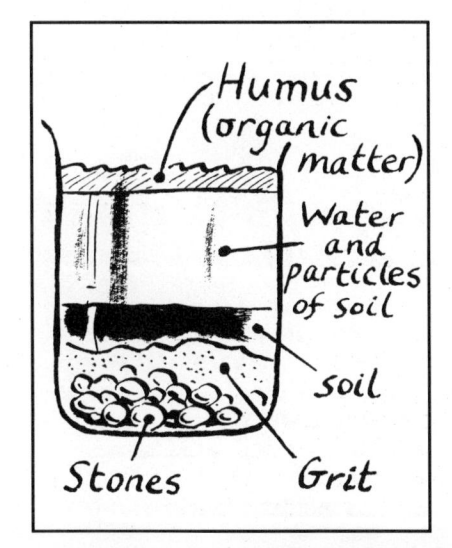

How much water is in the soil?

The children might notice that some plants grow in one area but not in another. While they might predict that it has something to do with the light, they may also notice a difference between the moisture in the soil of the two areas. Ask the children to design a fair test to see if there is a difference. Get them to suggest a prediction which contains a reason indicated by the word 'because'. For example, 'I think that the soil near the hedge will be wetter than the soil in the open because the plants shade it from the sun,' or 'I think that the clay soil will contain more water because the water sticks to the particles more than in sandy soil.'

The children should dig up some soil from the two sites ensuring that it is taken from the same depth and place it in a polythene bag. Back in the classroom they should weigh out exactly 100g (to avoid complicated mathematics) of each soil type and place them on a metal tray or piece of paper. The soil should be spread out as much as possible to ensure that it dries completely. The soil and container is then placed in a warm place, possibly close to a radiator, but safe so that it is not disturbed or any soil lost. Alternatively, the soil could be placed in an oven at a low temperature.

After a day or so the soil should be re-weighed and the amount of water in each soil type calculated. More able children could express the result as a percentage.

Soil testing

Soil test kits and soil meters may be obtained from most good garden centres and ironmongers, as well as school equipment suppliers. Some of these kits test exclusively for pH (acidity and alkalinity) while others test for pH and soil minerals. One of the most widely available makes is Rapitest.

Using a soil test kit

This simple procedure involves the addition of soil test solution to a small amount of soil in a stoppered, plastic tube. The mixture is then shaken and the ensuing colour analysed according to a colour chart. The kit is able to detect pH differences within the range pH 4.5 to 7.5, in 0.5 intervals, and is easily used in the field. A plant pH preference list is given for over 300 garden plants.

Both teachers and children often expect large pH differences between soils such as clay, sand or loam, but frequently this is not the case. Most soils will be in the range of pH 6.0 to 7.0. It is possible to test soil solutions with universal indicator paper or solution, but this usually produces results which show little difference. This is because the universal indicator paper or universal indicator solution generally in use in primary schools works over the entire pH range from 1–14 or 1–11. A narrower range is required, for example pH 6–8, to test more accurately for soil acidity and alkalinity.

Using a pH meter

A Rapitest pH meter is a quick and relatively inexpensive method of obtaining pH readings in soil, although the soil must be moist to obtain accurate readings. The probe of the meter is pushed into the ground to a depth of 10 to 12cm and is then rotated to ensure effective contact with the soil. After one minute of acclimatisation the reading may be recorded.

Using a light and moisture meter

A combined light and water meter may be used to measure qualitatively the amount of light falling on plants and the amount of water in the soil. The meter has two scales. The bottom scale is a light reading scale and the intensity of the light is indicated by letters from A (low) to H (high). To obtain a reading, slide the switch to 'light' and, holding the meter adjacent to the top row of leaves of a plant, direct the 'light window' on the meter to the brightest light source. Record the meter reading.

The top scale is a moisture reading scale and is numbered from 1 (dry) to 10 (wet). To obtain a reading, slide the switch to 'moisture' and place the probe into the soil near to the roots. Record the meter reading at least twice.

A combined light and water meter may also be used to identify when indoor plants require watering and the nature of the light regime that they need. Finding the optimum conditions for plants will induce strong, healthy growth and prevent scorching or over-watering. A table indicating the minimum light requirement and the meter scale at which different species of indoor plants should be watered accompanies the kit.

Testing for minerals

A Rapitest Soil Test kit may be used to test for potash and the minerals nitrogen (nitrates) and phosphorus (phosphates)

as well as for pH. Again, the procedures are relatively simple, if a little fiddly and time-consuming, but will allow the children to determine the pH of the soil and whether the soil contains high, medium or low levels of nitrogen, phosphorus and potash (potassium oxide). After obtaining the results, the children could consider whether fertiliser should be added to the soil in the school garden or flower beds, and if so, which type is needed.

Soils with a high acidity are conducive to the growth of rhododendrons and azaleas, while other plants thrive on lime-rich soils. Nitrogen is important for strong stems, and for the deep green colour of healthy leaves. Phosphorus stimulates early development, root growth and flowering. Potash is important in fruit and flower development and promotes resistance to disease.

Recording the weather

Young children should be encouraged to record the weather on a regular basis using a mixture of bought and home-made apparatus. As the children get older this can involve more quantification of temperature, rainfall and wind speed.

Invicta Plastics (see *Resources* page 162) makes a range of equipment to support teaching about weather. This could be the starting point for investigations into climate and the effect it has on people and vegetation. These resources include a weather board on which to record the day's weather, a weather vane, an anemometer, a rain gauge and a maximum and minimum thermometer.

Weather board
Invicta Plastics (see *Resources* page 162) produce a durable weather board which encourages children to observe and record the weather on a daily basis. The day, date, month, wind strength and description of the weather are shown on rotating dials. Temperature, wind direction and type of cloud are shown by pointers.

A home-made weather board could be made by the children with relative ease, particularly if some of the information was provided by means of cards fitted into slots as well as rotating dials.

Weather vane
These instruments work on the principle that a large, freely-rotating arrow comes to rest pointing into the wind. These can usually be hand-held or may be attached to a post. A compass is required to enable the user to point the north point of the weather vane towards the north.

Children may make a weather vane as indicated in the diagram below. It is important that the frictional force between the balsa wood, dowel and beads is reduced to a minimum. They should mark north, south, east and west accurately on the container. The children should set up the vane away from buildings, ensuring that the north mark on the vane faces north on the compass. Ask them to record the wind direction at the same time each day over a specified period.

Anemometer and wind speed indicators
Plastic anemometers and wind speed indicators can be purchased at a reasonable price. Anemometers (which can be hand-held or fixed to a post) may give direct readings of wind speed in metres per second and relate these to the appropriate point on the Beaufort scale – a chart which indicates wind speed on a scale numbered 0–12, with a description of the wind and its effects at each point.

Sampling, collecting and other environmental techniques

Wind speed indicators are hand held instruments which measure wind speed. Wind direction is indicated by an integral compass.

Alternatively, the children can make their own wind speed indicator as shown in the diagram below. The instrument is unable to measure the actual speed of the wind but is able to measure relative wind speeds. Ask the children to record the maximum deviation of the flap on the side of the box on a particular day. By looking at the effects of the wind in the environment, such as leaves blowing and small trees swaying, and comparing this evidence with the Beaufort scale, the scale of the children's device may be calibrated into an actual speed. Ask the children to record the maximum wind speed at the same time each day.

Rain gauge

Invicta's cone-shaped, plastic rain gauge (see *Resources* Chapter 13) is relatively cheap to purchase. The gauge may be secured in the ground by a plastic spike which may be removed if required. Four plastic side supports add to the gauge's stability. The gauge is graduated in millibars. A lid is supplied to prevent spillage, for example, when being carried back to the classroom.

Measuring temperature

A number of thermometers can be used to measure temperature, each of which can be used for a specific purpose. The children should become familiar with as many of these as possible. Four such thermometers will be discussed here, namely a normal 'wall' thermometer, a 'laboratory' thermometer, a maximum and minimum thermometer and a Thermostik, all of which measure in degrees Celsius.

'Wall' and 'laboratory' thermometers

The traditional 'wall' thermometer which is contained within a small wooden or plastic mount may be used to record daily temperatures at a fixed time each day to give an indication of the changes and trends in the weather. Alternatively, a 'laboratory' thermometer may be used for the same purposes. For safety reasons red spirit thermometers should be used in preference to potentially harmful mercury-filled thermometers.

Maximum and minimum thermometers

These should be used if the school is recording the highest and lowest temperatures each day. The maximum and minimum temperatures are recorded by markers which can only be moved from these points by a magnet or by tilting the thermometer. From this data, graphs can be drawn, the highest and lowest temperature for each month established and the average maximum and minimum temperature for each month calculated. Recording can be on a long-term basis so that the results of one year can be compared with the results of previous years.

Thermostik

The Thermostik is a durable thermometer with no glass or mercury but is as accurate and sensitive as mercury and glass thermometers. This thermometer may be used both indoors and outdoors. It is ideal for taking soil temperatures due to its strong metal probe, and water temperatures due to its ability to float. Its rotary scale reads from –10 to 120 degrees Celsius. A loop in the plastic case allows string to be attached so that the temperature of water in a pond may be measured without any danger of losing the Thermostik.

Survey and recording techniques

Making maps

Sketch maps

A sketch map can give useful information about the extent and shape of an area under study and show key features and details which might later be investigated, such as different vegetation or houses and a church etc. Children should be encouraged to draw the sketch map to scale; some limited measuring might be useful here, if only to compare the width of the pond with the length, by using standard paces. The sketch map could be compared at two different times of the year, for example a pond in the winter and also in the summer.

Map enlargement

Children might prefer to produce a more accurate map by map enlargement. While this can be carried out efficiently and accurately on an enlargement photocopier, older children might be able to increase the size of a map through scale drawing. This tends to result in roads which are rather wide, due to these being originally enlarged by the cartographer.

Compass bearings

Maps and sketch maps should be accompanied by their orientation relative to north. Always pack a compass in the school 'field bag'.

Obtaining information from people

The children may wish to survey the public or their class colleagues to obtain information about their preferences, likes, dislikes and opinions. While the preparation, discussion, public interaction and collation and interpretation of results is worthwhile in itself, it is more relevant if the actual questions are such that they produce valid, accurate information. This can only be obtained through careful planning and by careful questioning.

The following points need to be taken into account when surveying people's views.
- Make sure the children understand the point of the exercise and that they have a clear understanding of the information they require.
- Encourage them to ask clearly worded questions which will give them the information they require.
- Do not let them ask too many questions.
- Consider whether a questionnaire should be used by the 'interviewer' or given to the interviewee. Will the conversation be recorded?
- If a questionnaire is to be used by the interviewer it should be easy to complete, for example using short responses or ticks and crosses.
- Discourage the children from asking people their age. If age is considered important, such as in a survey of leisure facilities in a town where different age groups might have different views and preferences, they should ask which age group they belong to (10–15, 15–20, ...60+ etc.).
- Plan in advance what is to be said to people, including what to say if they refuse to speak to you (as is their right) and after talking to them.
- Will the children need to carry any identification? Should they tell people the purpose of the interview?
- What equipment will be needed on the day of the survey (pen, pencil, paper, questionnaires, tape recorder)?

The following techniques could be used to obtain information from people. Each technique has its strengths and weaknesses.

Street questionnaire

This is by far the easiest technique to carry out and is highly recommended as it produces a large amount of relatively reliable data, very quickly. Questions are pre-prepared and answers can be quickly filled in by the interviewer or an assistant. The questionnaire should be photocopied and a different sheet used for each interviewee unless it is very simple, for example, using a series of yes or no responses recorded in separate boxes as ticks or crosses.

Back in school the children can compile the results and produce histograms of their findings. They might like to include the age range or sex of the interviewees in the questions, but this will make the analysis of the data that much more difficult. They might like to inform the participants about their 'score' and possibly categorise it, but this would have to be done with a great deal of sensitivity and/or humour!

Questionnaire to be taken away

If a number of questions need to be asked or if the questions require more careful thought it might be useful to give people a questionnaire to take away and complete at their leisure. These could then be handed in to the school or to a shopkeeper who is sympathetic to the school and its work.

However, there are problems in getting these questionnaires back and a response of 10 per cent would be normal. This percentage may be improved by sending the questionnaires to an accessible group of people like shopkeepers or even better still to parents, relatives and friends. The non-random nature of this sample may be less important than the need to obtain a relatively high return of questionnaires without raising the costs.

Long and complicated questionnaires should be avoided as they are expensive to produce and the responses might be difficult for young children to analyse, unless ticks or restricted answers are required. You should think carefully about using this type, particularly if the children can obtain similar information with less difficulty.

Interviewing

More in-depth information might be better obtained through use of a pre-planned interview. These interviews might be divided into two categories:
- where information is required from a number of people about a local issue such as a plan for pedestrianising the High Street;
- where information is required and a known person has that expertise, for example information on the town 50 years ago.

With regard to the first category, interviews will probably need to take place on the street with people being stopped at random. Clearly, the nature of the weather, how preoccupied the person is and whether the person has strong views on the matter will all affect the length of the interviews. It might be useful to use a tape recorder, in which case the children must ask the interviewee's permission to use it and ensure that the location for the interview will not be too affected by traffic or other noise.

Back in school, the tapes can be played back and the main points of people's arguments, for example for and against pedestrianisation of the High Street, can be collated and displayed. A role play activity might follow.

The second category will again require a pre-planned interview but possibly the person could be interviewed in their home, at work or be invited into school. The interview might take place in front of the whole class so that everyone can hear it and possibly ask their own questions after the formal interview has finished. In view of the fact that the interviewee would have had time to prepare what she wants to say, it would be hoped that she would talk for some time without having to be prompted by another question.

Dating houses

It is not easy to date houses and other buildings as often they have been modified over the years. However, a number of features and the overall style allow buildings to be dated within periods of history.
- Tudor houses (1500–1602) have timbers visible on the outside. The upper storeys are wider than the storey below and their tall chimneys are decorated with spiralling bricks.
- Stuart houses (1603–1713) are typified by their sturdy appearance. They are built of stone and have large cornerstones and square chimneys.
- Georgian houses (1714–1836) are characterised by having squarish windows often with twelve small sections. The houses have three storeys and are generally brick built. Chimneys are tall and elegant and doors are decorated with pillars and porches.
- Victorian and Edwardian houses (1837–1913) are plain in comparison with the previous period houses, often being built of red brick, but with ornamental brick patterns near the chimneys, guttering and windows. Many towns have rows of Victorian terraced houses.
- Houses between the wars (1914–1945) were built with few frills and tend to be neat and utilitarian. Bay windows were popular during this period.
- Post-Second World War houses (1945–1980) appear modern but show signs of general weathering. The gardens are mature.
- Modern houses (1980–today) appear not to have been affected by weathering. The gardens are immature with young trees. Many modern houses do not have chimneys.

CHAPTER 3

Organising environmental activities

Many of the activities in this book involve taking classes to a number of locations outside the school grounds. Clearly, this will need careful thought and much detailed planning if the visit is to be purposeful, useful in educational terms, safe for the children and will not involve permanent change to the particular environment under study. The planning for any such visit might generally include the following:
- arranging and making a preliminary orientation visit;
- clarifying aims and objectives;
- gaining permission from the head teacher and/or governing body;
- making detailed arrangements for the visit;
- undertaking preparatory work in school prior to the visit;
- scheduling the day of the visit;
- undertaking follow-up work in school.

BACKGROUND

Making a preliminary orientation visit

Preliminary orientation visits are extremely time-consuming given the existing heavy demands on teachers' time. However, they are essential if the educational objectives are to be met and the time, effort and expense involved in any such visit are to be fully justified.

Initial contact will need to be made with appropriate personnel, for example, the supermarket manager, the farmer or the warden of the nature reserve. This should initially be by letter or a telephone conversation, followed up with a visit to discuss more detailed arrangements. These discussions should include details such as size of group, age of the children, programme for the visit and purposes of the visit. Permission should be sought if photographs are to be taken or interviews of customers are to be carried out.

These preliminary visits also give the teacher the opportunity to see the environmental context, to identify problems and possibilities, to talk to people who might be involved in the visit and to locate amenities. For example, if a class of children is going to investigate an oak tree in groups of four, a visit will allow the teacher to locate seven or eight suitable oak trees which are relatively close together.

Additional information which might be obtained could include:
- the time it takes to get from the school to the site of the visit;
- points of interest along the route;
- access restrictions, such as opening hours and availability of guides or wardens;
- admission charges;
- grouping of children given the restraints of the site;
- safety considerations;
- sensitive areas which might be damaged by the children;
- location of toilets;
- location of a possible place to eat lunch should the weather be inclement;
- plans or photographs of the site which would be useful either to the teacher for planning or to the children in their introductory work prior to the visit;
- any printed information produced by the organisation.

A letter confirming arrangements should be written after this preliminary orientation visit.

Clarifying aims and objectives

Aims and objectives need to be clearly defined prior to the visit, not only to enhance teaching and learning, but also to justify to the head teacher and the governing body the necessity and value of the visit. In common with other planning for classroom studies, objectives should be considered in terms of:
- knowledge and understanding;
- skills;
- attitudes, such as co-operation or perseverance.

These objectives should also relate to environmental issues and any statutory curriculum regulations.

Failure to clarify objects prior to the visit will probably lead to poor planning and a lack of focus on the day of the visit, thus reducing the children's opportunities for learning.

Gaining permission

Not only is it common courtesy to keep the head teacher informed of the visit, but it is also prudent in that she might be able to offer advice on legal and other matters. It is advisable to document details of the trip in writing, including objectives, potential costs and destination. This information should be updated at suitable periods prior to the visit.

Making detailed arrangements

Well-thought out arrangements will go some way to ensure that the day is a success, even if the reaction of the children and the weather are beyond the teacher's control! Some schools are involving parents more in the administration of school visits but many teachers will want to retain this time-consuming aspect as administrative and educational decisions often go hand-in-hand. Nevertheless, parent helpers could be extremely helpful, for example, in obtaining quotations and making travel arrangements while still leaving the educational decisions in the hands of the teacher.

The arrangements should include the following points:
• Obtain quotations, book transport and organise departure and return times. Ensure that other requirements are clarified (e.g. transport the children from Site 1 to Site 2 at 1.30 pm).
• Plan the day with precision but with some flexibility to take into account journey times, meal and toilet stops and the number of activities the children are to complete.
• Estimate the full cost of the visit, including transport, entry fees (if applicable) etc. Calculate the cost per child.
• Write to the parents informing them of the date and purpose of the visit, the estimated cost and the date by which payment is required. A pro forma requiring the signature of the parent or guardian giving permission for their child to participate should accompany the letter.
• Consider the day of the trip. If the visit takes place on a Friday, any plant material collected will have deteriorated by the following Monday, while any animals may be placed under stress which could lead to death.
• Invite parents to accompany the children on the visit ensuring that the adult:child ratio is suitable for the nature of the visit and within the LEA and school guidelines.
• Confirm to parents final details of the visit in writing, including departure time (if earlier than the normal start to the school day), time of arrival back in school (if later than the normal end of the school day), refreshment and money requirements and advice on clothes to be worn.
• Arrange a meeting to brief parents accompanying the visit and to explain further the itinerary, the purposes of the visit, your expectations of them and the children and safety considerations. This will help to make them feel more involved with the day and hopefully will lead to more effective learning by the children.
• Keep the head teacher informed of all arrangements by passing on copies of letters etc. Ensure that the visit is covered by existing insurance policies within the school or LEA.
• Develop a detailed programme for the day using the information gained from the preliminary orientation visit. This should include the activities to be carried out, the size of the groups involved, the amount of adult support needed, approximate timings for the activities and safety considerations which need to be relayed to children, teachers and parent helpers.
• Confirm travel arrangements 24 to 48 hours prior to departure.

Organising environmental activities

Preparatory work in school

Visits are expensive, both in financial terms and in curriculum time. To maximise learning potential, the children should be involved with work prior to the visit and with follow-up work after the visit. Such preparatory work might include the following.

Purposes and objectives of the visit

Making the purposes and objectives of the visit clear to the children will focus their minds on the activities they will be undertaking and convey to them the importance of the visit.

Conservation

The importance of causing minimal damage to woods, hedges, fields and freshwater habitats should be stressed to the children. Discuss the need for careful collection of specimens or no collection of specimens without permission from the teacher.

Producing materials

The time prior to the visit may be used to produce materials necessary for the day of the visit. For example, this might include designing a questionnaire (see Chapter 2) to find out where people do their grocery shopping, whether they use the bottle, can or paper bank or if they are green gardeners. This type of work will further involve the children in the 'ownership' of the visit and help them to think about the environmental issues involved.

Equipment and resources

Children could be shown how to use some of the equipment prior to the visit to enable more accurate recording on the day. For example, practise using a sound (decibel) meter to compare the noise levels of different vehicles and sounds in the town or using a pH kit to test the acidity of soil.

The children could also be involved in collecting the appropriate equipment together and checking that all the contents of the school's field bag (see Chapter 2) are present.

Arrangements for the day of the visit

It would be advisable to discuss the arrangements for the visit, particularly with the older children. This might include destination, activities, refreshments, money, clothing and group membership. Behaviour should be discussed, particularly if safety is an issue, for example on an industrial site, or if there is a danger of plant or animal life being disturbed or people being inconvenienced. Thorough preparation by both the teacher and the children and a clear understanding of, and involvement in, the work will help to reduce inappropriate behaviour. All aspects of safety should be considered and made clear to the children.

Records and recording

Some discussion of the need to make detailed and accurate records should take place with children prior to the visit. This might include maps, sketches, pictures, annotated diagrams, notes and photographs. A video camera and/or audio cassette player might be useful in recording the environmental context for later reference.

Safety

Children should be adequately supervised at all times and should use appropriate protective clothing (for example, plastic/rubber gloves when handling waste materials or soil) where necessary. They should also be made aware of the dangers present on busy streets, the countryside and ponds and rivers.

Codes of behaviour

Teachers should be familiar with the Wildlife and Countryside Act of 1981, while the children should be made familiar with the Country Code and/or the Outdoor Studies Code. The Country Code of the Countryside Commission is as follows:
• Guard against fire risks;
• Fasten all gates;
• Keep dogs under proper control;
• Keep to paths across farm land;
• Avoid damaging fences, hedges and walls;

- Leave no litter;
- Safeguard water supplies;
- Protect wildlife, wild plants and trees;
- Go carefully on country roads;
- Respect the life of the countryside.

The Outdoor Studies Code is as follows:
- Plan and lead excursions well;
- Take safety seriously;
- Choose and use your area carefully;
- Respect ownership;
- Think of other users of the countryside;
- Leave the area as you found it;
- Do not collect unnecessarily;
- Safeguard rare species;
- Give no one cause to regret your visit.

The children could make posters to illustrate one or more aspects of these behavioural codes.

The day of the visit

A successful day is more likely if the planning and preparation is sound and the children have been involved as much as possible. There are a number of points to consider on the day which will add to the smooth running of the visit.
- Ensure that a first aid kit and all the resources (field bag) are placed on the coach and are carried to the environmental site.
- Ensure that those children who suffer from travel sickness are suitably treated and that they are able to sit near the front of the bus where they can view the road.
- Ensure the safety and good behaviour of the children at all times on the visit, including during the bus trip.
- Restrict eating and drinking to official meal stops and times.
- Regularly check the numbers in the party, on arrival, on departure and after each activity.
- Brief the children clearly and fully so that they may work as independently as possible.
- Ensure that all the equipment is taken off the bus and that it is checked at frequent intervals; it is relatively easy to lose even larger items of equipment in the long grass and leaf litter of natural habitats.
- Allocate each group or groups of children to an adult, preferably someone who is familiar with the activities to be undertaken.
- Carry out agreed procedures concerning road safety and movement around urban environments at all times.
- Issue the children with some form of identification, details of the itinerary and instructions for what to do in an emergency.
- Ensure that the children thank their hosts for the visit and also show their appreciation to people who have given their time to be interviewed etc.
- Consider the needs of the children e.g. recreation breaks and toilet stops.
- If the visit has been well planned, the children should be able to start work relatively quickly. Ensure that the equipment is stored centrally and that the children are encouraged to return it once they have used it.
- Try to organise the activities so that all the groups are in view of the teacher, even if there are other adult helpers present. The teacher should circulate frequently to ensure that problems and misunderstandings are dealt with quickly and to ensure that the children do not follow the wrong thread of the activities that they have been set.
- Ensure that collection of specimens is kept to a minimum so that only material that will be used back in school is removed from the site.
- Tidy up the site after use, replacing soil and turf and collecting any litter which might have been dropped.
- Equipment such as pitfall traps which will be left in the field for some time should be hidden from obvious view. Their position in the habitat should be recorded so that they are not lost. These should be emptied regularly to ensure that animals are not subjected to cruelty.

LEAVE THE COUNTRYSIDE AS YOU FOUND IT!

Follow-up work in school

Follow-up work could take up a fairly extensive period of time, depending on the nature and scope of the environmental visit and the interest and motivation of the children. Follow-up work might include any of the following activities.

Discussion

It is important that the children fully understand the follow-up work they have to carry out and the end product, whether it be a display or an individual or group 'report'. Follow-up work should commence with a discussion of the activities carried out in the environment, the specimens which have been collected and suggestions for future work.

Observation, drawing and identification of materials

In order that animals can be returned to the wild as soon as possible and plants can be studied before they deteriorate, it is important that observational work is carried out without delay. Bear in mind that visits late in the week might prevent this from taking place. Encourage the children to draw large pictures with a sharp pencil and annotate them as much as possible. Ensure that a number of simple keys are available, for example those in *The Clue Books* (Oxford University Press), so that the children may identify plants and animals.

Returning living specimens to the wild

Demonstrate good practice by, wherever feasible, returning living specimens to their natural environment as soon as possible. Living specimens should preferably be returned to the exact location from where they were collected.

Completing drawings and maps

The children will probably need to complete a number of drawings and maps which they started in the field. This might involve converting a rough sketch into an accurate drawing, for example a house or a map.

Analysing surveys and collecting results

The children will need some time to analyse their surveys and to collect their results. They will probably need some assistance in collating their findings and deciding on the best way to record these results in a graphical form. Can the results be presented in more than one way? Does the bar chart clearly state the question that was asked? Are these results what the children expected? Would they like to carry out a further survey on the basis of these findings? Do they want to communicate the results to anyone? Would the local paper be interested?

Drawing conclusions and identifying areas for further investigation

The children should be encouraged to make inferences from their results and to consider the reliability and validity of their findings. For example, why do many younger people use organic garden methods than older people? This might well involve some form of written work to add to the graphical and pictorial data already prepared.

Display, presentation and discussion of findings

This is a most important aspect as it serves to summarise the visit and allows the teacher to assess and evaluate the quality of the learning which has been taking place. It also allows those children who have difficulty in writing and graphical skills to contribute on almost equal terms. Display and individual or group presentations of the activities undertaken will allow children to compare findings and to gain an overall picture of the work undertaken. Encourage the children to ask each other questions and to give clear responses.

Older children should be helped to understand that the validity of this data will depend on the numbers sampled and the accuracy and rigour with which that sampling was carried out.

Another class, parents or parent helpers could be invited to see the display and listen to the presentation.

Letters of appreciation

At some stage during the work, the children should be encouraged to write letters thanking those people who helped to make the visit a success. This could include any organisation or individual involved in a visit, such as the warden of a nature reserve, the bus driver or owner, and parent helpers.

If appropriate, individuals could be invited to look at the display the children have created or hear their presentations. The children should appreciate that a little courtesy goes a long way and costs nothing, except the effort of writing a letter and the price of a stamp!

CHAPTER 4

Planning a trail through the local environment

A trail is a planned, self-guided tour where a predetermined route is normally followed in order to find out more about the environment. There are typically a number of stops along the route where information is given about particular features of interest, or activities are undertaken in order to increase knowledge of the environment. Trails can be developed both through the natural and built environments, and trail booklets, route maps and fixed information boards are usually provided.

Trails are ideal for conveying information and stimulating interest about many aspects of the environment. If they are to reach their true potential, they must provide variety and foster an enquiry-based approach to environmental work. Planning a trail through the local environment is an ideal way for children to gain first-hand experience of investigations outside the classroom and to develop new knowledge and skills whilst studying an area in depth. Children will learn to care for and value the environment once they have had the opportunity to find out more about it through the trail. Positive, caring and responsible attitudes can be developed through such experiential work.

BACKGROUND

Purpose of the trail

Before designing a trail, it is important to clarify aims and objectives. What is the purpose of the trail? These aims can be clarified through asking such questions as:
• What concepts and knowledge can be developed by the children through designing and following the trail?
• Which skills is it intended the children will use and develop? These could be subject-based skills such as identifying plants or animals or personal skills such as working in groups or problem-solving.
• What type of environment will be used? This could be the natural or built environment or a mixture of both.
• Are there any particular aspects of the environment that should be studied, such as trees, buildings or animals?
• What age groups or ability range is the trail aimed at?
• How long will the trail last?
• What safety precautions need to be considered?
• What knowledge and skills might be required by the children beforehand?

The local environment

This could be the school itself, the school grounds, or areas within easy walking distance of the school. It is appropriate to plan trails for younger children in the school grounds. Much work of interest lies within the school gates, even in a tarmacked playground.

There are obvious advantages in planning a trail in the school grounds rather than looking further afield. The problems of safety and supervision are reduced. The site can be easily visited by both the teacher and children, and there could be considerable savings of time and money, when the trail is being designed and when it is in use. The school grounds are a familiar environment for the children. Children from other classes in the school can work conveniently on the trail. Features within the school grounds can be conserved and managed by identifying them as wildlife havens. The trail can be used easily in different seasons of the year, when different plants or animals may be present, or features may be different. For example, by studying trees at different times of the year, the children will be able to identify leaves, winter twigs, seeds and fruits, and in winter, the shape of the trees and patterns of the branches. In the spring and summer months, there will be a wider variety of insects, birds and flowers. If the trail is in the school grounds it will be easier to site stopping places where particular features can be studied, and new stops can be added at other times.

Moving beyond the school grounds, there is also excellent potential for designing a trail. The children could investigate the built environment – shops, houses and other buildings, and examine them from an historical and scientific perspective. The local church and churchyard can provide an interesting focus (see Chapter 12 – The churchyard). Traffic surveys at particular points could be undertaken. A simple map could be constructed, and the position of buildings and shops of different architectural styles, street furniture, and types of trees on the route marked on the map.

Trail booklets

The style of trail booklets will vary according to the age, knowledge and ability of the children who will be using the trail. These could be designed and written by the children. If appropriate the booklet could be accompanied by an audio cassette tape of sounds from along the trail.

The booklet should encourage an investigative approach rather than just giving factual information. Where questions are asked, it is important that the children are given some guidance as to how to find the answers. This could be done by providing simple drawings of plants, leaves or animals to accompany the questions. Encourage the children to make connections and to relate different parts of the trail to each other. Comparing and contrasting habitats is a helpful technique. Such questions which encourage thought, such as, 'Why do you think that...?' are useful. Questions aimed at helping children develop their powers of observation should be used. It is important that the children do not feel that the tasks or questions are too difficult or the trail will lose its appeal for them.

Useful questions
• How many different shrubs can you see growing in the hedge?
• How many different wild flowers can you find?
• What is the difference between...?
• What colour are they?
• How tall do you think the tree is?
• What sounds can you hear?
• Is it wetter or drier here?
• Can you suggest why this might be?
• Where else on the trail have you seen...?
• How does the vegetation on the path differ from that underneath the trees?
• Have you seen any signs of birds, squirrels and...?
• Can you see where else this... grows?

The children should be encouraged to make sketches of some of the sights they see along the trail.

You may wish to refer in the booklet to investigations which can be carried out when the children return to school, for example, you may wish them to investigate such aspects as: growth of plants under different conditions, or conditions which cause rusting of metals. The children might need to do some extra research using reference books.

Layout and presentation of the booklet is important. It must not be intimidating to the user and it must also look attractive and appeal to the children. It is a good idea to help the children to personalise their own booklet.

A space for their own name and class details can be provided. Spaces for the children's sketches can be built into the booklet. Make sure the language used in the booklet is appropriate to the age of the children using it. If a map is included in the booklet, it should be clear, simple and easy to follow. Any safety issues should be highlighted clearly in the booklet.

A trail is an ideal way to explore a range of aspects related to the environment. Such a planned route provides opportunities for a variety of themes to be developed. A trail could focus on one theme, such as the plants, or buildings along the route, or a general study encompassing several themes relating to the environment could be undertaken. The following themes, or combination of themes, are suggested for investigation along a trail.

Buildings

If the trail is in the school grounds then the school building can provide an ideal start. The exterior of the building has endless possibilities. The construction materials can be investigated. The children could look for brick, stone, wood, plastic, glass, concrete or metal. Help the children to link their observations to environmental factors by asking them questions such as: Why do you think this material was used to construct this building? Is the material available locally (for example, clay – brickworks)? Does the material used relate to the period of construction of the building, (for example, concrete – the 1960s)? The use of wood, type and bonding of bricks, shapes of windows, roofing material, and various structures on the building such as weather vanes or lettering could all become part of the trail.

The children could make rubbings of lettering or other interesting surfaces. Is there anything else on the outside of the building such as pipes or guttering? The children could look to see if the windows are double-glazed. Are there signs of weathering of the bricks or stone? Is there other evidence of weather such as rotting window frames or rusting metal?

Architectural features of a building can be studied. The style of windows, doors or roofs often give clues as to the age of a building. The children could compare a modern building with an old building and could make sketches to identify differences. Different types of houses could be studied, such as terraced, semi-detached and so on. The children could look for the presence or absence of television aerials and satellite dishes.

Most buildings abound with ledges, cracks, crevices, and window sills. They are a haven for wildlife. Birds nesting on buildings include starlings, sparrows, blue tits and house martins. Roof spaces provide nesting sites for swifts, swallows, house sparrows and starlings. Moss, lichens, ivy and Virginia creeper can be found on walls of buildings.

Other buildings such as huts may also prove to be of interest.

Walls

Walls may provide a fascinating study. The children could consider the following questions. Which direction does the wall face? Where is shade provided by the wall?

What material is the wall made of? What flora and fauna can be found on the wall, between the cracks on top of the wall? Lichens on a wall may indicate the degree of air pollution. What plants grow at the bottom of the wall? Are they in the shade or the sun? Is the wall a valuable habitat for plants and animals? Do a number of species live in it? If not, why could this be? The children should consider such aspects as age, niche diversity and availability of water.

Other boundaries

These could be hedgerows, gates, or a line of shrubs or trees. Direct observation of birds and some mammals inhabiting the hedgerow may be possible (use a tape recorder to record sounds). Birds' nests should be left undisturbed. Pitfall traps (see Chapter 2 – Sampling, collecting and other environmental techniques) could be set up for invertebrates, or they could be collected from the shrub layer by shaking the branches whilst holding a tray beneath them. Searching through the leaf litter on the ground will reveal minibeasts such as spiders, woodlice and beetles.

The children could measure the length of the hedgerow and count the trees and shrubs along its length. Younger children could simply record the occurrence of trees and shrubs in every metre of hedge. They could sort the leaves collected from the ground to establish tree type in the area. The hedgerow could be dated (see Chapter 7 – Farms, activity 4) by counting the species of trees and shrubs in a given length.

Boundary fences could be examined for material of construction, evidence of decay such as rotten wood, patterns of wood grain and height of fence. Has the rotting wood provided a habitat for any organisms?

Birds

A study of birds could be a focus for the trail. Bird identification can be carried out, and bird movements and territorial behaviour can be investigated. A nest box could be easily built as part of the trail and observations could be made of bird visitors and their feeding habits.

Minibeasts

Children could search on different parts of the trail for minibeasts and record numbers of species and types of habitat in which they are found. Encourage the children to search in leaf litter, under stones or in rotting wood, in hedges or along paths and walls. The children might wish to investigate types of butterflies seen on the trail (see Chapter 12 – The churchyard). Can they tell the difference between a moth and a butterfly? They might find caterpillars on leaves and buds. A simple identification guide to minibeasts should be provided.

Trees

Trees and shrubs are excellent subjects of study. Trees can be observed throughout the seasons. Tree identification, shapes of twigs and leaves, measurement of height of trees (see Chapter 2), types of fruits and seeds, trees as nesting sites, comparison of evergreen and deciduous trees, making leaf-prints are all aspects of the study of trees which could be included in a trail (see Chapter 9 – Woodlands).

Planning a trail through the local environment

Flowering plants

Different types of plants can be identified and recorded at various points along the trail. These will obviously vary season by season. Bluebells and Celandine might be seen in spring. Also in spring look for tree seedlings such as sycamore. In early summer, dandelions, buttercups and daisies will be common. A comparison might be made of an unmown and a mown area of grass, or a trampled area and an area that has not been disturbed. Growth forms of plants in the two areas could be compared. Plants growing in sunny and shady areas can be compared, as can those growing in damp and dry areas. The trail could identify different habitats for different species of plants. These habitats could be cracks in paving stones, under hedgerows, on walls or fences, grassy areas, flower beds or in the shade of trees. The children will need a simple guidebook to help them identify any flowers they may encounter on the trail.

Roads and traffic

A traffic survey could be undertaken. This could even be done from inside the school grounds by looking out from the playground on to the road. Care must be taken to ensure that the children remain within the limits of the school grounds unless properly supervised.

The number of cars travelling between fixed points along a road in say five minutes could be counted. This investigation might be carried out by different children using the trail at different times of the day, and their results can be compared. Recording sheets can be designed by the older children, and younger children could be given a simple sheet which just requires a tick for each car seen. The children can then draw bar charts from their results to work out how busy the roads are. Further details which might be recorded are: colour of cars, model of cars, and number of passengers. Parked cars can also be surveyed.

Opportunities arise here to raise important environmental questions such as problems associated with excess traffic or the provision of adequate car parking spaces and problems of pollution from vehicles.

Recording results

The children can record their findings in the trail booklet, but there are other ways of recording their trail experience which should be considered. Younger children, particularly, may benefit through recording their ideas on an audio cassette tape which could be played back in the classroom. A photographic record can also be made. This, along with a tape, can provide an invaluable, accurate record of the trail visit. Drawings, bark rubbings, plaster casts, record sheets and maps might also be used. Be careful about collecting material to bring back into the classroom. Many wildflowers are protected and animals such as minibeasts should be handled with care and returned to the place where they were found. A display can be created in the classroom to make an attractive record of the trail visit.

Engage the children in a discussion of the environment through which the trail has passed, and relate their observations and questions to relevant environmental factors. For example, the children might wish to consider the variety of habitats they have seen, the way in which they differ and what influence (if any) human activity has had upon them. They should also think about evidence of change in the environment over the years that they have witnessed along the trail. Is this change for the better or has it had a detrimental effect on the surroundings? This could lead into a further discussion about how the local environment could be improved for wildlife, the local community, children and those with disabilities.

CHAPTER 5

Shops and shopping

Shopping is an activity with which all children are familiar. They will have accompanied their parents to the local shops or wheeled a trolley around the supermarket shopping for food. This chapter aims to introduce a number of the environmental aspects associated with the supermarket and supermarket shopping. Younger children could begin by comparing shopping behaviour in the past with that of today. This will inevitably draw attention to the difference in packaging and they can then consider issues associated with the presentation and protection of the products. One of the ways of preserving food products is by using additives. It is important that the children understand the range of additives put into food and the possible risk associated with them. Organically-grown food stuffs are free from such additives but the cost associated with producing food in this way needs to be considered. The advantages and disadvantages of these two approaches to food production provide the basis for a lively class debate.

Supermarkets react to the preferences and needs of their customers by providing environmentally-friendly products. It is interesting for children to investigate the popularity of these products and to explore the benefits associated with them. Supermarkets are not suitable for all shopping needs. Top-up shopping at convenient local shops is another important type of shopping. This leads to a comparison of these two types. What are their benefits? What are their disadvantages? Is there an ideal type of shop which can cater for all needs?

More and more superstores are being built on the edges of town so it is not longer necessary to travel into the centre of town for a main shopping trip. In this respect, children need to consider the changes in shopping habits and factors such as provision of parking space for cars. The activities in this chapter could all be based around a single class visit to a supermarket with possible follow-up visits by smaller groups if desirable. A member of staff from the local supermarket could be invited to talk to the children at school about particular aspects of their work.

Shops and shopping

BACKGROUND

Shops and shopping — topics:
- Pollution
- Eco-friendly products
- Packaging
- Changes in shopping habits
- Types of shops
- Organic foods
- Recycling
- An environmental survey
- Food additives

	Progression in teaching and learning	
Theme	**Activity number and details**	
	Key Stage 1 (P1–3)	Key Stage 2 (P 4–7)
Conservation	Conserving resources (3), (8)	
Environmental change	Comparison of specialist shops and supermarkets (1) Comparison of shopping habits in the past and present (2)	Changes in shopping habits – the advent of 'convenience' shops (7)
	External environment – landscaping and provision of facilities (8)	
Plants, animals, and their habitats	External environment – landscaping (8)	
Pollution	Packaging as contributing to pollution (3) Food additives as pollutants (4) Pollutant-free supermarket products (5) Environmentally-friendly supermarket products (5)	
		Use of fertilisers, herbicides and pesticides – organic products (6), (8)

58 Chapter 5

ACTIVITIES

1. Where can we buy it?

Theme
Environmental change.

Age range
Five to seven.

Group size
Whole class and individuals.

What you need
Photocopiable page 172 (listing types of products and shops where products can be purchased), pencils.

What to do
Talk to the children about times they have been shopping with their parents for everyday items such as food. What sort of goods have been bought? In which shops have they bought these goods? Discuss the range of shops which stock items such as different kinds of food and other goods that are used every day. Give the children photocopiable page 172 and explain that they are going to match up the product with the shop where it can be bought. They can tick the appropriate column to indicate the particular shop where items can be purchased. They could draw or colour in a picture of each type of product and add their own items to the list.

At the end of the activity, bring the groups or class together for a discussion of their results. They will now know that supermarkets stock most everyday items, whereas some shops such as greengrocers specialise in only one type of goods.

Content
The purpose of this activity is to help the children consider the variety of goods that we use every day and to develop an understanding of specialist shops and shops such as supermarkets which stock a range of goods. This activity focuses on the child's immediate social environment and considers some of the material needs of society.

Subject links
NC geography and English
Scottish 5–14 social subjects

2. What's in a shopping list?

Theme
Environmental change.

Age range
Five to seven.

Group size
Whole class.

What you need
Shopping lists from the 1940s/50s and the present. The past lists could be obtained from older relatives, such as grandparents or through a local museum or historical society.

What to do
Ask the children to talk with older relations (such as grandparents) to find out about shopping habits in the past. Alternatively, invite an older person into the classroom and encourage the children to ask him or her questions about shopping such as:
• What types of shop did people visit – supermarkets or specialised shops such as grocer and greengrocer?
• Was food delivered to the home by the shopkeeper?
• Where did food come from – local sources or delivered from long distance sources?
• How was the food transported to the shops?
• What goods did he or she purchase?
• How were they sold and packaged?
Help the children to compare past shopping practices with those of today.

The children could compare two shopping lists, one from the past and one from the present day. Encourage them to look for the main differences. The children could use reference books to find out answers to such questions as: How was the food bought in the past? Were items such as butter or sugar packaged or bought loose? Are more items pre-weighed and pre-packaged now? Ask the children to compare the contents of the shopping lists. Do we tend to buy much more processed food now such as beefburgers or crisps? Which list do they think reflects a healthier diet? Were people able to buy frozen food in the past?

The children could recreate a shop of the past in the classroom and take the roles of shopkeeper and customers.

Content
The children will appreciate through this activity the changes that have occurred in shopping habits over time.

Subject links
NC history and English
Scottish 5–14 social subjects

3. Wrapping it up

Theme
Pollution; Conservation.

Age range
Five to eleven.

Group size
Small groups then whole class.

What you need
A range of packaged household goods including fresh, perishable food and frozen food. Packaging should include a variety of materials such as paper, plastic and metal.

What to do
Following a visit to a local supermarket, discuss with the children the amount of variety in packaging of household goods. Why do they think that so much packaging is needed? What happens to the packaging when the products are opened? What do they think the packages are designed to do, in terms of the customer? Does colour and brightness affect the choice of goods? Ask the children which bag of sweets they prefer and why.

The children should sort through the packaged goods and classify them into types of packaging such as paper, plastic, metal or cardboard. They could then identify the packaging which could be recycled or those goods which have unnecessary packaging on them. Older children should consider the reasons why foods and other goods are wrapped in layers of packaging and whether the type of packaging has been chosen for a particular purpose, for example, plastics which are impervious to water vapour are appropriate for chilled and frozen foods.

Ask the children to think of ways of cutting down on packaging (supplying products as concentrates or providing refill packs, packing goods in recyclable materials, using plastic cartons as storage containers at home). The results of these discussions could be presented at a class assembly or the children could make posters giving facts about packaging so that the other children in the school could make up their own minds about the value of packaging.

Further activity
The children could use reference books to investigate methods of packaging in the past. Which goods were sold without packaging? How were the goods transported safely to the home?

Content
The purpose of this activity is to raise the children's awareness about the issue of packaging. It is important that the children understand some of the benefits which packaging brings as well as the problems in terms of production and waste materials.

Packaging is necessary on some goods, particularly some perishable foods which may dry out or become infected if exposed to the air. These foods are kept fresh by being sealed in plastic packs which contain mixtures of gases such as nitrogen, oxygen and carbon dioxide. Some foods give off strong smells and packaging is necessary to prevent contamination of other foods. There is also a convenience factor in that products are weighed and priced beforehand in containers. Information about ingredients is provided on packaging as is information on use, cooking time and storage. Most packaging prevents contamination or breakage. We can reduce waste resulting from packaging by buying products in packaging made from recyclable materials and returning these materials to collection points such as paper and bottle banks.

Subject links
NC science and English
Scottish 5–14 science

4. Adding it in

Theme
Pollution.

Age range
Five to eleven.

Group size
Pairs or small groups.

What you need
Labels from packet or canned foods, pens, paper, photocopiable page 173, icing sugar, colourings and flavourings, egg whites, mixing bowl, paper sweet cases.

What to do

A visit to the local supermarket is a good starting point for this activity. Discuss with the children that certain substances called additives are added to food to preserve it or to add flavour or colour. The children can investigate which foods contain additives by comparing the labels on different packet or canned foods. All processed food must list the ingredients used in their manufacture. Give the children some of the labels (a few per group) and ask them to list the additives which each food contains.

Only permitted additives may be used in foods. European countries have given these additives numbers which have the letter 'E' in front of the number. The children could find out information about the main groups of additives and use photocopiable page 173 to translate the 'E' numbers.

Many supermarkets now publish information leaflets which give details of the main groups with lists of 'E' numbers and the names of the additives.

Encourage a class discussion on the advantages and disadvantages of additives in foods.

This activity can be used for Key Stage 1 children by focusing on colouring and flavouring additives. Discuss with the children which coloured sweets they prefer. Do the different colours make any difference to the taste? The children could make their own coloured sweets using icing sugar, egg white and different colourings or flavourings. Which of their sweets do they prefer? Does the colour make a difference to their choice?

Safety

Great care must be taken here because a few children are allergic to additives. It is sensible to write to parents before this activity is carried out to gain their permission for the children to taste the sweets. Stress to children the importance of hygiene in preparing food. They should wash their hands thoroughly before preparing food.

Content

Additives generally fall into the following main groups:

- **Preservatives** are added to food to prevent or slow down the growth of bacteria and moulds on it.
- **Antioxidants** are additives which help stop food decaying through oxidation (the bacteria which cause food to decay need oxygen). Fatty foods are prevented from becoming rancid and fruit is prevented from browning.
- **Emulsifiers** help substances like oil and water mix together.
- **Stabilisers** are often used with emulsifiers to prevent the ingredients separating out again once they are mixed together.
- **Colourings** make food more attractive or restore the original appearance of foods once they have been processed. Both natural colourings (such as beetroot red) and artificial colourings are used.

• **Flavourings and flavour enhancers** are added to foods to restore flavours after processing. Flavour enhancers make the existing flavour of food stronger. The most well known of these is monosodium glutamate (MSG) which occurs naturally in seaweed.

Some people are allergic to certain additives and so it is important that they know which foods contain these substances so that they can avoid them.

Subject links
NC science
Scottish 5–14 science and health education

5. Eco-friendly shopping

Theme
Pollution.

Age range
Five to eleven.

Group size
Pairs or whole class.

What you need
Clipboards, paper, pencils or pens.

What to do
Arrange to visit, as a group or as a class, the local supermarkets to investigate the range of products which the shops promote as being 'environmentally friendly'. Before the visit discuss with the children why they think these products are now being sold. Discuss the problems associated with using products which are not designated as being 'environmentally friendly'. During the visit ask the children to look out for symbols on shelf-strips or products that label products as having an added environmental benefit, for example, organic foods, or foods having had an unfriendly ingredient removed, for example, phosphate. Does the shop have an alternative range of household products such as phosphate-free washing powder, non-chlorine bleach, paper products which have a modified bleaching process, or pump-action aerosol sprays?

Ask the children, in their pairs, to examine the different products. What is it about these products which makes them environmentally friendly? How do the prices of the products compare with the prices of products without these environmentally friendly labels? Encourage the children to ask the supermarket staff about these products – are they as popular as non-environmentally friendly products? What do the labels say are the main environmentally friendly features? The children could collect labels from these

Shops and shopping

products and make a display for the classroom. They could also research the potentially harmful effects of certain components of supermarket products.

Encourage the children to undertake appropriate action as a result of carrying out this activity. These could include asking parents or carers to:
• buy alternatives to aerosols – pump-action sprays, stick or roll-on deodorants, polish from a tin;
• buy recycled paper products;
• choose organically-grown foods.

Content
A range of environmentally friendly products has been introduced by large supermarket chains. Phosphates are used in many detergents as water softeners. These phosphates, if they get into lakes and reservoirs can promote the growth of algae which, when they die, are broken down by tiny animals and fungi. These use up oxygen from the water, causing the water life to die. The algae also cause problems in the water supply by blocking filters.

Some disposable nappies are now being made without using chlorine-bleached cellulose pulp. These bleaches were used to produce a whitening effect of the material which is more aesthetically pleasing but can cause pollution effects in the locality of manufacture. Some bleached products contain dioxins (chemical substances which are harmful to humans), although the traces are so small there is virtually no risk.

Alternatives to aerosols are pump-action sprays which do not use chlorofluorocarbons (CFCs) (see Chapter 1 – Pollution). Other alternatives to aerosol deodorants are roll-on or stick deodorants.

Subject links
NC science and English
Scottish 5–14 science

6. Grow it naturally

Theme
Pollution.

Age range
Seven to eleven.

Group size
Whole class discussion with younger children, class debate with older children.

What you need
A selection of organically and non-organically grown fruit and vegetables, appropriate reference books for research.

What to do
Start with a visit to a local supermarket which stocks organically grown produce. Set the children the task of comparing prices of fruit and vegetables which are organically grown with those which have been sprayed during their growth. Why are the organically grown products more expensive? Do they look any different in appearance?

On returning to the classroom encourage the children to use reference books to research the positive and negative aspects of spraying chemicals on to food and organise a class debate on this topic. Make sure children are aware of the various issues involved such as health reasons, risks associated with the use of chemicals. These risks are pollution of water, hazards to people who are handling the chemicals, and the killing of other species by the pesticide. The advantages of such chemicals are the increase in yields of crops, and the maintenance of quality of crops. Help the children to distinguish between pesticides (chemicals that are aimed at killing pests, for example, weeds, fungi and harmful insects), and inorganic fertilisers (those chemicals applied to crops to improve their growth). A vote could be taken at the end of the debate to see how many children favour organic methods of farming.

Content
This activity can be used to raise the children's awareness of the issues associated with the spraying of pesticides, herbicides and fertilisers on to crops.

Foods are sprayed to minimise loss of the crops to pests, and to ensure a high quality. Organically grown foods have no pesticides, herbicides or inorganic fertilisers sprayed on to them during growth. They are healthier to eat but are more expensive to buy because there can be a significant loss of the crop to pests and disease. There are no easily visible differences between organically and non-organically grown fruit and vegetables.

Subject links
NC science and English
Scottish 5–14 science and health education

7. Shopping for convenience

Theme
Environmental change.

Age range
Nine to eleven.

Group size
Pairs or small groups.

What you need
Maps of the local area, clipboards, paper, pencils, rulers.

What to do
Encourage the children to discuss the advantages and disadvantages of shopping at supermarkets compared to corner shops which stay open till late or shops at petrol stations. Issues such as convenient location, range of products, ease of parking, time wasted waiting in long queues as opposed to more friendly, one-to-one service should be raised.

The children could mark on a map of the local area sites where supermarkets and convenience stores are located. Which is the most common type of shop? The

Shops and shopping

children could try to find out when new supermarkets were built, either from their own knowledge or by asking parents, relations and friends who live locally. How close are their homes to these shops? Which shops are more convenient? The children could carry out a survey to compare the use of a supermarket to the use of a small corner shop in the same area. They should ask why customers choose to visit one particular shop in preference to another. They could compare product prices and range of products in the two types of shop.

Further activity
A recent change in shopping habits has been consequent upon shops opening on Sundays. Discuss with the children whether they have been shopping on Sunday. They could carry out a class survey to see how many parents, friends and relatives now shop on Sundays in preference to weekdays. Remember, if necessary, to be sensitive to the religious aspect of this issue.

Content
Whereas in the past more shopping was done in small specialised shops such as the greengrocer, the butcher or the baker, today supermarkets cater for the majority of our shopping needs. Some smaller shops, however, are being used as 'convenience' stories for 'top-up' shopping and therefore stay open for longer hours. People also use shops at petrol stations for 'top-up' shopping and for buying goods such as snacks and drinks.

There has been an increase lately in the use of these smaller shops for convenience shopping. As people's hours of work have become more flexible, it is often easier to stop off at the local small shop on the way home either to buy food and household goods which have been forgotten in the big supermarket shopping expedition, or to save time which is wasted queuing at check-outs. The car driver has to buy petrol on a regular basis and the shop at the petrol station provides a range of goods which are available late in the evening.

Often large supermarkets are built out of town centres and the smaller local shop is much closer to home and thus more convenient to use. The environment of the large supermarket does not encourage social contact whereas the smaller convenience store encourages more of a community spirit.

Subject links
NC geography and English
Scottish 5–14 social subjects

8. Green supermarkets – a whole investigation

Theme
Conservation; Pollution; Environmental change.

Age range
Seven to eleven.

Group size
Small groups or whole class.

What you need
Paper, pens, clipboards, a tape-recorder, a camera (optional).

Planning and preparation

This activity focuses on a whole investigation of environmental aspects of supermarkets. The children will examine the ways in which such shops take action to care positively for the environment and they will carry out an environmental audit. This investigation may require several visits to the chosen supermarket. Initially, a visit by the whole class could be undertaken and then small groups could carry out different aspects of the audit in follow-up visits. Alternatively, a comparison of two supermarkets may be undertaken, possibly one nearer the town centre and one located on the outskirts of the town.

Initially the supermarket managers should be contacted and permission gained for the children to carry out the survey. Try to arrange for the children to have the opportunity to talk to both supermarket staff and to customers.

Discuss with the class the possible actions which a supermarket chain could take to care for the environment. Raise the issue of whose responsibility it is to solve environmental problems and take positive steps to conserve resources and to improve the environment. Encourage the children to recognise that we all play a part in improving the environment, and it is not just large industries who should take an environmental responsibility.

The first visit to the supermarket will raise the children's awareness of aspects which they will want to explore in more depth. On returning to the classroom, identify with the children these aspects and divide the class into groups to examine each of these issues more closely. The children should decide how they are going to proceed. Will they need to interview customers? If so, what questions will they wish to ask? Interviews/questionnaires should be designed in advance. How will they record answers to the questions? Is tape-recording the interview a good idea? – some people might not feel relaxed if their answers to questions are taped. Encourage the children to design tables and charts on which to record data to be collected on visits. They may wish to appoint one of their group as the official photographer (permission must first be sought from the supermarket manager if the children intend to interview customers and make a photographic record).

Investigating

Once the practical details are planned, the programme of visits should be undertaken. Encourage the children to include the following issues in their investigation:

The external environment

The children could sketch a map of the external environment of the supermarket. This will include the lay-out of the car park. Are there enough car-parking spaces for the numbers of customers using the store? Are there designated spaces for disabled people? Is the car park clean and free from litter? The children could locate the sites where there are litter bins – are there enough? Has

Shops and shopping

the opportunity been taken to plant trees, shrubs and other vegetation to improve the appearance of the car park and the store? Are pedestrians routed away from areas where car exhaust fumes would be most prevalent? Is planting used to absorb harmful fumes and protect people? Does the store have a policy whereby delivery vehicle drivers are prevented from leaving their engines running? Is there a petrol station, and if so, does it stock unleaded petrol? The children could carry out a survey to compare numbers of customers buying leaded and unleaded petrol.

The building
Does the building itself look attractive – does it fit in with surrounding buildings? Do the architectural features have a particular character? Is the heat extracted by refrigeration used to heat the shopping area?

The trolleys
Does the store manage to control the use of trolleys, for example through a deposit system? Have the children seen trolleys from the supermarket away from the site itself?

Products sold
Does the supermarket stock organically grown foods or products which have an 'unfriendly' ingredient removed, for example, phosphate-free detergents? Does the store make a positive effort to reduce excess packaging on products? What sort of packaging is it? Can the packaging materials be recycled? Do customers prefer to buy products in concentrated form or in refill packs? How many customers prefer to buy products made from recycled paper?

Recycling
The children could find out whether the supermarket has a recycling policy. What does it do with all the cardboard boxes in which the food arrives at the store? Does the store provide biodegradable plastic bags or does it encourage customers to bring their own bags or boxes to the store? Are bottle, paper and can banks provided in the car park? If so, how many customers use these daily – a survey could be carried out to answer these questions.

Recording and communicating
The results of the investigation should be analysed by the children. Histograms, graphs and pie charts can be drawn to show results of surveys. Posters can be made to illustrate the store's environmental policy. A large map of the car park and external environment of the supermarket could be displayed (can the manager provide plans to assist in this?) Recommendations for the future could also be made. The work could be presented as a class assembly to which members of the supermarket staff and parents could be invited.

Subject links
NC science, geography, mathematics and English
Scottish 5–14 science and social subjects

CHAPTER 6
Streets and transport

The focus for this work would be a visit to a local street, preferably in a local town or city. Further visits might be necessary depending on the nature, breadth and depth of the study. A large village might be suitable depending on its amenities.

All children will be familiar with the bustle of a street but few of them will have stopped to consider the structure and nature of the street, the many activities taking place, the numerous people carrying out their occupations, far less the environmental issues which the street context raises. It is important that all the activities in the street are suitably supervised and that the children remain on the pavement at all times and are aware of the dangers of traffic in a busy street.

The three main environmental themes, Conservation, Environmental change and Pollution, will all be covered in these activities.

Depending on the location and type of street, the number and type of vehicles will vary. Children could carry out a survey of the vehicles in the street and possibly the people and attempt to answer such questions as, 'What is each vehicle carrying?' and 'What are the people doing?' Vehicles help us move about and bring food to the shops in the street but consume energy and pollute the environment. This might lead to older children considering the merits and disadvantages of private and public transport. Any visit to a busy street is accompanied by a substantial amount of noise and sounds, some of which are 'safe' sounds (for example, a pedestrian crossing signal) while others indicate potential danger (for example, a car reversing). As well as noise pollution, the children could survey the litter which is produced by the bustle of activities on the street. Away from the roads, the street will be fronted by a range of buildings some of which will house the people using the street and some of which will be shops, serving the community and receiving the goods brought in by lorries and vans. Children could be encouraged to distinguish old and new buildings, to indicate their preferences and to be introduced to the role of planners and conservationists in the aesthetic nature of the street. Towns and streets need to be planned to the smallest detail. Children may consider small details such as the positioning and number of litter bins, and progress to studying larger issues such as the course of rain water from the moment it hits the roofs, pavements and roads, disappears out of sight into drains and then joins streams and rivers, thus preventing the formation of large puddles and floods.

Within the nature and life of the street the three recurrent themes are clearly visible but interwoven. One only has to venture out into the street and be confronted by a wealth of environmental issues.

Streets and transport

BACKGROUND

Pollution
- Traffic noise
- Safe and dangerous sounds
- Litter (types)
- Organically grown foods
- Bottle banks
- Unleaded and leaded petrol
- CFCs

STREETS AND TRANSPORT

Environmental change
- Litter bins
- Drains and drainage
- Bottle banks
- Street design and planning
- Safety and pedestrian crossings
- Safety and speed limits

Conservation
- Bottle banks
- Buildings old and new
- The street now and in the past
- Energy outlets
- Energy waste
- Public and private transport

	Progression in teaching and learning	
Theme	**Details of activity and activity number**	
	Key Stage 1 (P1–3)	Key Stage 2 (P4–7)
Conservation	Identifying old and new buildings (4) Identifying energy sources (5) How environmentally friendly is our street? – A whole investigation (10)	Comparing old and new maps of the street (8) Is good use made of energy? – role of public transport (9)
Environmental change	Provision of litter bins (2) How environmentally friendly is our street? – A whole investigation (10)	Getting rid of water from the street to prevent floods (7) Comparing old and new maps of the street (8)
Pollution	Vehicle survey (1) Types of litter pollution (2) Safe and dangerous sounds (3) How environmentally friendly is our street? – A whole investigation (10)	What makes the most noise pollution? (6) Is good use made of energy? – role of public transport (9)

ACTIVITIES

1. Vehicle survey: what passes?

Theme
Pollution.

Age range
Five to seven.

Group size
Whole class or half class divided into small groups.

What you need
Chalkboard or large piece of paper, clipboard, paper, pencil.

What to do
Prior to the visit, talk to the children about the types of traffic they might find on the street. These could be listed on the chalkboard or on a large piece of paper. Help them to design a recording chart for their vehicle survey. They could draw pictures of the vehicles they think they might see prior to the visit, with drawings and names down the left-hand side and a space to tick or write comments down the right-hand side. There should be some space left at the bottom of the sheet to fill in vehicles spotted in the survey but not anticipated beforehand.

Assemble the children on the street and tell them to record the numbers of the different types of vehicles they see travelling down the street on their sheet by placing a tick against the appropriate form of transport. Types of transport spotted that are not already on the sheet could be added to the bottom or a separate note taken on the back of the sheet. If the street is busy and sufficient parental help is available, the class could be divided so that half records the traffic in one direction, while the other half records the traffic in the opposite direction.

Back in the classroom the children could add up the total numbers of each type of vehicle observed. Bar graphs could then be produced. The results could be discussed and questions raised such as those below:
- Which type of vehicle was seen the most?
- Which type of vehicle was seen the least?
- Why might this be?
- Why were there few or many lorries?
- Why were there few or many tractors?
- Was there a difference between the number of vehicles travelling up and down the street?
- Which types of vehicles use petrol and diesel and produce pollution?
- Which types of vehicles do not use petrol and diesel and do not produce pollution?

Further activity
A survey of people on the street could be undertaken to find out what they are doing, for example, shopping, involved with work, out for a walk and so on.

Alternatively, the number of pedestrians could be surveyed. How many have dogs? How many have prams? How many have children?

Content
The discussion could focus on the nature of the journeys being made. Some people are probably going shopping while others are driving their car to work. Lorries are transporting food and materials to where they are needed. Tractors are being used to take livestock to

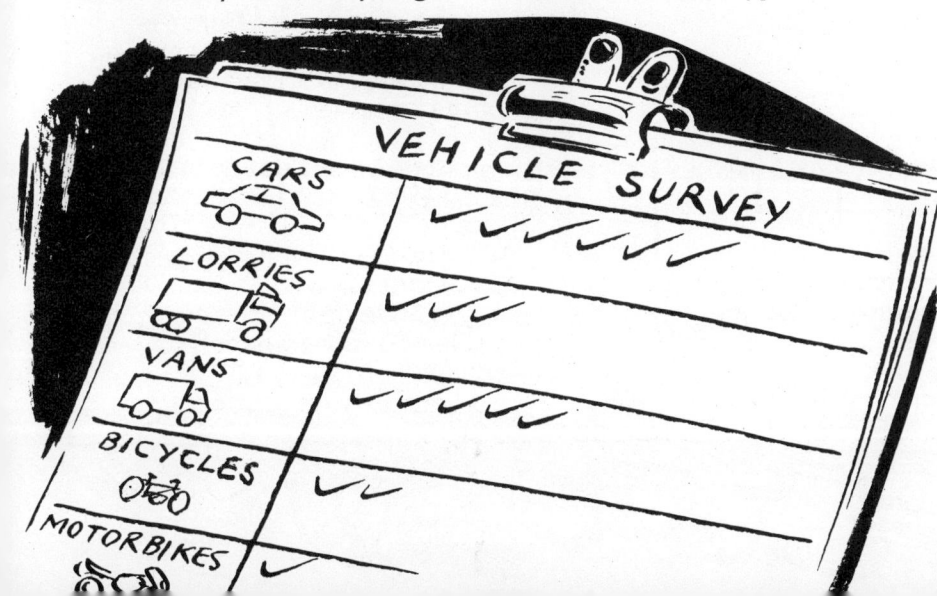

market or food to the animals. The postwoman is delivering letters on her bicycle. Vehicles such as cars and lorries use fuel and produce pollution, while vehicles such as bicycles do not. Do the children think that the vehicle use they see is justified?

Subject links
NC geography
Scottish 5–14 social subjects

2. Litter, litter everywhere?

Theme
Pollution; Environmental change.

Age range
Five to seven.

Group size
Whole or half class.

What you need
Clipboards, simple outline maps of the street, one for each child, paper, pen or pencil.

What to do
Once in the street, ask the children to mark on their maps the position of the litter bins. Get them to carry out a safe litter search identifying the places where litter has been dropped. They might use a colour code to identify the type of litter e.g. crisp packets, cigarette ends, cans and ring pulls, tissues, sweet papers etc. and could consider how they would indicate the amount of litter that they find, for example by putting a red dot on their map for every crisp packet they find. When they have finished their litter survey ask them the following questions:
• What types of litter were found?
• Where was the most litter found?
• Are more litter bins needed?
• Should they be fitted with lids?
• Should the litter bins be relocated?
• Why do people drop litter so close to litter bins?
• Are separate bins provided for cigarettes?
• Is it safe to put lighted cigarette ends into litter bins?
• What observations might they like to pass on to the local community or Council?

Further activity
Back in the classroom, ask the children to think what the street might have looked like one hundred years ago, before the motorcar was invented. Would there have been crisp packets and tin cans in the street? What types of 'litter' might have been in their place (horse droppings, human effluent)?

Safety
It is important that this activity is suitably supervised and that children stay on the pavement at all times.

Content
Humans and their activities produce a wide variety and a great deal of waste. It is each individual's responsibility not to drop litter but to take it home with them or place it in the litter bins provided. Councils have a responsibility to provide litter bins in streets and other public places. It might be considered dangerous to put a lighted cigarette in a litter bin, but are there any alternatives? It is an offence to drop litter and a fine might result if the perpetrator is caught.

Subject links
NC science, history
Scottish 5–14 technology, health education, social subjects

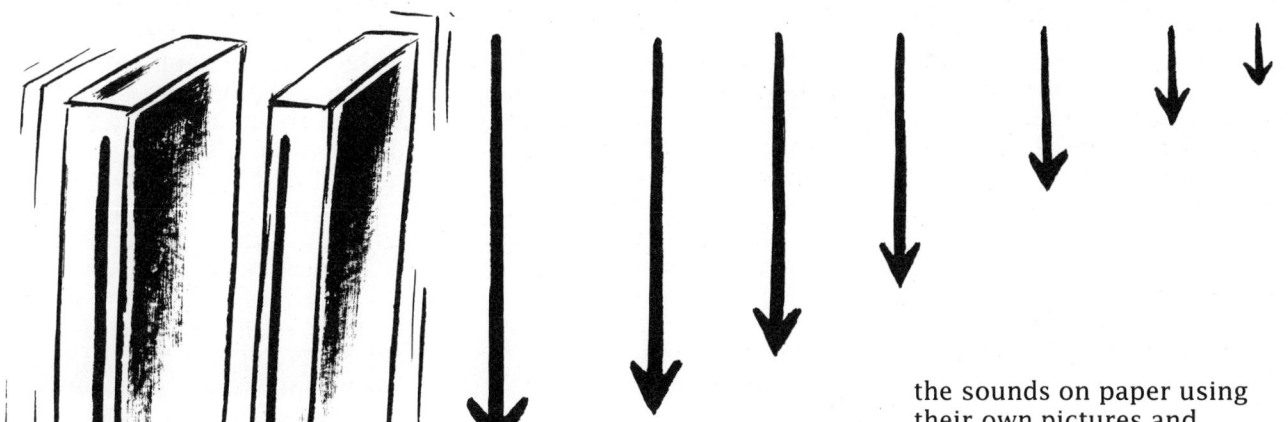

3. Safe and dangerous sounds in the street

Theme
Pollution.

Age range
Five to seven.

Group size
Whole class or half class in the street; small groups back in the classroom.

What you need
Clipboard, pencil, paper, cassette recorder(s), blank tape(s), percussion instruments.

What to do
Once in the street explain to the children that they are going on a 'sounds walk' and that they will need to be quiet and listen carefully to the sounds and noises around them. Divide the class into smaller groups if sufficient supervision and tape cassettes are available. The sounds that they identify will be recorded on the cassette recorder. However, ask the children to make a note of the sounds they hear as well, either in writing or pictures, or both, and number them so that they can make reference to them back in school.

Back in school, reinforce the children's findings by listening to the tape recording the children made. Discuss the sounds from the point of view of safety, identifying the 'safe' sounds such as people talking, music playing and the sound of a pedestrian crossing telling people that it is safe to cross. Also discuss those sounds that might mean danger, such as a car engine getting louder (and therefore closer), the sound of a police car siren, or the sounds of building work.

Using the human voice and a variety of percussion instruments, tuned and untuned, ask the children, working individually within their groups, to make their own versions of the street sounds. Ask them to 'record' the sounds on paper using their own pictures and symbols as indicated above. This shows a Year 2 child's interpretation of music blocks imitating footsteps in the street becoming quieter as the arrows get shorter. Each symbol can represent a different sound and hence instrument and the noise level might be represented by the size of the symbol.

When each child within the group has completed this, ask the children to produce their street symphony on a long strip of paper, by combining the music from their individual contributions. They may then perform their composition in front of the rest of the class or other classes.

Further activity
The activity above could be reinforced by the Oxford Primary Music Tape (Oxford Universtiy Press) which includes a number of familiar sounds. Alternatively, the cassettes prepared by the children could be played a few days after the 'sound walk' and the children have to attempt to identify the sounds. Encourage the children to make a sound tape in the school environment or in the home environment. Can the other children identify the sounds? Which ones did they have difficulty with?

Content
The children have experienced a range of sounds in the street environment and will be aware of their causes and uses. They will have investigated making sounds in a variety of ways and across a range from soft to loud. They should be encouraged to appreciate that while some sounds are 'dangerous' sounds (for example, a car revving), other sounds are relatively 'safe' (for example, sound on a pedestrian crossing indicating when it is safe to cross). Some loud noises can be annoying and frightening, for example, a motorbike accelerating.

Subject links
NC science, music
Scottish 5–14 science and health education

4. Is it old or is it new?

Theme
Conservation.

Age range
Five to seven.

Group size
Small groups in the classroom; whole class or half class out in the street.

What you need
Photographs of local buildings and houses of different ages (for example, modern, Victorian, Georgian, Elizabethan), clipboards, paper, pencils, card and glue.

What to do
In the classroom, show the children the photographs of the houses and other buildings and discuss with them their similarities and differences. Which is the oldest? Which is the most modern? Introduce appropriate vocabulary such as new or modern and old. Working in groups, ask the children to discuss and compare the photographs of the houses with their own houses. How are they alike? How are they different?

Help the children to produce a time-line of the photographs and relate this to their experiences such as, 'built since they were born' or 'built before granny was born' and so on.

Out in the street, ask the children to identify whether buildings are 'new', 'old' or 'very old'. Ask them to sketch a new and an old building and then to say why they think it is old or new.

Further activity
Back in the classroom the children could make a model of one of the houses or other buildings. With help they could date it and draw attention to important architectural features of the building.

Content
Encourage the children to be aware of the technological and historical significance of the changes in the design and construction of buildings. New materials such as plastics and absence of chimneys due to central heating are indicative of modern houses. Brick replacing local stone (in a comparison of two areas, for example) indicates the change to new materials (or that local resources of materials have been depleted) and improved transportation from other localities.

Changes in the design of houses occur as people's views and preferences alter.

Emphasise that it is possible to date buildings by their design and the materials from which they are constructed.

Subject links
NC history, art and technology
Scottish 5–14 social subjects and technology

5. Lots of energy

Theme
Conservation.

Age range
Five to seven.

Group size
Whole or half class.

What you need
Clipboards, paper, pen or pencil, photocopiable page 174, reference books on energy.

What to do
Talk to the children about objects in the classroom and in their homes which require 'energy' to work. How does a portable computer game work? How can they see at home at night? The discussion could be broadened to include such questions as, how do they travel to school or to the nearest town?

Provide each child with photocopiable page 174, then take the children into the street. Ask them to identify as many objects and vehicles as possible which are using energy. The children should tick those objects and vehicles already drawn on the sheet and add pictures of any others they find.

Back in the classroom ask the children to divide these objects into sets on the basis of the type of energy which they use, such as mains electricity, batteries or fuels. Talk to the children about where this energy comes from. Explain that energy sources such as petrol (which is produced from oil) and mains electricity (which is produced mainly from gas and coal) are expensive, are in short supply and should be used carefully. The children should consult the reference books and choose one type of energy and show, with the aid of a simple flow chart, where/how it begins and then ends up in its final form.

Further activity
Ask the children to suggest why there are so many bright lights in the shops? Are they all needed? Who thinks they are needed? Develop this idea by asking the children how they may save energy in school and at home.

Content
In the street there will be numerous examples of energy being used such as fuel (petrol and diesel) in vehicles; electricity to light shop windows and signs; coal, oil, gas or electricity to provide heating. Mains electricity is generated from coal, gas and nuclear fuel in power stations. These fuels are burned to heat water which produces steam which in turn powers a generator which generates the electricity. The energy in these fuels is thus changed into the energy present in electricity. In the shops the children might see items which have batteries as their energy source. Emphasise that it is important that energy is not wasted as it is expensive and in short supply.

Subject links
NC science
Scottish 5–14 science and technology

6. What makes the most noise?

Theme
Pollution.

Age range
Seven to eleven.

Group size
Whole class or half class.

What you need
Clipboard, paper, pen, if possible a sound level (decibel) meter.

What to do
Talk to the children about sounds and noise. What is a sound and what is a noise? Is one person's pleasant sound, another person's unpleasant noise? References could be made to types of music or children playing near houses. Introduce the idea of noise pollution and elicit examples from the children.

Ask the children to consider the street they are studying and to suggest examples of possible sounds and noises that they might hear. Once on the street, ask the children to write down all the sounds/ noises that they hear as they walk up and down the street. Suggest that they might like to devise and define a scale to estimate the volume of the sound/noise. This might be indicated by a numerical scale, for example, 1–5 or by abbreviations, for example VN – very noisy; N – noisy; FL – fairly loud; Q – quiet; VQ – very quiet. How could they make this a fair test? For example, suggest that they would need to be the same distance from the sound, they would need to face it and the same person would need to make the estimation. They might also be encouraged to classify the types of sounds that they hear. A table such as the one below might be constructed:

Sound/noise	Type of sound/noise	Noise level
Lorry	Vehicle	N
People talking	Human	VQ
Digging up the road	Machines/tools	VN
Pedestrian crossing	Machine	Q

Alternatively, it might be possible to gain more quantitative results by using a sound level meter (decibel meter), which could be borrowed from a local secondary school.

Further activity
The children could similarly investigate sounds in their school environment or a more rural environment and make contrasts and comparisons.

Content
The children will be introduced to the concept of noise pollution and the obtrusive nature of some sounds in the environment and will look for specific examples in a street environment. Concepts such as loudness and pitch of sounds should be emphasised and this should lead the children to the question of acceptable and unacceptable levels of noise.

Subject links
NC science
Scottish 5–14 science and health education

7. Where does the rainfall go?

Theme
Environmental change.

Age range
Seven to eleven.

Group size
Whole class or half class.

What you need
Clipboards, paper, pencils.

What to do
Prior to the visit, encourage the children to observe what

Water vapour cools down and forms clouds

Water evaporates and rises

Rivers take the water back to the sea

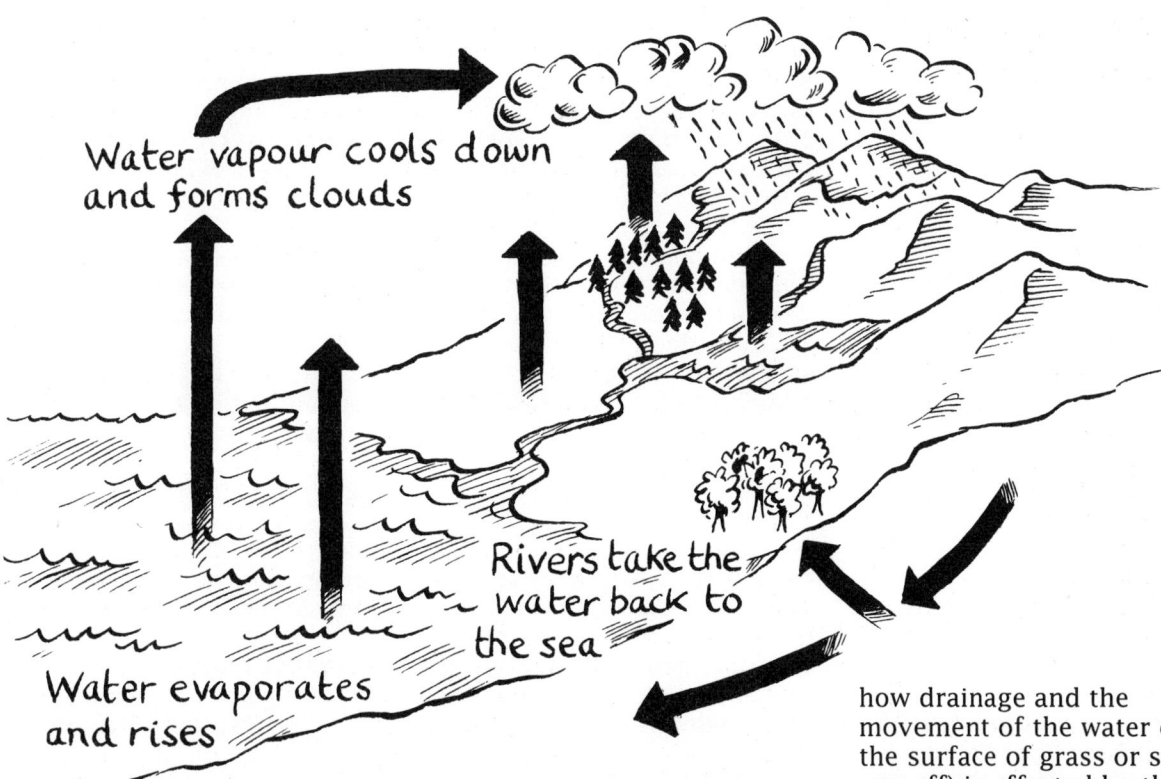

happens to the rainfall around their school or at their home. Where does it go after it falls on the roof? Where does it go after it falls on the road, lawn or soil? Ask the children to consider where the rain goes to when it falls on the street and the buildings on the street.

When the children are assembled on the street ask them to observe the buildings and roads, and pose the question, 'Where does the water go to?' Ensure that they identify the guttering, downspouts and the drains they lead in to, on and around the buildings. Switch their attention to the roads and to the drains which are fed from water in the gutters. Ask them to sketch a picture of the street showing the path taken by the rain after it has fallen on the buildings and roads.

When the children are back in the classroom they could be asked to consider where the water goes to *after* it passes down the house and street drains. Introduce the ideas of culverts leading into streams and sewers, leading to sewage works and finally into rivers. Also ask the children what happens to the rain which falls on the hills, fields, lawns and soil. Consolidate the notion of drainage into small streams eventually, and later into rivers which flow into seas.

Using these ideas the children could add a rural scene to their urban scene to complete their understanding of the concept of rainfall and drainage.

Further activity
Children should investigate the effects of water (drainage) on different surfaces such as grass, sand, soil and tarmac. They could also investigate how drainage and the movement of the water over the surface of grass or soil (the run-off) is affected by the angle of the slope. This can be carried out by using the same apparatus as in activity 6, Chapter 7.

Content
The children should be able to describe what happens to rainwater when it falls on buildings and the land and trace its route, with assistance, to streams and rivers via the drains. Depending on the age and ability of the children, the elements of the water cycle could be introduced, though many children will find the physical processes of the cycle (precipitation, evaporation, condensation) difficult. These concepts can be reinforced by using a simple diagram of the cycle (see above).

Subject links
NC science, geography and technology
Scottish 5–14 science, social subjects

Streets and transport

8. Going back in time on the street

Theme
Environmental change; Conservation.

Age range
Seven to eleven.

Group size
Small groups.

What you need
Two large-scale maps of the local street and surrounds which is being studied, one from the past and one from the present preferably 50 to 100 years apart, paper, pencils or pens, chalkboard and chalk or large piece of paper, an illustrated history of the area to supplement the information on the maps (optional), reference books on the period of the older map.

What to do
Ask the children to study the maps carefully in their groups, in turns, and to document any changes between the past and present maps. When they have done this, produce a class list on the chalkboard or on a large piece of paper.

Discuss with the children the likely reasons for the changes between the two maps. For example:
• Why has the number of houses increased or decreased?
• Why is there no railway station on the recent map?
• Why are there new streets on the more recent map?
• Why was there no car park on the old map?
• Why has the canal been breached by roads?

As an alternative, if there is no up-to-date map of the street, the children could attempt to produce their own, discussing the features that would have to be included.

Further activity
Ask the children to imagine what life would have been like at the time of the old map. What would the people be wearing? What would be the chief form of transport? What sounds and smells might be noticed if one was standing in the street? What games might the children be playing in the street? Why might it be safe to play in the street? They should refer to reference books to see how accurate they were.

Content
Depending on the circumstances, ensure that issues such as population migration, improvement in transportation, movement of shops out of city centres and pedestrianisation etc. are raised and discussed.

Subject links
NC geography and history
Scottish 5–14 social subjects

9. Energy usage: should we use public or private transport?

Theme
Conservation; Pollution.

Age range
Seven to eleven.

Group size
Whole or half class.

What you need
Clipboards, paper, pencils or pens.

What to do
This activity offers children the opportunity to compare the number of people travelling in a unit of public transport, for example a bus, with the number travelling in a unit of private transport, for example a car. It enables the children to compare the approximate energy usage of each form of transport and decide for themselves about energy wastage in this context. The public should be interviewed to ascertain which form of transport they use and what they see as the advantages and disadvantages of it.

Arrange to visit the street at a time when some form of public transport is expected. Tell the children, prior to the visit to the street, that they are going to carry out a census on the type of vehicles travelling down the street in one or both directions. Tell them that they are also going to record the number of people travelling in each vehicle, though point out that this could be difficult in a busy street with fast-moving vehicles, so an estimate might need to be made. Before they visit the street ask them to design a table on which to record their findings. Encourage the children to think about the types of transport they are likely to see. Will they all be motorised? In addition, encourage the children to interview some of the travellers from both public and private transport asking them how they have travelled and why they have travelled in the way they did. (This could be carried out at a bus stop or a car park). What are the advantages of using this form of transport?

Visit the street and tell the children to record the data on the tables which they have produced and carry out the interviews.

Back in school collate the findings and find out how many of each vehicle type were observed. What is the average number of people in each vehicle type?

Talk to the children about public and private transport and ask them in their groups to list from their interviews and their own experience, the pros and cons of both. Which do they think is more cost effective in terms of energy usage and why? Which is more convenient? Which do they think produces less pollution per passenger journey? When is private transport slower than public transport? What other problems are associated with private transport in towns and cities?

Further activity
Ask the children to think about ways of cutting down their use of car travel. Would it be safe to walk to the local shops rather than asking parents or guardians to take them in the car? Would it be healthier for them?

Content
In some rural areas the number of passengers carried by public transport may be low. However, in most cases public transport is more energy efficient and causes less pollution per passenger journey, as more passengers are carried per vehicle despite the lower mileage per gallon of buses and trains. However, private transport is often more convenient though parking in urban areas may be problematic, expensive and there is always the risk of car crime. Some people prefer to walk or travel by bicycle thus using little or none of the world's consumable energy resources and causing little or no pollution.

Subject links
NC science
Scottish 5–14 science, technology and health education

10. How environmentally friendly is our street? – A whole investigation

Theme
Conservation; Environmental change; Pollution.

Age range
Five to eleven.

Group size
Whole class or half class divided into groups.

What you need
Clipboards, paper, pencils or pens, copies of the local street plan if available.

Planning and preparation
This investigation may involve a number of visits to the street either as a whole class, half of the class or in groups depending on staff and parental supervision. It would be advisable to inform certain traders and officials of the intended visit, so that they may be made aware of it and prepare for it so that maximum benefit may be obtained. For example, the local greengrocer could be informed that you want him/her to show the children those 'organic' products which have been grown without the aid of chemicals.

Discuss with the children how the architects and planners who design the street, and the shopkeepers who trade in the street can make it a more environmentally friendly place to visit. Explain that the term 'environmentally friendly' means trying to improve the environment or not harming it. List the key issues which the children raise in the discussion. People contacted prior to the visit might depend on the responses from the children, but it should be possible to anticipate the major points as listed later.

Discuss with the children the issue that while local government planners and local traders have responsibilities to protect, maintain and improve the environment, each and every person can influence how 'environmentally friendly' a street becomes by their actions (not dropping litter, keeping their surroundings tidy and well kept) and what they purchase (insisting that shops sell free range eggs and organic products). Once this background discussion has taken place and the contacts have been made, the visit may proceed. The children will be documenting their findings by drawing pictures and making notes, using a copy of a street plan if available. These findings will be shared with the whole class on return to the classroom. The children should have included the following aspects as the key issues to investigate.

The children could find out whether there is a speed limit imposed in the street thus slowing down the speed of traffic. This might have to be found out indirectly if the street is long and walking the distance to speed limit signs is too far. If there is no speed limit do the children think there should be one? Who could this be suggested to? Where would it start and end? Whether or not there is a speed limit, ask the children if the street is easy to cross. Is there a pedestrian crossing on the street? Where is it positioned – in the middle of the street or at a busy access point? If a pedestrian crossing is absent, do the children think there should be one and where should it be positioned? Ask the children whether now they think that the street is a safe, environmentally friendly street.

The car park
The children could sketch a map of the position of the car park in relation to the street. Is the car park convenient for the street? Are there reserved places for disabled persons? Is access for cars and pedestrians easy and safe? Are there sufficient litter bins in the car park? Is the car park concealed by trees to make the area look more attractive and to reduce noise? If there are, they could add tree symbols to their sketch map. Ask the children whether now they think that the car park is a safe, environmentally friendly place.

The buildings
Do the children find the buildings in the street pleasing to look at? Which ones do they like and dislike? Do any new buildings fit in with the architectural design of other, older buildings on the street? Is access to the buildings easy and convenient for older people, disabled people or for those with prams? Do the children think that the street has pleasant, environmentally friendly buildings?

The bottle bank
The children could investigate the provision of recycling facilities near the street and then report their findings later to the rest of the class. Is there a bottle bank in the car park or near one of the local shops? Are many people using it? Why do they use it? How many of the children's parents use the bottle bank? What happens to glass bottles if they are not recycled? Are any other items recycled at the same place, for example, tin cans, paper. Is the street environmentally

friendly on recycling waste materials?

Litter bins
The children could investigate the provision and location of litter bins on the street. Is the street dirty? Are the bins full? Are there enough litter bins? Where are they located? Are they in appropriate places? How often are they emptied? Should more bins be provided? Where would they locate them? How often is the street cleaned? Ask the children if they think that the street is an environmentally friendly place regarding litter and litter bins.

The petrol station
Visit a nearby petrol station and explain to the children that lead in petrol pollutes the atmosphere and grass verges and can affect health. How many pumps sell unleaded petrol and how many pumps sell leaded or diesel? How many people fill up with unleaded petrol and how many do not within a given period? Ask some of the people why they are using or not using unleaded petrol. Is the petrol station an environmentally friendly place? Are all its customers being environmentally friendly?

The shops
Talk to the children about food that has been grown using fertilisers and pesticides and food which has been grown organically using manure and with no potentially harmful chemicals. Visit a greengrocer's shop and ask the shopkeeper does s/he sell organically grown food? Why does s/he sell or not sell it? Is it more expensive? Do people ask for it to be provided? Ask the children whether they think that the greengrocer's shop is trying to be 'friendly' to the environment.

Visit a chemist or grocers shop and look for the presence of CFCs (see Chapter 1, page 13) in hairsprays and other aerosol products. Are alternative products stocked so that the customer has a choice? Ask the children whether they think the shop is trying to be 'friendly' to the environment.

Visit a shop which sells matches. Are some makes of matches made from wood from sustainable forests (see Chapter 2, page 24)? If not, ask the shopkeeper why s/he does not stock such matches. Are the makes of the matches 'friendly' to the environment?

Recording and communicating the findings
Back in the classroom the results of the investigation may be considered further by the children, in groups. On a large map of the street they could indicate by pictures and/or writing those parts of the street that were 'friendly' to people and the environment and those parts that were 'unfriendly'. They could also include their results and conclusions next to each context which they have considered, for example, shops, bottle bank, petrol station, speed limit and so on. The children's ideas to improve the environment could also be included.

The final discussion should include the idea that most improvements to the environment cost money and that many people do not want to pay more unless they think it is harming them a great deal.

Subject links
NC English, mathematics, science, geography and history
Scottish 5–14 science, social subjects, technology and health education

CHAPTER 7

Farms

In approximately 3000 BC during the new Stone Age, some 5000 years after the last ice age, people in Britain ceased being wandering hunters and became growers for the first time. These changes were introduced long after Britain had become an island, by immigrants from the Continent who brought with them cattle, sheep and grain. They obviously needed fields for their animals and crops, and therefore cleared parts of the forest using fire and stone axes. Thus farming began on these islands.

Forest clearance has continued to this day and was accelerated when new industries required wood and charcoal to burn in furnaces, prior to the mining of coal on a large scale. Today, some three quarters of the land is used for farmland, and areas of extensive woodland are limited.

Because so much of the countryside is farmland, management and care of the environment are critical to the survival of wildlife. Further stress on the countryside was brought about by the need for Great Britain to produce more of its own food in order to become more self-sufficient, particularly after the Second World War and with the rise in population after the war. The situation has been further complicated by entry into the European Union and compliance with the Common Agricultural Policy. Subsidies awarded per hectare planted and other policies have led to more intensive farming, resulting in hedges being removed, more chemical fertilisers being used to increase yields and herbicides and insecticides being applied to weeds and rough areas to enlarge the area for crops and to reduce pests. At the same time marsh areas have been drained, heath and woodland areas destroyed and rough grasslands removed and replaced by arable land or pasture. While such practices have undoubtedly led to cheaper food and prosperity in the farming industry, wildlife has suffered as a consequence.

Children might view a farm from the point of view of its cuddly animals such as calves and lambs, its scary animals such as bulls, boars and geese, the impressive nature of machinery, and the wonder of its produce such as large, brown free-range eggs. While many children will not be familiar with the workings of a farm, particularly if they live in an urban environment, even fewer will be aware of the complex environmental issues with which the farmer is faced on a regular basis. It is important that the tension between farm productivity and environmental care is considered as a difficult issue with no easy solutions. A totally 'green' farm would probably result in less food being produced which would in turn make the produce more expensive to buy. However, there would be great benefits to wildlife. As more organically grown produce reaches the supermarkets, the consumer may at last have a real choice.

This chapter introduces children to the difficult environmental issues facing farmers as they manage an industry upon which both ourselves and wildlife are often dependent. It is important that teachers approach these issues carefully with skill and tact and with as much factual knowledge at their disposal as possible.

BACKGROUND

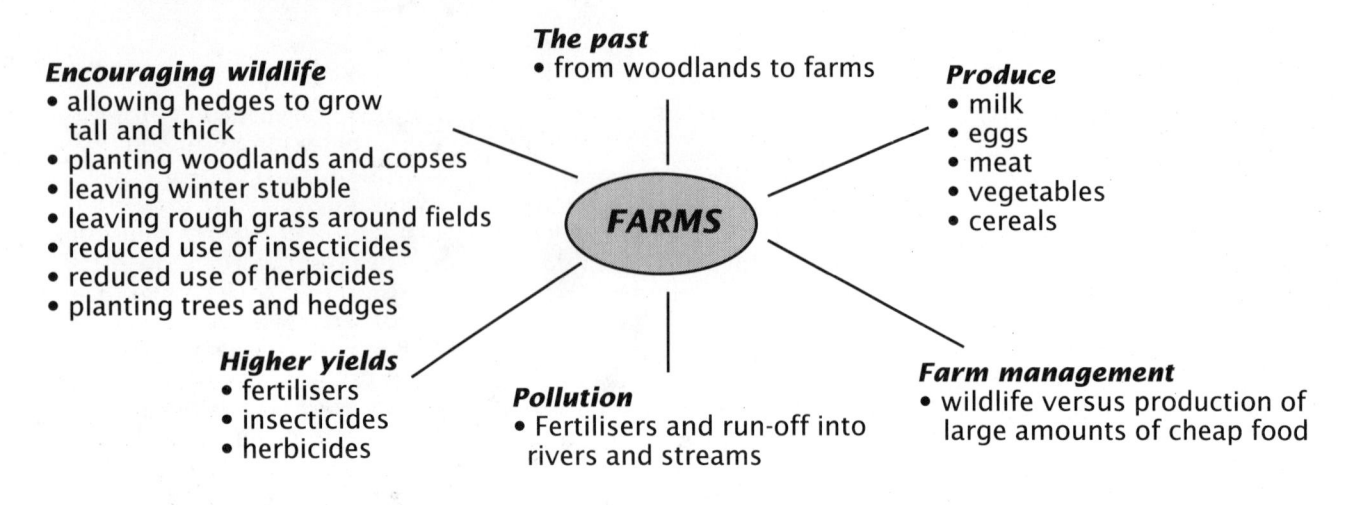

The past
- from woodlands to farms

Encouraging wildlife
- allowing hedges to grow tall and thick
- planting woodlands and copses
- leaving winter stubble
- leaving rough grass around fields
- reduced use of insecticides
- reduced use of herbicides
- planting trees and hedges

Produce
- milk
- eggs
- meat
- vegetables
- cereals

FARMS

Higher yields
- fertilisers
- insecticides
- herbicides

Pollution
- Fertilisers and run-off into rivers and streams

Farm management
- wildlife versus production of large amounts of cheap food

Progression in teaching and learning		
Theme	**Details of activity and activity number**	
	Key Stage 1 (P1–3)	Key Stage 2 (P4–7)
Conservation		Barn owls (7) Farm management (8)
	Coppices and woods (3) Hedges and wildlife (4) How environmentally friendly is the farm? – A whole investigation (9)	
Environmental change	Farm produce (1)	Farm management (8)
	Farming in the past (2) Hedges and wildlife (4) How environmentally friendly is the farm? – A whole investigation (9)	
Plants, animals and their habitats	Hedges and wildlife (4)	Barn owls (7)
	How environmentally friendly is the farm? – A whole investigation (9)	
Pollution		Fertilisers and productivity (5) Fertilisers in the streams and rivers (6)
	How environmentally friendly is the farm? – A whole investigation (9)	

84   Chapter 7

ACTIVITIES

1. What does the farm produce?

Theme
Conservation; Environmental change.

Age range
Five to seven.

Group size
Whole class organised into small groups.

What you need
An organised visit to a farm, tape recorder (optional), pencils or pens, paper, clipboards.

What to do
Prior to the day, contact the farmer to explain the purposes of the visit. Also, explain to the children that they are going to find out what the farm produces, the reasons why these foods and materials are produced on this particular farm and to whom they are sold. Point out that they will need to make a record of the food and materials the farmer produces. Hopefully, the children might be able to take small samples of some of the produce back to school with them.

During the visit, ask the farmer why particular crops are grown and animals are reared on the farm. This might well be dependent on the local climate.

Ask the farmer where and to whom the produce is sold. Is it sold locally? Ask the children if they have woollen goods (from sheep's wool), flour (from wheat) and vegetables such as beans and sprouts, in their homes. Where did they come from? Did they come from farms via the shops? Ensure that the children list or draw pictures of the animals, plants, materials and food produced by the farmer.

Safety
Farms can be dangerous places so ensure that children do not wander off unsupervised.

Content
Clearly, the food and materials produced on the farm will be dependent on the location of the farm, the climate, current agricultural regulations and financial incentives. Milk cattle might be kept because of relatively warm, but not too wet, weather; while a sheep farmer might explain that high ground, poor soils and wet, cold weather make sheep the most suitable animals to rear.

Farm crops include plants such as cereals which produce food (flour) and bedding (straw) for animals, sugar beet which is made into sugar and a number of vegetables such as potatoes, beans and cabbage. Animals such as sheep are kept for wool and meat, while cattle produce beef, milk and leather for shoes etc.

It is important to make clear the link between the foods and materials in the children's homes and the food and materials produced on the farm. Reference should be made to shops as the intermediaries in the process. Some food comes from abroad and the children's parents may well grow fruit and vegetables in their gardens and allotments.

A great deal of land has to be used to produce food. A long time ago this land would have been covered in trees, but gradually humans cut down the trees so that they could farm and produce food.

Subject links
NC science and geography
Scottish 5–14 social subjects

Farms 85

2. What was the farm like long ago?

Theme
Environmental change.

Age range
Five to eleven.

Group size
Whole class organised into small groups.

What you need
Video showing the felling of a forest or woodland to generate farmland (optional), recent and old maps of the area, copies of photocopiable page 175, an organised visit to a farm.

What to do
Prior to the visit, show the children the video. When they are at the farm, ask them what the land would have looked like a long time ago before the farm was established. Point out any remnants of woodland and relate them to stories with which the children might be familiar, such as Robin Hood and Sherwood Forest.

Ask the children why they think the trees were cut down. Was this a good thing? Who might benefit from cutting down trees and who or what might not? Ask the farmer whether any trees have been cut down in recent years. Has the farmer planted any trees in recent years? If so, why? Are trees beneficial to a farm?

Older children could look at old and recent maps of the area, showing the retreat of woodlands in recent times. Ask them to compare the maps on photocopiable page 175. These show a farm in recent times and in 1740.

This investigation could be widened into an in-depth study of Food and Farming (History, Extension Study Unit 1) to include domestication of animals, enclosures and clearances acts and the impact of machinery on agricultural practices.

Further activity
The children could be introduced to further ways in which people have changed the environment, such as constructing buildings, building roads and motorways, developing areas of farmland for golf courses and leisure activities, and industrial uses, such as quarrying and factories.

Content
The children will have been introduced to one way in which people have changed the environment for a specific purpose. The development of farming could be compared with the decline of British woodlands to provide a variety of food for an ever-increasing population.

Subject links
NC history and geography
Scottish 5–14 social subjects

3. Coppices and woods

Theme
Conservation.

Age range
Five to eleven.

Group size
Whole class.

What you need
Visit to a farm, interview with the farmer, clipboards, paper, pens or pencils.

What to do
Prior to the visit, talk to the children about the farm and the animals and crops they might see. Also discuss with them the range of wild animals that might live in the hedgerows, coppices and woods. Remind younger children of stories they have read, such as *Peter Rabbit*, *Charlotte's Web* and *George's Marvellous Medicine*. While at the farm, walk around the wooded areas and ask the farmer which wild animals live

in the small woods (coppices) and hedgerows. If appropriate to their abilities, ask the children to list these animals. Why are they found there?

Older children could be asked to discuss and write down the factors which are important to the animals' survival in the woodland. Get the children to ask the farmer why there are not more wooded areas on the farm. Would this be beneficial to wild animals? Were there more wooded areas in the past?

Back in the classroom, younger children could draw pictures of a wood and the wild animals which live there. Older children could discuss intensive farming and conservation and the importance of coppices and small woods for the welfare of wild animals.

Content
Intensive farming has changed the landscape. Woods and hedges have been cleared and wet areas have been drained, forcing wild animals away from farmland to find new homes. These changes in farming practice have been carried out to increase the size of fields so that large machinery can be used with more ease. This in turn has reduced the habitats of a number of wild animals such as foxes, rabbits, hares, squirrels, owls, pheasants and partridges, as well as numerous small birds and insects.

Wooded areas provide animals with food, shelter, nesting or den sites. Wet areas and ponds, seen less often on farms in recent years, offer habitats for frogs, newts and birds as well as water for many animals.

Subject links
NC science and history
Scottish 5–14 science and social subjects

4. Hedging our bets

Theme
Conservation; Environmental change.

Age range
Five to eleven.

Group size
Whole class divided into small groups.

What you need
An area of farmland with both hedgerows and modern fencing, plastic specimen containers, magnifying glasses, reference books about plants and trees, pens or pencils, paper, tape measure, display materials.

What to do
Carry out a survey on an 'old' hedgerow, preferably on a farm, or in the school grounds or near to the school if a farm visit is not possible or convenient.

Ask the children to identify and draw as many different types of plants as they can see. The children could also hunt for insects and other animals, trapping them in clear plastic containers and observing them closely through magnifying glasses before drawing them. Talk to the children about the importance of hedges as places where insects and other animals live, as well as the variety of plant species in and at the base of the hedge. Does the farm have many hedges or does it have fences? Is a fence a good place for insects and other animals to live? Are there many places for insects to live on the farm? Is there any difference between the bases of hedges that have been treated with weedkiller and those which have not?

Older children could be asked to divide their plant list into woody and non-woody plants, thus emphasising the difference between the tree species present in the hedge and the herbs at the base of the hedge. Ask them to measure a 10-metre portion of the hedge and draw a plan of the tree species present (see below). The children could compare the insects and other animals living in or near the hedge with those inhabiting a length of fence.

Talk to the children about their findings and the plants and animals they have found. Explain the importance of hedges as homes for wildlife, such as plants and insects as well as birds and small mammals. Relate this to the modern agricultural practice of providing large fields so that machinery may be turned more easily and so that all available land is used for crop production.

Back in the classroom, ask the children to collate their findings on a large separate display of a hedgerow or on a general farm display.

Further activity
It is possible to estimate the age of an 'old' hedge by the number of tree species found in a stretch of approximately 30 metres. As a general rule, each tree species found adds 100 years to the age of the hedge, though scientists differ in their views on ageing hedgerows. For example, a 100-year-old hedge in certain circumstances could have as few as one species or as many as four species. The hedge sampled should be well-established and not just recently planted with mixed species by the County Council!

Content
Hedgerows are an important habitat (home) for a variety of wildlife, but modern farming practices such as uprooting hedges and spraying the bases of hedges destroys these homes. Some birds such as the Cirl Bunting are on the decline while animals such as the fox are finding urban as well as rural habitats.

Subject links
NC science
Scottish 5–14 science

5. Fertilisers: increasing the yield

Theme
Pollution.

Age range
Seven to eleven.

Group size
Small groups.

What you need
A visit to an arable farm, two seed trays or margarine cartons per group, poor soil or spent compost, pea or cereal seeds, liquid fertiliser, pens or pencils, paper.

What to do
This activity should be started at the beginning of a term or half-term of suitable length. Following a visit to a farm which grows cereals or vegetables, and a discussion with the farmer about the use and advantages of fertilisers, explain to the children that they are going to investigate the long-term effects of fertilisers on the growth of plants. While the seeds will germinate within one to two weeks, the effects on growth may not be seen for several weeks.

Talk to the children about how a fair test may be carried out. Consider the variables such as the soil/compost, amount of water, number of seeds, presence or absence of fertiliser, heat and light (position of seed tray when germinating and growing). Ask them to predict what will happen and why.

Sow the seeds at a relatively high density in the soil/compost so that they will compete for the available nutrients in the soil. Poor soils or spent compost should be used so that when the fertiliser is applied greater differences may be seen between the plants that have received fertiliser and those that have not. Cover the seeds with soil/compost and get the children to water both trays with an equal amount of water. When the plants have germinated, apply fertiliser to one of the trays, following the manufacturer's instructions. Apply further applications of fertiliser on a regular basis. Ask the children to observe, measure and record the growth of the plants and describe any noticeable differences.

Discuss the results of the investigation on a weekly basis. The children could produce graphs of their results and document qualitative changes in pictures and writing.

Further activity
Add fertiliser to a small area of the school playing fields or lawns and observe and record the effects, compared with areas which have received no application. This method is likely to produce quicker, more reliable results than the method above but does not involve the children in such a sophisticated, interesting fair test.

Safety
Ensure that the fertiliser is stored safely, that fingers are kept away from mouths and that hands are washed thoroughly. Solid fertiliser lodged in finger nails can be painful and potentially dangerous.

Content
Fertilisers contain a number of minerals which contribute to healthy plant growth. Of these, nitrogen, usually in the form of ammonium salts, and phosphorus, usually in the form of phosphates, are perhaps the most important, but magnesium is important for the production of the green pigment, chlorophyll, in plants.

In the above investigation, the presence of fertiliser in poor soil/compost should lead to healthier (greener) plants, which may be taller and produce a greater weight of seeds, if the investigation can be sustained for a considerable length of time. The plants growing with no fertiliser may show signs of yellowing of the leaves and a lower yield. Fertilisers are beneficial to plant growth but may be harmful to the environment (see activity 6).

Subject links
NC science
Scottish 5–14 social subjects and health education

6. Fertilisers and run-off into water

Theme
Pollution.

Age range
Seven to eleven.

Group size
Whole class working in small groups.

What you need
Seed tray, soil or compost or turf of grass, dye, water, watering can with a fine rose.

What to do
Talk to the children about why gardeners and farmers add fertilisers (liquid and solid) to the soil and ask them what might happen to the chemicals. Will all the chemical reach the soil (have any of the children seen a farmer applying fertiliser on a windy day)? Is all the chemical used up in the soil? Will some run off in the rainwater and drain through the soil to reach

streams, rivers, lakes and seas? What effect will it have in the water?

Place some compacted soil or compost in a seed tray, leaving a gap of approximately 5cm at one end. Alternatively, cut a piece of turf from the grass and place it in a seed tray, ensuring that a gap of approximately 5cm is left at one end (see below). Fill a watering can partly full with water and explain to the children that the water represents rainfall. Add a dye to the water to simulate an application of fertiliser.

Ask the children to water the soil or turf and to observe closely what happens. As more water is added, the children should see the water seeping out from under the soil, demonstrating how fertiliser drains through the soil and joins the water courses, such as streams and rivers.

Discuss with the children what is happening to the fertiliser. Explain to them that some of it drains through the soil and into the streams and rivers, from which much drinking water is taken. Discuss with the children the effects of fertiliser in the water. They might have heard of lakes with enormous growths of algae which have been poisoning sheep or lakes which are rich in nutrients but poor in oxygen.

Further activity
Provide the children with articles on eutrophication of water and discuss its effects. Remind the children of the results of their investigation into the effects of fertilisers on plant growth. With this background information, get them to discuss whether fertilisers should be used by farmers and gardeners. Ask them if they would use fertilisers in their gardens.

Safety
Care should be taken to keep the dye away from clothing.

Content
While many modern fertilisers are active for relatively short lengths of time and have their effect in the soil, depending on the soil dynamics, some drain through the soil and sub-soil and eventually end up in the rivers and lakes. Lakes are particularly vulnerable to the effects of nitrogenous and phosphate fertilisers as the concentration builds up relatively rapidly. This richness or 'eutrophication' of the water may lead to explosions in the algae population because of the favourable, nutrient-rich growing conditions, leading to so-called 'algal blooms' (profuse presence of algae on the surface of the water). The increase in algae on the surface of the water reduces the amount of oxygen in the water, because oxygen is prevented from dissolving into the water from the air. This may lead to the death of other freshwater plants and animals such as fish, which require plentiful supplies of oxygen. In addition, the algae may be poisonous and potentially dangerous.

Subject links
NC science and geography
Scottish 5–14 social subjects and health education

7. Where have all the barn owls gone?

Theme
Conservation; Environmental change.

Age range
Seven to eleven.

Group size
Whole class working in small groups.

What you need
Clipboards, paper, pencils or pens, pictures of barn owls, a farm visit, reference books.

What to do
Ask the children if they know what a barn owl looks like. Have they ever seen one? Show the class a picture of a barn owl. The following types of questions could act as a stimulus prior to visiting the farm:
- Where do barn owls live?
- What do they feed on?
- Why have the numbers of barn owls decreased from 18,000 pairs in 1920 to 5,000 pairs in 1987?

At the farm, get the children to ask the farmer whether there are any barn owls on the farm. If so, have they nested? Where do they nest? Where do they roost? Are they beneficial to the farm? If the farm does not have any barn owls ask the farmer why this is the case. Did the farm have barn owls in the past? Does the farmer store grain? Does the farmer have any old grassy meadows on the farm?

Back in school, the children can research more about the life and likes of the barn owl and relate this to the occurrence or otherwise on the farm visited, remembering of course that one farm is a small sample. They could also plot the following data on a bar chart or graph to show the changes in barn owl population numbers over the last 70 years.

1920	18,000 pairs
1930	12,000 pairs
1940	11,000 pairs
1960	9,000 pairs
1985	4,400 pairs
1987	5,000 pairs

(Data from *The Royal Society for the Protection of Birds*)

Consolidate the children's understanding of the demise of barn owls this century. Can they think of any reasons for the upturn in numbers during the late 80s?

Further activity
Ask the children to research more about barn owls. How many young do they produce? What is their distribution? Collect some barn owl 'pellets' and dissect them to reveal the bones of small mammals. Place the bones in bleach for a short time and display them.

Safety
Thin plastic gloves should be used when dissecting owl pellets. This might be an activity to be carried out by the teacher.

Content
Barn owls used to be quite common in the United Kingdom. Farmers allowed them into their barns because they caught mice and rats which ate the stored grain. The owls nested in hollow trees in the hedgerows and hunted small mammals in the meadows. Meadows are uncommon today. In the United Kingdom we have lost 95 per cent of old meadows and 41 per cent of rough grazing land since 1945. Because these areas have been lost, barn owls seek food on other grassy areas like playing fields which support very little prey. They also seek food on dangerous roadside verges which has led to a doubling of deaths of the owl since the 1950s. Modern buildings are more secure and allow less access for barn owls. More rough grasslands, the habitat of small mammals, will help barn owls rear more young. Recently there has been a rise in numbers which seems to be due to improving weather conditions and the presence of less pesticide residues in barn owl habitats.

Subject links
NC science
Scottish 5–14 science

8. Production or wildlife: is it a choice?

Theme
Conservation; Environmental change.

Age range
Seven to eleven.

Group size
Whole class and then pairs.

What you need
Copies of photocopiable pages 176 and 177, crayons, pens and paper.

What to do
Talk to the children about the important role of farms and farmland in our countryside. Ask them about the different habitats offered by the farm environment, which include grasslands (cultivated and rough), crops, hedges, woods and coppices, ponds and buildings etc. Explain that some animals and plants are adapted to live in these particular environments and that any change to them will risk their survival.

Explain to the children about intensive farming and the effects it has had on the countryside. For example, many hedges have been removed to make larger fields, woods and coppices have been removed, and wet areas and marshes have been drained. Cereals are sown in autumn rather than the spring to increase yields and these and other crops are given fertilisers to increase production further and are sprayed with various chemicals to prevent disease. All these measures have had an effect on wildlife. For example, the numbers of three farmland birds (barn owl, cirl bunting and grey partridge) have declined dramatically over the last 30 or 40 years.

Remind the children that farmers have a role to produce food and to make money like all other working people, but that many people feel they have a moral obligation to look after the environment.

Ask the children to work in pairs to think of ways of improving the farm shown on photocopiable page 176, to encourage the return or retention of the three birds, details of which are given on photocopiable page 177. Explain that the children will need to read photocopiable page 177 to find out about the habitats of the birds and the management strategies which can be used. Tell them that they can only make one change per year as changes are time-consuming and costly. As each change is made they should modify the farm map as appropriate (for example, colour in a hedge with a crayon), indicating the year of the change. Which changes might they implement early on to ensure that there is a chance of all three birds returning as quickly as possible to the farm? Which management strategies would not affect the return of the birds to any great extent?

Ask the children to present their management plan to the others in the class, explaining the reasons for their decisions. Have they realised that some strategies are long-term and will not produce instant results (e.g. planting hedges and allowing hedges to grow), while others are relatively short-term and could produce a swift return of some of the birds (e.g. ploughing stubble into the fields in spring not the autumn)? Hopefully, some of the children should appreciate that more than one condition needs to be fulfilled before the birds will return. Clearly, the longer term strategies need to be put in place first.

Talk to the children about the improvements that they have made to the farm. Discuss with them the drawbacks from the farmer's point of view in terms of a smaller area of crops, a lower yield and therefore less income.

Content
Three quarters of our countryside is made up of farmland. Since the Second World War there has been a need for farmers in Great Britain to produce more food and so more land has been changed from, for example, woodland, rough grass or marsh into arable land or pasture. Farming has become even more intensive since we joined the Common Market of the EC, with subsidies being given to encourage farmers to cultivate land and produce yet more food. However, in recent years, farmers in the EC have been producing more food than can be eaten. To remedy this situation, farmers have been provided with less subsidies, quotas of dairy cattle have been produced and areas of farmland can no longer be cultivated. This provides farmers with the opportunities to let land go fallow, and to have more woods and coppices on the farm.

In the activity above, the children should be made aware that birds have more than one need in terms of habitat. For example, the cirl bunting requires both thick overgrown hedges and winter stubble. Ensure that the children are aware that farmers will suffer financially if they carry out some of the environmentally friendly measures. In the short term at least, farmers could perhaps be given subsidies to encourage wildlife rather than producing food that no one can afford to eat. However, that might mean more taxes!

Subject links
NC science, geography
Scottish 5–14 science, social subjects

9. How environmentally friendly is the farm? – A whole investigation

Theme
Conservation; Environmental change; Pollution.

Age range
Eight to eleven.

Group size
Whole class divided into small groups.

What you need
Clipboards, paper, pencils or pens, copies of photocopiable page 178.

Planning and preparation
This activity needs to take place at a farm and organising an interview with the farmer would be most beneficial. It might also be useful to discuss the purpose of the activity

What the farmer has done to the environment	Points given	Points taken away
Farmed the land	(10)	
1a. Planted a hedge recently	1	
1b. Removed a hedge recently		1
2a. Allows hedges to grow tall and thick	(1)	
2b. Allows hedges to be cut regularly		(1)

Figure 1

with the farmer, explaining that it is an exercise designed to help children understand the costs of wildlife conservation to the farmer as well as the advantages to the wildlife.

Prior to the visit, the children need to be given some background about the criteria for judging the extent to which a farm is environmentally friendly or not. They will need to find out about a number of issues, either from a class discussion or through guided research. Previous work on conservation of wildlife, use of pesticides and use of artificial fertilisers will aid their knowledge and understanding. In this way, a list of criteria for an environmentally friendly farm could be developed prior to the visit, but be prepared to add to it once the children have visited the farm and carried out some of the earlier activities in the chapter. A checklist like the one above and on photocopiable page 178 might be developed, or alternatively, the children can produce their own.

Investigating

The children could fill in their checklist sheets by circling the appropriate score on the score sheet as indicated in Figure 1. The farmer has been given a starting bonus of 10 for farming the land. During their guided tour of the farm, the children could ask the farmer for clarification of any points about which they are uncertain.

Recording and communication

Ask the children to add up their score of points given and then to add up their score of points taken away. Subtract the latter from the former.

A score of 0 might suggest that the farm was not at all friendly to the environment, while a score of 20 might indicate a farmer who manages the farm with concern for wildlife in mind.

A score of around 10 might indicate a farmer who has attempted to balance a friendly approach to the environment with the need to produce a great deal of food cheaply. If the relationship with the farmer is well established, the results of the environmental survey could be discussed with him, so that he could justify management of the farm.

Back in school, the children could comment further and write about the environmentally friendly nature of the farm. This work could be added to any display work produced during the farm visit.

Subject links

NC science, geography
Scottish 5–14 science, social subjects, health education

CHAPTER 8

The garden

Looking after a garden is an important way of helping children to develop a sense of trusteeship and a caring attitude towards the environment. From an early age children show a keen interest in living things. Through the garden children can develop their knowledge of animals and plants, and by watching plants grow they will learn to treat living things with care and consideration. Above all, they will discover that gardening is fun.

Through the activities in this chapter, children will learn about a variety of seed types, the conditions that plants need to grow and how to propagate plants through cuttings. They will increase their knowledge about different types of plants such as herbs and wild flowers and gain practical experience of using organic matter to help plants grow by making a compost heap.

There are many ways of attracting wildlife to a garden and children can learn how to provide appropriate habitats to encourage birds and insects to visit their garden. Knowledge can be gained about aspects of the environment which are being affected by human activity, for example the removal of peat for use as a growing compost. The children should become aware that alternatives to peat are available.

By carrying out the activities in this chapter the children will further develop the four identified themes.

The garden

BACKGROUND

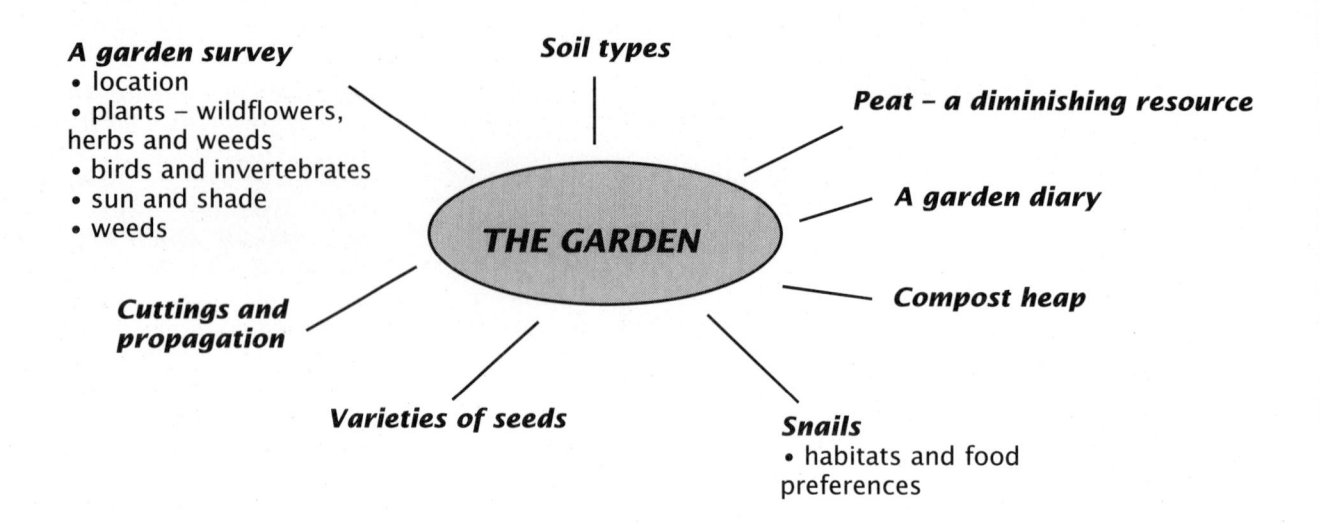

A garden survey
- location
- plants – wildflowers, herbs and weeds
- birds and invertebrates
- sun and shade
- weeds

Soil types

Peat – a diminishing resource

A garden diary

THE GARDEN

Compost heap

Cuttings and propagation

Varieties of seeds

Snails
- habitats and food preferences

	Progression in teaching and learning	
Theme	**Details of activity and activity number**	
	Key Stage 1 (P1–3)	Key Stage 2 (P4–7)
Conservation	Plant and propagation (3) Organic gardening (9) Growing wild flowers (9)	Peat substitutes (5)
Environmental change	Keeping a diary (9) Choice of site and planning a garden (9)	
Plants, animals and their habitats	Biodiversity of seeds (1) Snail habitats and food preferences (2) Soil invertebrates (7) Garden birds (8) Garden plants (9)	Soil types and conditions for growth (6)
Pollution	Weed control – alternatives to herbicides (9)	Alternatives to fertilisers (4)

96 Chapter 8

ACTIVITIES

1. Assorted seeds

Theme
Plants, animals and their habitats.

Age range
Five to eleven.

Group size
Individuals or small groups.

What you need
Seed catalogues containing information on and pictures of common garden flowers, empty seed packets, adhesive, paper, pens.

What to do
The purpose of this activity is to help children understand both the nature and variety of seed types which will serve as an introduction to the concept of biodiversity (see Chapter 1 *Environmental issues*). Ask the children to work in groups and cut out information and pictures from the catalogues on different types of seeds. They can look for instructions on soil conditions and on when and where to plant the seed, for example, in the sun, in the shade, in damp or dry soil, in the spring or in the summer. Do the seeds need a lot or a little amount of water for growth?

They can then group their seed pictures and packets into different types, for example, annuals, biennials and perennials. It is important to introduce and explain these terms at this stage. Ask the children to make a chart of their pictures to record the results of their classification. They could make a chart such as the one below with their pictures illustrating the flowers which will be produced from the seeds.

Content
Annuals are plants that complete their life cycle in one year. Examples of these are nasturtium, sunflower, sweet pea, Californian poppy.

Biennials are plants that flower and fruit in the year after they are sown and then die, for example, honesty, wallflower.

Perennials flower in the season after they are sown and go on flowering year after year, for example, Michaelmas daisy, lupin, delphinium.

Subject links
NC science
Scottish 5–14 science

Name of plant	When to plant	How to plant	Other facts
violet	Feb – April	Sow thinly and cover with a fine layer of compost	Keep moist
flax	March – May	Cover lightly with fine soil	Keep moist. Support with twigs if necessary

2. Snail-biting!

Theme
Plants, animals and their habitats.

Age range
Five to eleven.

Group size
Small groups or whole class.

What you need
Large covered container – for example, an empty fish tank – a selection of different types of leaves from around the school, a number of snails, collecting trays.

What to do
The purpose of this activity is to investigate where snails are found and their food preferences. Tell the children that they are going to collect some snails from around the school. Snails range in size from 2–3cm down to others less than 1cm. It is likely that most of the snails found by the children will be of the smaller species. Snails should be carefully picked up between finger and thumb and gently placed in the collecting tray. The best time to do this is after rain. Snails can be found under stones and wood, and in leaf litter. After collection make sure the children wash their hands. Discuss with the children the food which snails eat such as leaves and other parts of plants and tell them that they are going to find out which leaf type snails like the most. When the children have finished observing the snails they should return them to a shady and safe part of the playground.

The children should collect five different leaf types, one of which should be a lettuce leaf, and place them inside a suitable container side by side. This is a good opportunity to think about fair testing, for example, size of leaf. They should then place the snails inside the container, being careful to spread them out. Discuss with the children the type of environment that snails prefer, for example, dark, damp places. Place the container inside a dark cupboard.

Discuss with the children that snails, like humans, prefer certain foods to others. The children can check the container every day to see which leaves have been eaten and they can record their results in the form of a table or chart. Run the activity over no more than three days.

Content
Snails eat leaves and other vegetation, and they prefer some types of vegetation to others. They seek a variety of habitats in which to hide away during the day, preferring to feed at night. There are a number of snail species which might be found in and around the school, most of which do not cause any damage to garden plants and vegetables.

Subject links
NC science
Scottish 5–14 science

3. Cutting it fine

Theme
Conservation.

Age range
Five to eleven.

Group size
Pairs or small groups.

What you need
Softwood plant – for example, rosemary or geranium – scissors, plant pot, cutting compost, polythene bag, elastic band, watering can.

What to do
This activity will help the children to understand that plants can be propagated from cuttings. Discuss with the children that plants can be formed not only from seeds but also from other parts of the plant, for example, the stem. Each group can take a plant such as a geranium and cut a small part of the plant stem (about 10cm) from just below a leaf. The children can then pull off the bottom leaves from their cutting. They should then take some special cutting compost, and place it in a plant pot with the cutting. They can cover the cutting with a polythene bag secured with an elastic band and place the pot in a warm place out of direct sunlight. The polythene bag ensures that the cutting does not lose too much moisture.

The children can make observations of the plant over a period of time and water it when necessary, until more leaves begin to grow on it, when they can re-pot it and take it outside.

Content
A cutting is a part cut from a plant, for example, part of the stem, which can be grown into another plant by making a cut in a particular place on this host plant and slotting the stem piece into it. Plants can be reproduced to form identical copies of themselves by using cuttings. This can be an important means of conserving species both in the garden and in the wild.

Subject links
NC science
Scottish 5–14 science

4. Making a compost heap

Theme
Pollution; Conservation.

Age range
Seven to eleven.

Group size
Whole class.

What you need
Vegetable peelings, tea leaves, grass cuttings, vegetable leaves, hedge clippings, plastic sheeting or a piece of old carpet, planks of wood and wooden posts, hammer, nails, bricks (or ready made tumble compost bin/plastic dustbin), calcified seaweed or other activator (obtainable from garden centres), spade, water, watering can, household rubber gloves.

What to do
This activity will help the children to understand that the creation of compost prevents loss and wastage of organic plant material and fertilises the soil for new plant growth. Recycling the material avoids unnecessary pollution. This activity will also help the children to understand how nutrients can be added to the soil without using artificial fertilisers and that compost is a natural fertiliser.

Discuss with the children the benefits of adding compost to the soil and how plants can be grown without the use of chemical fertilisers. Tell the children that they are going to learn how to make compost. A purpose-made compost container such as a plastic dustbin or a tumble compost bin can be used. Alternatively, a simple compost container can be constructed using wooden planks secured to corner posts and lined with bricks. One side should be readily removable so that when the compost is ready to be used it can be easily lifted out without having to dismantle the whole container. It should be

The garden

approximately 1 metre square and should have gaps for ventilation.

The children can build their compost heap by adding layers of the ingredients (peelings, grass cuttings, activator and so on). The layers should be packed tightly and watered to keep the heap moist. Tell the children to cover the top of the heap with plastic sheeting or a piece of old carpet to keep out the rain and keep in the heat. The compost must be turned every three weeks. The compost heap must be left for several weeks or a few months (depending on the season) before the compost can be dug into the soil.

Content
Compost is a major source of nutrients for a garden. The organic material rots and produces a compost which has a balanced amount of the nutrients and minerals required for healthy plant growth. The temperature in the compost will rise as the material decomposes. The compost should be turned over regularly so that the outside edges are moved into the centre and air is mixed through the heap to allow decomposition to take place. The compost needs an activator such as calcified seaweed to speed up decay. The compost can be used in the Whole investigation to fertilise the garden or given to someone in the community for their garden, for example, an elderly person.

Subject links
NC science
Scottish 5–14 science

5. For peat's sake!

Theme
Conservation.

Age range
Seven to eleven.

Group size
Small groups or whole class.

What you need
Packet of seeds (choose a variety that is simple to grow, i.e. one that has a high percentage germination rate), seed trays or cottage cheese or margarine tubs, samples of peat substitutes (obtainable from a garden centre), watering can, bucket of soil, trowel, weighing scales.

What to do
Explain to the children that peat is a soil material and not a type of soil. It is the organic remains of plants which have been partially decomposed. The aim of the activity is to compare different peat substitutes and their effect on seed growth.

The children can plant the seeds in the peat substitutes mixed with soil and compare rates of growth. A control should be provided containing soil only, i.e., no peat substitute. They should provide the same conditions for all of the seeds, for example, same amount of light, same temperature, same amount of water, equal weights of soil and peat substitutes. Measurements of seedling height should be taken at different times. Other measurements could include counting the number of leaves and assessment of general health of plant and its colour.

It is important that the children design an appropriate recording sheet to note both quantitative (for example, seedling height) and qualitative data (for example, general plant health). This should be drawn up before the experiment is carried out. Help the children to prepare histograms to illustrate their results.

Further activity
The children should locate on a map areas of peatlands such as those at Chartley Moss, Hatfield Moors, Shapwick Heath, Wicken Fen and

6. Seeds and soils

Theme
Plants, animals and their habitats.

Age range
Seven to eleven.

Group size
Small groups.

What you need
Two packets of different seed types (choose a variety which is easy to grow, i.e. has high percentage germination rate), seed trays or cottage cheese or margarine tubs (any containers used should be identical in size and shape), samples of soil collected from different areas (use stony soil, sandy soil, clay soil, and compost), measuring cylinder, weighing scales, pens, pencils, paper.

What to do
This activity helps children to understand that plants need different conditions for growth. Soil type is an important factor in growth. Explain to the children that soils are formed by the erosion of different rocks. Explain that there are various types of soil, for example, sandy soil, clay soil, and explain that different plants grow better in different soil types.

Ask the children to weigh equal amounts of each soil type using the scales. The children should put a measured amount of each soil type into a container. They should then plant an equal number of different seed types in each type of soil.

Explain to the children the importance of having all the conditions the same for a fair test, including the same amount of water, the same light and temperature conditions. The seeds should be put in the same place and be watered regularly. The children can measure the growth of the seeds over a period of time by measuring the height of the seedlings and by counting the number of seeds which have germinated. The children can then see which seeds grow best in which type of soil. The children should record their findings through a diary by using recording sheets that they have designed themselves.

Content
There are many different types of soil, for example, clay soil, sandy soil, depending on where you are. Different types of plants grow better in different types of soil, e.g. some plants will grow better in clay soil than in sandy soil, and others will grow better in sandy soil than in clay soil.

Subject links
NC science and geography
Scottish 5–14 science and social subjects

Woodwalton Fen in England, and Borth Bog, Loch Garten Nature Reserve in Scotland and Insh Marshes in Wales. The children should find out why these areas are so important.

Content
Peat is added to the soil for use as a compost supplying valuable nutrients to help plants grow. Alternatives to peat are now available and one such alternative is coir which comes from coconut palms.

In addition to being a valuable material resource, peatlands are unique wetland habitats supporting a diversity of plants and animals. Such habitats are virtually irreplaceable and with continued peat extraction, are becoming very rare.

Subject links
NC science and geography
Scottish 5–14 science and social subjects

The garden

7. Animals in the soil

Theme
Plants, animals and their habitats.

Age range
Five to eleven.

Group size
Small groups or pairs.

What you need
Collecting trays or specimen containers, large pieces of white paper, trowels, buckets for collecting soil, plastic spoons or pooters, hand lenses, paper, pencils, large tank (covered) in which to put animals in the classroom.

What to do
The purpose of this activity is to observe some of the animals which are commonly found in garden soil. Through this activity the children will be able to understand that there are a variety of animals which live in the soil. Simple observations can be made by the younger children on such aspects as patterns of movement and characteristics of the animals. Older children can go on to identify the animals and make drawings of them in order to develop the skills of detailed observation.

The children could compare and contrast the different animals, and could construct tables showing similarities and differences.

Allow the children to search for minibeasts in the school grounds. They should dig up small amounts of soil from different parts of the ground, and they should bring the soil back into the classroom and spread it out over collecting trays or large pieces of white paper. Tell the children to separate the soil particles and look for animals present in the soil. They can put any animals they find into the covered tank. They should be very careful not to damage the animals as they transfer them. The issue of sensitive handling of animals should be discussed with the class. All animals should be returned to the wild after observations have been made.

The children can work in small groups or pairs to make detailed observations of the animals which they find. Ask the children such questions as:
• What colour is your minibeast?
• What shape is it?
• Does the minibeast have wings?
• What does the minibeast's body look like?
• Is the body surface dry or slimy, rough or smooth?
• Is the body divided up into parts?
• How many legs does your minibeast have?
• How does your minibeast move?
• Does the minibeast move slowly or quickly?
• Which direction does the minibeast move in?

Encourage the children to make detailed observations with the hand lenses provided. They should draw large pictures of their animal and older children should label some of the features and describe the appearance of the animal.

Content
The children will have found out that there are a wide variety of animals which live in the soil and will have identified some similarities and differences between them. They will also have learned about their behaviour and how we should care for animals.

Subject links
NC science
Scottish 5–14 science

8. Birds in the garden

Theme
Plants, animals and their habitats.

Age range
Five to eleven.

Group size
Small groups or pairs.

What you need
Notebooks, pencils, a camera, a rubber dustbin lid to use as a bird bath, a simple tray mounted on a post for use as a bird table, plastic mesh bags, nut baskets, shallow containers for bird food, a range of bird foods (unsalted peanuts/monkey nuts, bird seed, bread, water), reference/guide books identifying types of birds. Binoculars may be useful but are not essential.

What to do
The purpose of this activity is to study the behaviour of birds which visit the garden or school grounds. The study could take a term or even longer (use the autumn and spring terms). Younger and older children can take part in this activity though the older children may make more sophisticated observations. Making a simple bird table to attract the birds is advised (see activity 9, A whole investigation). Site the bird table if possible outside the classroom window. Food can be placed on the table either loose or in small containers, or it can be hung from the bird table in net bags. Food can also be put on the ground at the base of the bird table in small, shallow containers.

The children should observe the different species of birds which visit the bird table. They should note which birds feed on the table and which feed on the ground. Food preferences should be noted and related to the shape of beak of the different species. The children should observe times of feeding – do the birds feed throughout the day or do they have mealtimes? Simple recording sheets should be designed by the children. Photographs of the bird visitors could be taken by the children.

A simple bird bath can be made using a shallow dish or an upturned rubber dustbin lid so that there is a 'deep' end and a 'shallow' end (the handle causing it to tilt at an angle). The children should watch the birds bathing. They should consider the following questions. Which species bathe, and do they bathe more when the weather is warmer and drier? What depth of water do the birds prefer? How do the birds dry themselves after bathing?

The children should observe closely the birds' drinking habits. Ask the children to make observations of the way the birds drink. Which species drink the water provided? What sort of behaviour do they exhibit between each sip? Do birds drink at any time of the day?

The children should study the way birds move. Which birds walk and which birds hop?

All of this information can be collected together and put up as a classroom display made up of pictures the children have drawn of the birds they have seen feeding, with some information about their behaviour. The children could present the results of their investigation at a school assembly.

Further activity
The children could write to the RSPB (see *Resources*, Chapter 13 for address) to obtain further information about garden birds. A member of the local RSPB could be invited

into the classroom to talk to the children about local birdwatching activities.

Content
The children will find a variety of birds are attracted to their bird table. Ground feeding species are blackbirds, dunnocks, thrushes and robins. Birds which feed from the bird table are blue tits, sparrows, great tits and greenfinches. Blue tits and greenfinches prefer the peanuts and sunflower seeds. Dried fruits such as raisins are enjoyed by blackbirds and robins. Fat is enjoyed by tits, small seeds such as millet attract house sparrows, dunnocks and finches. Food put on the ground should be spaced out so that more birds can feed at any one time. The shape of the beak is a guide to the sort of food and how a bird eats. Birds that eat insects have thin, pointed bills. Seed-eaters have bills that are pointed at the tip and are broadest at the base. The bills of finches are adapted to cracking seeds.

Birds enjoy bathing and drinking all the year round. Birds move on the ground in different ways. Starlings walk whereas sparrows, thrushes and blackbirds hop.

Subject links
NC science
Scottish 5–14 science

9. The garden – A whole investigation

Theme
Conservation; Environmental change; Plants, animals and their habitats.

Age range
Five to eleven.

Group size
Whole class and groups.

What you need
Garden implements, seeds (flower/herb), reference books on flowers, herbs and weeds, plastic sheeting or old carpet pieces, a wooden post and flat piece of wood to make a bird table, bird food, paper, pens, pencils, a camera.

Planning and preparation
This whole investigation is adaptable for a range of different types of garden which could be established in the school grounds, for example a herb garden or a wild flower garden. Only a small patch of land is required. It will be necessary to seek permission from the headteacher before embarking on this activity. The investigation could continue throughout a term or preferably over a school year.

Choosing a site
Choosing a site for the garden is important and there are a number of factors to consider which need to be discussed with the children. A south-facing garden will receive more light and the site should be well-drained. Shelter is also important. A garden plot near a fence or near shrubs will trap the warmth from the sun and will provide protection from wind and rain. After this discussion the children could weigh up the advantages and

disadvantages of a site location.

Once the patch of land has been chosen, decisions must be made by the children on what type of garden is to be developed, for example, herb garden or wild flower garden, and whether they will be carrying out investigations such as a weed study, observing garden birds or undertaking a garden survey of minibeasts, plants and animals. A visit to a local garden centre could be arranged in order to find out the range of plants/seeds available.

Investigating

Weeds in the garden
Weeds are plants growing where they are not wanted. Not all weeds are problems. Some attract insects such as bees, butterflies and lacewings. Weeds can also be controlled by planting plants close together in the ground. This will result in the weeds being smothered. Examples of common garden weeds are plantains, chickweed, nettles, groundsel and dock.

An investigation can be carried out by the children to ascertain where weeds are more likely to grow. The children can compare different areas of the garden for weed growth, for example a shady area, or a sunny exposed area. Alternatively, two areas can be compared, one where preventative measures such as mulching are taken to control weeds and another where no control measures are taken. The children will need to dig two plots identical in area and position and then clear the land of weeds. Before doing so the children should attempt to identify as many different weeds as they can. They should refer to reference books to help them and list the weeds they find. They should try to remove all the roots with a digging fork and hoe. Mulching means covering the ground in order to deprive weeds of light and air to make sure the weeds do not survive. The mulch could be pieces of old carpet or plastic sheeting or tree bark.

Make a wildflower garden
Encourage the children to make a wildflower garden. Discuss with them the fact that many wildflowers are under the threat of extinction and stress that they should not pick flowers in the wild. The children could learn to identify the flowers by sowing the seeds and cultivating their wildflower garden. (There are seed suppliers who specialise in wildflower seeds.) The children can grow their flowers and take photographs of them to be used as a record and identification guide. Growing flowers from seed will take a number of weeks. The flowers will attract insects such as bees and butterflies and other helpful insects such as ladybirds that control pests. They can measure the height of their plants as they grow and make a record of their observations.

Plant a herb garden
Discussions could centre on the use of herbs in the past and present for medicinal and culinary purposes. Ask the children to name some herbs which they will be familiar with from their kitchen at home. The children can plant herbs in their garden plot or inside the classroom in plastic margarine tubs or larger containers. If planting the herbs outside, ask the children to design the layout for their herb garden. Some herbs can be sown as seed, for example chives and dill, whilst others

can be re-potted from cuttings. A range of herbs can be grown such as parsley, mint, thyme and rosemary. Encourage the children to water the herbs regularly and to snip them to stimulate new growth.

Birds in the garden
Birds can be attracted to the garden by a bird table and a regular supply of food. The children could construct a simple bird table using an upright post topped with a flat piece of wood (RSPB offers advice on the construction of bird tables). Discuss with the children the type of food they should put out to attract the birds. Encourage the children to observe the birds that visit the garden. They will be able to identify common species and note their feeding preferences in a note book and where they feed (ground feeders or on the bird table). The children could make their own birdseed cake to attach to the bird table.

A garden survey
Once the garden is established the children could carry out a survey. Help the children to decide how they are going to carry out their survey and what the purpose of this survey will be. Will they be looking for the most common plants and animals to be found in their garden? (See activities 7 and 8.) They will need to draw up a simple plan of their garden in order to map out whereabouts in their garden the plants and animals are to be found.

They could divide the garden area into different sections and different groups of children could survey each section. Encourage the children to look carefully at all aspects of the garden and to turn over twigs and leaves in order to discover more, such as the presence of minibeasts in the leaf litter.

The children should design their own recording sheets on which to record their data. A minibeast survey could be carried out in two different parts of the garden such as a sunny area or a damp, shady area. They could collect data about the plants, minibeasts, the soil and the birds.

A classroom garden
If the school grounds are such that it is difficult to find a suitable site for a garden outside, many useful investigations can be carried out indoors by establishing a classroom garden. The children can grow plants from seeds, they can take leaf and stem cuttings and propagate plants, and create mini-wildflower or herb gardens. They will need to consider the best conditions required for the growth of their plants. Encourage the children to carry out simple investigations such as comparing the growth of plants in sunny and shady areas of the classroom. They could grow seeds such as mung beans, cress or alfalfa seeds on damp cotton wool placed in shallow dishes.

Recording and communicating

Keeping a diary
A garden diary can be kept over a period of time (preferably over one school year). Encourage the children to look for changes in the plants, numbers of minibeasts and birds over the seasons. The diary could be illustrated with photographs which the children have taken at regular intervals in the school year. They could present their findings in a school assembly at the end of the year and guided tours of their garden could be offered to parents on school open days.

Subject links
NC science and geography
Scottish 5–14 science and social subjects

CHAPTER 9

Woodlands

Most of the activities in this chapter will involve a visit or visits to a wood or wooded area. The majority of children have enjoyed exploring in a wood at some time during their lives. However, only a few will have much knowledge about common trees, flowers, birds and animals and most will not have considered the woodland environment from the point of view of its detailed and varied biology. It is therefore useful to introduce the children to the importance of conserving the animals and plants which reside in it. Every walk in the park or countryside is made far more interesting and meaningful for parents and children if they can identify and make sense of the natural world around them.

This chapter attempts to help teachers interest their children in the woodland environment by providing them with a number of practical activities which involve direct interaction with animals and plants. Depending on their age and ability, children will observe, identify and record tree leaves and tree twigs, explore the animals in the leaf litter and play 'detectives' to find animal tracks and signs and discover how they were formed. The older children will be able to take an historical perspective and look at coppicing, a vital industry to the local community, and consider the products obtained from it. From the past the children will consider an important issue of the present and the future – the implications of continuing to fell the rainforests. Arising out of the woodland investigation, a school or community woodland could be planned and planted and its management discussed and implemented.

Finally, the activities should lead the children to consider their own role in the conservation of woodlands. Vandalism of many urban and rural woods near to housing is a serious problem. Children can play their part in conserving the tree stock by not damaging trees, not playing near young saplings or cutting down trees and by collecting dead wood for Guy Fawkes night.

BACKGROUND

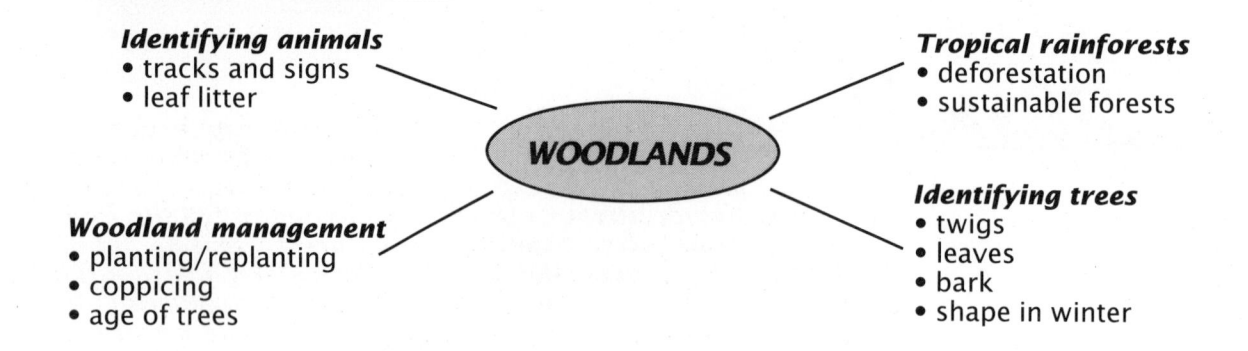

Identifying animals
- tracks and signs
- leaf litter

Tropical rainforests
- deforestation
- sustainable forests

WOODLANDS

Woodland management
- planting/replanting
- coppicing
- age of trees

Identifying trees
- twigs
- leaves
- bark
- shape in winter

Progression in teaching and learning		
Theme	**Details of activity and activity number**	
	Key Stage 1 (P1–3)	Key Stage 2 (P4–7)
Conservation	Tree identification (1) Twig identification (2) Animals in leaf litter (3) Animal tracks and signs (4) Tropical rainforests and deforestation (7) Study of an oak tree – A whole investigation (10)	Coppicing trees (5) Planning and planting a school wood (6) Green matches (8) Sustainable forests (9)
Environmental change	Tropical rainforests (7) Study of an oak tree – A whole investigation (10)	Coppicing trees (5) Planning and planting a school wood (6) Deforestation and rainforests (7) Green matches (8) Sustainable forests (9)
Plants, animals and their habitats	Animals living in leaf litter (3) Evidence of wildlife (4) Study of an oak tree – A whole investigation (10)	
Pollution	Study of an oak tree – A whole investigation (10)	Deforestation and rainforests (7) Green matches (8) Sustainable forests (9)

ACTIVITIES

1. Which tree?

Theme
Conservation.

Age range
Five to eleven.

Group size
Whole class and then individuals.

What you need
A visit to a wood or wooded area, secateurs, leaves, clipboards, paper, sharpened pencils, photocopiable page 179, reference books on trees.

What to do
During the visit to the wood with the younger children, collect a small number of leaves from different trees in the wood using secateurs for later study in the classroom. Explain to the children that the removal of plants should be limited and then only if they are relatively common. Back in the classroom, ask the children to draw carefully one of the leaves, observing its features.

Ask the children if they know the names of any woodland trees and, if they show an interest, help them to identify their leaves using the reference books. Ask them to write the name of the leaf next to their drawing. Display their drawings and compile a class list of the common trees found in the wood.

With the older children in the wood, ask them to identify the leaves of common British trees using photocopiable page 179. Back in the classroom they could colour accurately the pictures on the photocopiable page and label their drawings with any distinct characteristics. Further information could be added if the children carried out the further activities below.

Further activities
For younger children
• Paint the leaves on one side and use them to make leaf prints
• Whilst in the wood get the children to make bark rubbings using white paper and a soft pencil. Can the children identify trees from the bark pattern?
For older children
• Ask the children to produce a word key to identify their leaves.
• Using books, the children could research one tree in more detail, finding out amongst other things about its flowers, fruits and biological name.

Safety
Secateurs may be extremely sharp and great care must be taken in their use.

Content
The leaves from different trees may be identified by their colour and texture but particularly their shape. Most of the trees considered to be native to the British Isles emerged after the last ice age in approximately 6,300 BC.

These include: alder, birch, elm, lime, ash, cherry, hazel, oak, beech, elder, hawthorn, willow. The horse-chestnut was introduced later and the sycamore was a late arrival in 1210 AD.

Woods are often planted with non-native species which, like clothes, come in and out of fashion. For example, the Victorians planted a large number of coniferous Giant Redwoods (Wellingtonia spruces) to commemorate the Duke of Wellington and the Battle of Waterloo. The trees in the list above are all deciduous as they drop their leaves in winter. However, conifers may also be found in woods particularly yew and larch, the latter being a conifer which does actually shed its needles.

Subject links
NC science
Scottish 5–14 science

2. Winter twigs

Theme
Conservation.

Age range
Five to eleven.

Group size
Whole class and then pairs.

What you need
For the younger children, horse-chestnut twigs containing sticky buds, paper and pencils. For the older children, a variety of winter twigs which might include alder, ash, birch, beech, cherry, elder, elm, hawthorn, hazel, horse-chestnut, lime, oak, sycamore, willow, paper and pencils, photocopiable page 180.

What to do
With the younger children, show the whole class the horse-chestnut twigs and ask them what they are. Where has each twig come from? Alternatively, take the class to a nearby horse-chestnut tree and remove a few twigs with a pair of sharp secateurs. Explain to the children that the minimum of material should be collected and that a sharp instrument should be used.

Build up their understanding of the formation of a tree using such words as trunk, branches (large and small) and twigs, aided by a diagram if not in the field.

Divide the class into pairs and give them a 'sticky' bud. Allow them to examine the twig for some time but tell them not to damage it as they are going to draw it later. What have they noticed? What colour are the 'sticky' buds? Are they made up of one piece (bud scale) or more than one piece? Have they noticed anything else except for the 'sticky' buds? What do they notice on the rest of the twig? Can they see the shield-shaped marks with dots inside them? What do they think might have made those marks? What was on the twig in the spring and summer which is not there now? Tell them that these are the marks left when the leaves fell off. Ask the children to draw a large picture of the twig using a sharpened pencil, reminding them to add any details that they can see. Who is the most observant? Add a title to the children's work and form a display.

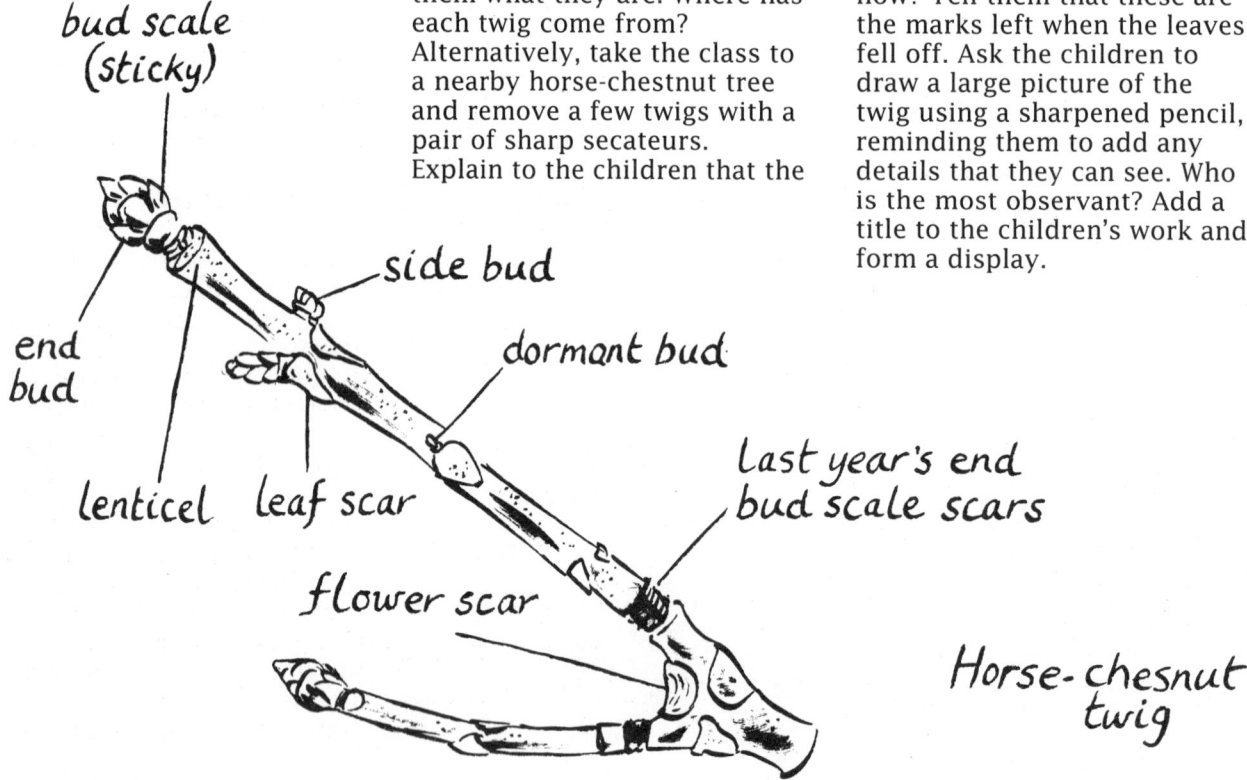

Horse-chesnut twig

With the older children visit the wood in the late autumn or during the winter and collect some twigs from common woodland trees. Talk to the children about the ethics of minimal collection of common plants and remind them that they should not pick plants that might be rare. Alternatively, the children could identify the twigs on the trees while in the wood.

Label the twigs (or the trees – see above) using a capital letter, A, B, C... and so on. Then ask the children to identify them using the pictures on photocopiable page 180. Following this activity, with some assistance, the more able children might be able to construct their own word key to identify the trees. An example like the one below using items from pockets (bunch of keys, coin, metal pen, plastic biro and top, ruler) might be helpful to the children. Explain to the children why there is a need to have a key to identify many plants or animals. Explain that the key asks questions (see example below).

Suggest that the children try not to use size in their key and use colour to distinguish the twigs only when the buds or the bark colour differ greatly from the buds or bark colour of the rest of the twigs.

When the children have finished using the key, ask them to draw a detailed diagram of a horse-chestnut twig using a sharpened pencil. Talk to them about the presence of two types of scars on the twig. Why might they be present? What was present previously to cause them to be produced?

Talk to the children about the importance of trees to the welfare of wildlife and the aesthetics of the natural landscape. How can they help? For example, they could make sure they do not damage trees in any way when playing and ensure that live, healthy trees are not cut down for bonfire night. They could also endeavour to plant new trees whenever possible.

Content
This activity will help children to become familiar with common British trees and enable them to observe plants more closely. The shield-shaped scars on the twigs are the leaf scars while the other scars which pass horizontally around the twig are the bud scale scars (girdle scars). The dots or pores on the twig are called the lenticels. These are small gaps in the bark where the cells are loosely packed allowing carbon dioxide and oxygen to enter and leave.

Subject links
NC science
Scottish 5–14 science

3. What's living in the leaf litter?

Theme
Conservation; Plants, animals and their habitats.

Age range
Five to eleven.

Group size
Whole class and small groups.

What you need
Equipment and materials for making a pitfall trap (see Chapter 2, page 34), white trays, see-through plastic specimen containers, magnifying glass or hand lens, pooters, books on minibeasts.

What to do
Pitfall traps are a simple and cheap method of sampling the animals which live in the leaf litter of woods or on the surface of the soil or grass. Using pitfall traps it is possible to sample the animals living in a particular area.

Ask the younger children

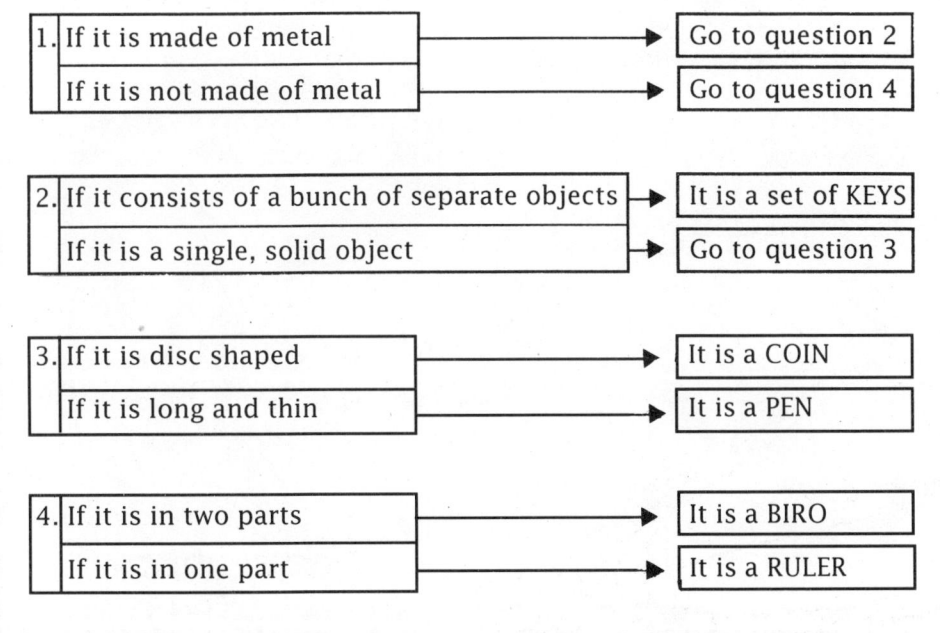

1. If it is made of metal	→ Go to question 2
If it is not made of metal	→ Go to question 4
2. If it consists of a bunch of separate objects	→ It is a set of KEYS
If it is a single, solid object	→ Go to question 3
3. If it is disc shaped	→ It is a COIN
If it is long and thin	→ It is a PEN
4. If it is in two parts	→ It is a BIRO
If it is in one part	→ It is a RULER

which small animals (minibeasts) they would expect to find on the surface of the soil and in the fallen, rotting leaves (leaf litter) on the floor of a wood. Make a class list of the suggestions (predictions) and display them. Show the children the pitfall traps and explain how they work.

Once in the wood discuss with the children where the traps will be placed to catch as many animals as possible. They might be located near a trunk, in open ground or in short vegetation. How can they make it a fair test? Using the trowel, carefully dig the container into the soil making sure that the rim of the container is level with the ground. If the class are visiting the wood for a day or less this should be carried out on arrival so that the contents may be examined prior to departure. Alternatively, they may be left overnight and collected the next day. Empty the contents of the pitfall trap into a white tray or into see-through plastic specimen containers and allow the children to observe them using magnifying glasses and hand lenses.

Encourage the children to draw animals of their choice. Help them to identify their animals from reference books if they show interest and collate the findings for the class. How does the list compare with the predicted list? Show the children pictures of the animals they have found and encourage them to read and find out more about them.

For the older children, explain the use of the pitfall traps prior to the visit and ask the children to think of an investigation they might like to carry out. This may need further consideration when they see the woodland environment at first hand. They might like to compare the animals found near the trunk, with those between the trees and those found in the undergrowth. Alternatively, they might like to see if more animals or more species of animals are found in the leaf litter of a group of oak trees compared with a group of sycamore trees and beech trees. Another investigation might involve the traps being given different baits. How would they ensure that the investigation was a fair test? Set up the pitfall traps as indicated in Chapter 2 (page 34). Ask the children to make predictions and to give reasons for their predictions. Using books get the children to identify and record their catch. Which group of invertebrates do the animals belong to? What did their investigation show? Was it as they predicted? Was it really a fair test? How might it be improved?

Content

Pitfall traps are a method by which animals that live on the surface of the soil or in the leaf litter may be trapped. The children will be able to appreciate the variety of animals found in this habitat. These animals are invertebrates (animals without backbones) and are mainly of two groups. The soft animals (snails and slugs) belong to the group called the molluscs while the others are insects, spiders and crustaceans and belong to the group called the arthropods (arthro = jointed; poda = legs; animals with jointed legs).

The animals are given some protection by the leaves placed in the pitfall container. Ensure that all the animals are returned to their natural habitat as soon as possible.

Subject links
NC science
Scottish 5–14 science

4. Tracks and signs

Theme
Conservation; Plants, animals and their habitats

Age range
Five to eleven.

Group size
Whole class and small groups.

What you need
Visit to a mixed deciduous woodland, plaster of Paris, small tins, water in a container, clean sticks, stiff paper or card, paper clips, paper, pencils, clipboards, rulers, photocopiable page 181, reference books on tracks and signs – for example, the *Oxford Clue Book* (see Resources, Chapter 13); in addition, paint and varnish which need not be taken into the field.

What to do
Whilst in the wood or prior to the visit, talk to the children about the larger animals which might be found there. This might be an opportunity to remind them that all living things which are not plants are animals, so the list should include members of the mammals, birds, reptiles and amphibians.

Ask the younger children which animals might be present in a wood. Do they often see animals when they walk through a wood? Why is this? Where have they all gone? Suggest to the children that there might be other ways of finding out which animals have been in the wood apart from seeing or hearing them. Can they think what this might be? How do they know if a mole has been in the garden? How do they know that a dog or fox has walked across the flower bed? Introduce the idea of animal tracks and signs. Using photocopiable page 181 encourage the children to observe the surroundings closely for animal tracks and signs. These might include footprints, fur, feathers, skins or egg remains, holes out of leaves, remains of nuts or cones, remains of snail shells, droppings, pellets of birds, damage to bark, holes in bark and nests. An earlier reconnaissance of the wood is advisable so that appropriate areas may be chosen for this activity.

The children could make a collection of some of the signs and sketch pictures of some of the others such as footprints and holes in the bark. Talk to the children about the possible animals or types of animals which have made the track or sign. The findings could be displayed with appropriate drawings and writing on returning to the classroom.

Introduce the activity to the older children in a similar way to that suggested above for the younger children. Using reference materials and with or without photocopiable page 181 (depending on ability), the children can explore the immediate area of the wood looking for tracks and signs and attempt to identify what caused it and what the sign actually is. Encourage them to measure and draw accurately what they find and to write down which animal they think has made the track or sign.

The children could make a plaster cast of a bird or mammal footprint using the plaster of Paris method described on page 35 of Chapter 2. Back in the classroom the shape of the footprint can be painted and the whole cast varnished. The children can display their finds and associated work when they return to school. This could be supplemented by a list of the animals whose tracks and signs they discovered.

Content

Tracks and trails should be found in most woods as long as the soil is wet. They can also be found in snow or sand. If the track has three toe-prints pointing forward and possibly one facing backwards, it is a bird. If the animal has one or two large toe-prints, it is a hoofed animal. A badger print has five toe-prints and a large pad print while a fox's print is pear-shaped. Nuts and cones are opened by mice, voles or fruit-eating birds such as finches and nuthatches. Holes in leaves are caused by caterpillars, adult insects or slugs and snails. Broken snail shells with jagged edges are caused by a vole or hedgehog if individual or scattered, or by a thrush if in a clump near a stone ('anvil') as thrushes take the shells in their beaks and smash them on stones to get at the snail inside. Pellets (round lumps usually containing feathers) have been disgorged by birds such as owls, rooks or jackdaws. Molehills indicate the presence of moles and damage to trunks may be caused by beetles (small holes and chambers in the bark) and woodpeckers. The bark of young trees may be stripped by hares, particularly if the winter is severe, while deer may tear bark off older trees. Axe marks are generally caused by children building dens or collecting wood for Guy Fawkes night!

Subject links

NC science
Scottish 5–14 science

5. Coppicing: once a way of life

Theme
Environmental change; Conservation.

Age range
Eight to eleven.

Group size
Whole class, then individuals.

What you need
Visit to a wood where there is evidence of coppicing, paper, pencils.

What to do
When in the wood, ask the children to observe the trunks of the trees. Most trees have a single trunk but some trees have a number of smaller trunks growing out from near the ground. Ask the children how this might have happened. Is this man-made or a natural phenomenon? Can they find any other trees like this one? Are they all the same species? Which species is it/ are they?

Establish that it is a man-made phenomenon (which will be obvious by the straight cut if the wood is currently being managed) and the technique is called *coppicing*. Why would people want to cut the tree in this way? Why isn't it allowed to grow to its full height? For what use might we need the cut wood? Talk to the children about the benefits of coppicing hazel to both man and the natural environment. Ask the children to draw a coppiced tree. Back in the classroom they could find out about and draw some of the products which were made/are still made from coppiced wood.

Content
Centuries ago hazel was found all over the countryside until oak trees became established, but it is still common in hedges and woods. It is also a very useful shrub because it grows quickly, starts to grow again as soon as it is cut down, is bendy and tough, produces early pollen for bees and produces nuts. Coppicing (from the French *couper* = to cut) has been an important occupation in Great Britain from Norman times until the early twentieth century. Hazel would be cut on a rotational basis every seven to fifteen years depending on the weather and soil fertility. Thus in a nine-year coppice a person would be responsible for coppicing all the hazel trees in an area of woodland in nine years, by which time the first area had grown again and was ready for cutting. Lime and ash trees have also been used in this way.

Hazel wood was used for making hurdles for temporary fences before the Enclosures Act (because there were few hedges and permanent fences) and for hoops for barrels and walls of wattle and daub. It is seldom used for this today although coppiced hazel is still used for wattle fencing, wind breaks, pea and bean sticks and rustic poles.

Woodlands

Not only did coppicing produce useful products but it allowed, as the hazel regenerated, for a variety of habitats in the wood, which encouraged different plants and animals. It was a deliberate management strategy for the benefit of man and other animals and plants, which is still carried out today for conservation and economic purposes.

Subject links
NC science, history
Scottish 5–14 science, social subjects

6. Planning and planting a school wood

Theme
Environmental change; Conservation.

Age range
Nine to eleven.

Group size
Small groups working in co-operation.

What you need
Plans or maps of the school, permission from the school and the groundstaff or relevant authority to create a small woodland area.

What to do
As the planting of a few trees, far less a wood, may not be possible for all schools, it might be that the activity could involve planning a woodland in the local community, rather than planning and creating one in the school grounds.

From the woodland work might arise the desire to have a small wooded area in the school grounds. Suggest this to the pupils after first establishing with the headteacher and other relevant authorities such as the groundstaff that it is feasible. Talk to the children about the idea and encourage them to raise the questions which will need to be considered and answered before a wooded area can be planted.

Who would they need to talk to or write to, to gain permission (headteacher, governors, groundstaff, local council)? Where would the small wood be planted? Should it be adjacent to a hedge, near people's houses, near the school drains, near another 'wild' area, in the middle or on the edge of the school grounds? Which trees should be planted? Should they be indigenous, deciduous trees, coniferous trees or ornamental trees? What is the age of the trees that are to be planted? Are the children going to grow them from seed or are they going to obtain them as young trees? Where will they obtain them from? Can they obtain them free from the local authorities or from conservation groups? Do they know how and when to plant them? How can they obtain this knowledge? Will they need to look after them once they are planted?

Provide the children with a photostat map or plan of the school grounds or ask them to draw their own. Working in groups, ask them to decide where the wood should be situated. Clearly, the size of the wooded area needs to be established in advance and should not be too large. In addition, the children will need to decide which trees they would like to plant and provide a plan of this, taking into account the fact that trees grow upwards and outwards! Each group should make a case for the area and against other areas and be prepared to put their case to the other groups. The headteacher and governors could be invited to this presentation. Once the area has been decided upon, plans can go ahead to obtain the trees and to plant them. Planting should take place in late February/early March before the trees have started to grow or in late autumn once the trees have stopped growing.

Content
The most fun and sense of achievement would be obtained if the children were to grow their trees from seed but this would result in small seedlings which would take a long time to establish. It is probably better to obtain more established young trees which could be supplemented by those grown from seed. The trees will certainly need watering if it is dry in the first spring and summer after planting until the root systems become established. In addition, the area immediately around the growing trunk should be weeded in order that competition for minerals does not occur. Leave the rest of the area to grow wild.

The project needs to be introduced as a long-term venture in order to avoid raising expectations of short-term results. In ten or twenty years the wooded area will become established but maximum tree size will not be reached for much longer. However, the children will have established a natural area in the 'barren' school grounds, provided habitats for animals and plants, helped to conserve tree species, added to the levels of oxygen in the atmosphere and provided trees that they and future pupils may study. They will have also learned how to plant and look after trees and be able to identify some of them. The children can feel justly proud of the fact that they will have contributed to conservation in their area.

Subject links
NC science
Scottish 5–14 science

7. Tropical rainforests and deforestation

Theme
Conservation; Environmental change.

Age range
Five to eleven.

Group size
Whole class and small groups.

What you need
Pictures of tropical rainforests, a video of a tropical rainforest if available, fish tank or propagator with lid, gravel,

charcoal, compost (preferably not peat-based), stones, exotic-looking plants such as coconut palms and rubber plants, atlases, photocopiable page 182, books on tropical rainforests.

What to do

Show the children the pictures of tropical rainforests and, if available, a video. Ask them if they know where the tropical region is found on the globe. Therefore, where would they find the *tropical rainforests*? Explain that the tropical region is hot. What would the weather (climate) be like in the region of a tropical rainforest? Explain that it would be hot and very damp.

Talk to the children about the fact that some of the tropical rainforests are being chopped down for timber and so that farming can take place. What would suffer as a result? What do they think about cutting down forests? Tell them that people are concerned because the rainforests are important for the stability of the world's climate (due to the large amounts of water associated with the trees and soil in which they are growing) and because parts of the trees are used for food and medicines.

Encourage the children to cultivate their own rainforest. In the bottom of a fish tank or propagator place some gravel and some pieces of charcoal and cover this layer with 6-8 centimetres of compost (not soil). Plant a number of exotic looking plants at a reasonable distance apart to allow for growth. Water well, cover with a lid and place in a sunny, warm position. The children have now created a mini rainforest of their own. All they have to do is water it when required.

Ask the older children what they know about rainforests. Why are people concerned about them? Why are they being destroyed? Introduce them to the areas of the world where rainforests are found. Working in small groups, give the children photocopiable page 182 and ask them to locate the countries where rainforests are found using an atlas. Raise the issue of climate in the region of the rainforests and ask them to first discuss then describe on paper what a walk through such a forest would be like. The children should research the importance of the rainforests in terms of the stability of the climate, the conservation of animals and plants and the possible economic importance of the plants as sources of food and medicines.

If appropriate, the children could set up their own class mini-rainforest as suggested above.

Content

The natives of the rainforests are being forced out from their natural homes because the forests are being destroyed. Half of the world's rainforests have been destroyed. They are being cut down to provide timber for countries around the world and to create more farm land to produce food. Most of the countries where the rainforests occur are poor and the population is generally rising rapidly, so they need to sell their natural resources and provide more food by creating more farmland.

The rainforests are important in controlling the climate around the world because the trees absorb the carbon dioxide in the atmosphere. Without these forests there would be a build-up in the levels of carbon dioxide resulting in an increase in the Earth's temperature – global warming. They are also important in providing us with oxygen. Trees take in carbon dioxide which we breathe out, and give off oxygen which we breathe in. We have not yet learned how to make best use of the variety of resources provided by the rainforests, which include food and medicines. Capitalising on the resources of the rainforests must be carried out in a sustainable way, so that we can reap the benefits without destroying the forests.

It should perhaps be pointed out to children that countries where rainforest resources are being depleted are merely repeating what was done in most Western, developed countries, i.e. cutting down trees. In Britain, the felling of trees provided more land for farming and industry, more food to feed an ever-increasing population and more wealth through industrial production.

Subject links
NC science and geography
Scottish 5–14 science and social subjects

8. Green products: green matches

Theme
Conservation; Pollution.

Age range
Ten to eleven.

Group size
Individual activity at home.

What you need
Packaging from so-called 'green' products including match boxes, product literature explaining why a product is green (see Resources Chapter).

What to do
Ask the children what they understand by the word

Woodlands **119**

'green'. What is meant by a 'green' product. A range of products claiming to be 'green' could be on display.

Ask the children for examples of green products; these might include washing powder, washing-up liquid, bleaches, various cosmetics and matches.

Ask the children (with assistance from their parent or guardians) to make a list of any green products they have in their house or that they see in the local shops, and to find any information explaining why the product is green. They should draw up a recording sheet to fill in this information, for example, a table divided into two, the left-hand column listing the names of products and the right giving reasons why it is green (according to the product label).

After a period of time discuss the class results. Children who have had difficulty in finding appropriate items could complete a recording sheet using the items on display in the class.

Further activity
Show the children the matchboxes and explain that certain matches are from sustainable forests and that some matchboxes are made from recycled board. Discuss these ideas with the children. What are the advantages of using recycled board? How does it affect conservation of resources and decrease pollution? What is meant by a sustainable forest? Get the children to play the 'sustainable forest game' (see activity 9).

Content
Products are said to be 'green' if they are friendly to the environment. This might be because their manufacture involves conserving natural resources or because their use reduces pollution or does not involve any pollution at all. Sometimes the extent of the 'greenness' is not made clear and one unpleasant chemical is replaced by another. Manufacturers' claims should be considered carefully.

Subject links
NC science
Scottish 5–14 science

9. The sustainable forest game

Theme
Conservation; Environmental change; Pollution.

Age range
Ten to eleven.

Group size
Pairs.

What you need
Photocopiable pages 183–185, preferably photocopied on to card, scissors, envelope or small plastic bag.

What to do
Tell the children that they are going to play the 'sustainable forest game' described below. Once they are familiar with the game you could ask them to design their own, having been introduced to the idea of sustainable wood resources.

Give the children photocopiable pages 183 and 184. Page 183 represents a mature forest where the trees are fifty years old and ready for harvesting. Ask the children to cut out the axe symbols, numbers, money tokens (£1000 and £100) and the time tokens indicating how much time has elapsed, on page 184. Put these in a safe place like an envelope or a small plastic bag. Finally, give the children the instructions for the game which can be found on page 185 and ensure that they read them carefully and understand them. The game is designed to cover a period of seventy-five years.

Provide the children with two challenges:
A To make as much money from the forest as quickly as possible.
B To ensure that the forest is sustainable and that a regular income is generated.

After the children have played the game, discuss the implications of the management strategies used in each challenge. With Management Strategy A, the children will have made a large amount of money quickly, but the forest is probably destroyed with little or no replanting. The forest is not sustainable with this sort of strategy. Much or all of the wildlife will have been killed because their habitats have been destroyed and the top soil washed away into the rivers by heavy rains, thus causing pollution. This happens because, as the trees and undergrowth plants are destroyed, there are no roots left to anchor and retain the soil. During the heavy rains the top soil is washed away into streams and rivers. This in turn can pollute the river water due to the presence of suspended solids, which is detrimental to the water supply.

With Management Strategy B, the children must chop down an area every five years and replace it immediately by replanting young trees. If this strategy is used the forest will be sustainable, because, by the time all the mature trees have been chopped down, the first area to be felled and replanted will have grown to maturity again. The children will not have made as much money as in the previous challenge, but they will have generated a steady, regular income and they will be producing a sustainable product, conserving wildlife and reducing possible pollution as the soil will not be eroded and washed into rivers and streams.

Content

A sustainable forest is one in which the amount of planting is equal or greater than the amount of felling. As one area is felled to meet commercial demands, an area similar to that is replanted, ensuring there is a continuity in cropping. For example, in simple terms, if a particular tree type takes fifty years to mature and the company who owns the trees wishes to crop the forest every year, then they must ensure that a *maximum* of one fiftieth of the acreage is felled and immediately replanted to ensure a sustainable crop. This ensures continuity of supply without the need to chop down extra trees which cannot be replaced.

Tree felling without replanting leads to loss of wildlife, erosion of soil and pollution of the water with soil particles.

Subject links

NC science and geography
Scottish 5–14 science and social subjects

10. Study of an oak tree – A whole investigation

Theme
Conservation; Environmental change; Plants, animals and their habitats.

Age range
Five to eleven.

Group size
Small groups.

What you need
Pens, pencils, paper, clipboards, magnifying glasses, pooters, plastic containers, reference books on trees, a camera.

Planning and preparation
An oak tree is an ideal tree for investigation as it has more species of animal associated with it than any other British tree. Hence, its study should be more productive than for other trees. Try to choose a tree or trees which has branches near to the ground so that the children can explore the leaves and twigs.

The study could be repeated, in part or in whole, at a different time of the year to see the contrast between the tree in the spring or summer and the autumn or winter. Photographs could be taken in each season as a visual record of the changes taking place.

Divide the children into small groups of three or four and assign each of them to start on a different activity. This should ensure that one part of the tree, for example, the trunk, is not over run by children, though this would be further helped by choosing two or more trees in close proximity. The children can then move on to the other activities, so completing their investigation of the tree.

Investigating

The whole tree
Standing at a distance, the younger children could attempt to sketch the outline of the tree and possibly compare it with another type of tree. The older children could repeat this but with more accuracy and could estimate the height of the tree using one of the methods described on page 32 of Chapter 2.

The trunk
The younger children could find out the girth of the tree by linking together their outstretched hands at waist height (handspans).

They could carry out bark rubbing using a sheet of white paper and a soft pencil. Small hands will find this difficult so it will help if one or two children hold the paper tightly while another child carefully shades with the pencil, to ensure that they do not rip the paper. They could comment on the texture of the bark and add this note to their bark rubbing. This could be extended for older children to compare 2 or 3 oak trees and other tree types. The crevices of the tree could be closely observed to see if there are any minibeasts present. These may be collected and examined using pooters (see page 34, Chapter 2) and magnifying equipment and drawn, with a description added. Finally, the younger children could look for animal signs such as birds' nests, woodpecker holes and holes caused by beetles.

The older children could use a tape measure to calculate the girth of the tree. This could lead to further investigations comparing height and girth of different trees. A bark rubbing could be carried out and compared to similar rubbings of other oaks and other tree types. The children could describe the texture of the bark and the shape of the bark pieces. Following this tactile experience the children could be blindfolded in turn and taken to a tree where they attempt to recognise it, or say whether it is an oak or not. Animals in the bark could be obtained using pooters, observed and drawn with the aid of magnifying equipment and later classified using their own or documented criteria.

Finally, animal signs could be detected, identified and documented on a picture of the tree.

Twigs and branches

The younger children could look at the texture of the twigs and branches and examine the colour. The older children could consider how the leaves are arranged on the twig. In both cases pictures may be drawn and descriptive comments added.

Leaves

The younger children could draw around a leaf or leaves. They could count the number of lobes or indentations on each leaf. Is it the same in all the leaves? Does it vary much? They could look for animals on the upperside and underside of the leaves. These may be collected using pooters, observed closely, described and drawn. Tell the children to look for animal signs on the leaves which might include damage to leaves, webs, marks and unusual structures such as oak apples, marble and other galls. These could be drawn and described and one or two galls opened to find the animal (grub) inside.

The older children could draw pictures of the shape of the leaves and measure the width and length of a number of leaves. What is the average length and width? Animals on the leaves could be observed, classified and identified using reference books. Animal signs could be located and identified. These might include rolled or eaten leaves indicating the presence of insects and oak galls, of which there are several types. These include oak apples, marble galls and cherry galls, which are growths produced by the oak tree to isolate the grubs of gall wasps. The children could make a limited collection of the galls, drawing those that interest them. Back in the classroom they can research the cause of the galls and how they are formed.

Under the tree

The younger children can place some leaf litter (leaves and decayed leaves) in a white tray and can use a pooter to isolate any animals. The animals can then be drawn and described and perhaps

Woodlands 123

grouped into sets. The leaf litter should be examined. What is it composed of? Are the leaves the same as those on the tree? How do they differ? Are other leaf types present? If so, how did they get there? Encourage the children to search for animal signs such as broken snail shells, opened nuts and fur. They could make a collection of these items to take back to the classroom.

The older children could extend the study of the animals found in the leaf litter by classifying them on their own or given criteria. They could also identify the animals using reference texts. They could then examine the leaf litter in more detail by carefully examining how it changes with depth, bearing in mind that by the end of the winter there will be little left in an oak wood. More decay should be seen nearer the soil due to the action of minibeasts, bacteria and fungi. This can then be related to the conditions needed for the decay of living (organic) organisms: temperature, moisture, air and decaying organisms. The older children could make a collection of animal signs and attempt to identify the items found and the animals involved.

Recording and communicating

A number of ideas for recording results have been given in the sections above alongside the activities. However, back in the classroom a display could be set up involving the children's drawings, observations and artefacts. This could be supplemented by further book-based research. The children in their groups could give a talk on their findings and what they have learned to the rest of the class and other classes. This information should then be retained for comparative purposes when the children examine the oak tree in a different season. A photographic record of the activities will serve to highlight and reinforce the seasonal changes and differences. This will also make the information more accessible to younger children who have been involved in the investigation at a more basic level.

CHAPTER 10
The school and home environment

The school and home environments are ideal contexts in which the children can be introduced to a number of important issues which affect their everyday lives. Most of a child's time is spent either at school or at home so respect for these environments and preventing waste provide important foundations for understanding the wider world outside.

Litter is a common problem in school grounds, whether it is dropped by the children or blown into the grounds by the wind. The children should be encouraged to address questions such as whether there are enough litter bins around the school and whether they are sited in the most appropriate places.

More than ever, schools are conscious of the high cost of energy to heat and light buildings. Children do not pay energy bills and to them the consequences of leaving doors open are not usually of great importance. However, a school policy on the closing of doors and windows and encouraging children to turn off water taps and lights will make them more aware of the high cost of energy and the need to conserve previous fuel reserves. Older children can be encouraged to consider energy saving in their own homes by investigating whether they have cavity wall insulation, double glazing, lagged pipes and hot water tanks, roof insulation and draft excluders.

Conservation of materials may also be considered frequently because primary teachers are experts at recycling boxes, clothes and plastic bottles, to name but a few. Stress the importance of using recycled items in the classroom and at home and explain the implications of conservation of materials, for example, recycling paper means cutting down fewer trees and also reduces pollution.

Environmental change can be observed by visiting sites near the school which have undergone some form of change, either favourable or detrimental to the environment. The same basic theme can be considered in different contexts, with children recording the weather, observing birds in the school grounds at different times of the year and pond dipping in the summer and winter. The effect of weather on the natural world may then be explored in relation to the seasons, life cycles, hibernation and migration.

The activities in this chapter will help children to understand further the complex issues concerned with environmental education in the familiar context of the school and to a lesser extent the home.

BACKGROUND

Litter
- from within the school
- from outside the school

Changes and the local environment
- favourable
- detrimental

Saving items for recycling
- newspapers
- paper/packaging
- bottles
- cans

Conserving fuel energy
- switching off lights
- closing doors and windows
- turning off taps
- cavity wall insulation
- double glazing
- roof insulation
- pipe lagging
- draft excluders

Changes and the seasons
- birds in the school grounds
- recording the weather
- pond dipping

Recycling items for school
- boxes/packaging
- plastic bottles/containers
- clothes
- silver foil

Reducing pollution
- conserving fuel energy
- reducing litter
- using recyclable items

(Central node: SCHOOL AND HOME ENVIRONMENT)

Progression in teaching and learning		
Theme	**Details of activity and activity number**	
	Key Stage 1 (P1–3)	Key Stage 2 (P4–7)
Conservation	Switching off lights, closing indoors, turning off taps (1) The school pond – A whole investigation (8)	Identifying and saving energy in the home; survey of measures taken to conserve energy (6,7)
Environmental change	Birds present in different seasons (5) Weather throughout the year/seasons (3) The school pond – A whole investigation (8) Is a site detrimental or advantageous to the environment? (4)	
Plants animals and their habitats	Birds present in different seasons (5) The school pond – A whole investigation (8)	
Pollution	Conserving fuel by being diligent (1) Where does litter come from? (2) Is the site detrimental or advantageous to the environment? (4) Identifying and saving energy in the home (6,7)	

126   Chapter 10

ACTIVITIES

1. Switch off, turn off, close!

Theme
Conservation; Pollution.

Age range
Five to seven.

Group size
Whole class initially, then in pairs.

What you need
Copies of photocopiable page 186, pens or pencils.

What to do
Talk to the children about how the school is kept warm. Show them the heating boiler, the radiators and the pipes. Relate it to their homes. How are their homes kept warm? Do they have central heating and/or gas, electric or coal fires or storage radiators?

Why does the school or their house sometimes feel cool or cold? Is it because the heating has not been on for long or has it not been turned on enough? Ask the children how much of the heat can be kept in the school or their homes. Ask them how it is possible for the heat to escape easily from the school and their homes. Lead the discussion around to the need to close doors (not just outside doors) to keep in the heat, and the need to have fresh air without letting too much heat escape through the windows.

Ask the children how else may valuable heat energy or electrical (light) energy be wasted in school and in their homes. Do they switch off their bedroom light when they leave the room or do they leave it on for when they return? Do they leave taps dripping, particularly the hot tap so that the boiler has to waste more fuel to heat more water?

Explain to the children that they are going to go around the school, checking whether outside doors are closed, whether windows are open unnecessarily, whether lights have been left on unnecessarily and whether any taps have not been properly turned off. Provide the children with copies of photocopiable page 186 and explain that they should work in pairs to fill in the location of any heat and energy loss. Warn your colleagues of the possible disruption to the rest of the school; you will need to decide whether the whole class

The school and home environment 127

carries out the activity together or whether it is advisable to spread it over the day or longer.

Talk to the whole class about the findings. Which doors were left open? Which lights were left on unnecessarily? Which cloakroom had the most taps dripping? Re-emphasise that these waste money and valuable fuels, and add to pollution because more fuel has to be burnt. Stress that cold water is also a valuable resource which should not be wasted.

Content
There are different forms of energy which include heat and light energy from the sun, chemical energy from fuels, sound energy, nuclear energy, electrical energy, moving energy and stored energy. When fossil fuels burn, the waste gases emitted include carbon dioxide, sulphur dioxide and carbon monoxide. If the fuel is not burnt efficiently, more carbon monoxide is produced.

Energy resources are expensive and it is important that they are conserved as much as possible. Heat rapidly escapes through open doors and windows. Lights and hot water taps left on consume relatively large amounts of energy. This also results in more pollution because more fuel has to be burnt and more gases are produced. Children might be nagged by their parents to close doors as doors left open make the house cold and consequently cost money which could be better spent on other things.

Subject links
NC science and geography
Scottish 5–14 science and social subjects

2. Where does litter come from?

Theme
Pollution.

Age range
Five to seven.

Group size
Whole class and individuals.

What you need
Photocopiable page 187, spirit marker pens, pens or pencils, plastic gloves, two containers labelled 'litter we dropped' and 'litter blown into the school grounds'.

What to do
Talk to the children about litter, asking questions such as the following:
• Where does litter come from?
• Do they like the sight of litter?
• How do they feel about dirty streets?
• How can litter be reduced?

Begin the activity by asking the children to carry out a litter survey in the school grounds using copies of photocopiable page 187. Ask the children to identify the types of litter and record the number of items on the sheet. The blanks in the left hand column may either be completed by the teacher or the children, depending on the amount of help required. The data may then be collated and simple bar charts drawn.

Follow this up by asking the children to try to find out from where the litter originates. Is it being dropped by the children or is it being blown into the school grounds by the wind? It might also be dropped by persons other than the children. Over the course of a week, get the children to use spirit marker pens to mark the labels of any items of food they bring to school, including sandwich wrappings and foil. Clearly, this will be time-consuming and would need the co-operation of all staff, perhaps within a whole-school mini-project. After a week, give the children plastic gloves and ask them to go out into the school grounds and each

Subject links
NC science
Scottish 5–14 science and health education

3. Rain, wind, hail or shine

Theme
Environmental change.

Age range
Five to seven.

Group size
Small groups.

What you need
Card, scissors, felt-tipped pens, Blu-Tack.

What to do
Ask the groups to take turns to record the weather on a daily basis over a period of time such as a week. To develop the idea of fair testing, encourage them to record the weather at the same time each day; just before or after lunchtime might be appropriate. The children can then record their findings on a daily and/or weekly weather chart. This could later be extended to a monthly chart.

Involve the children in the construction of some weather charts for use in the classroom. Older children could be encouraged to make charts with more than one symbol.

The temperature and wind directions could also be added. A daily chart would require cards with the day, date, weather type and related picture attached with Blu-Tack. The children could also fill in a weekly chart with symbols they have designed or drawn themselves. Words to describe the weather could also be

---

collect the first five pieces of litter they find. Provide two containers labelled 'litter we dropped' and 'litter blown on to the school grounds' and get the children to place the litter in the appropriate one.

When the children have collected the litter, add up the pieces and discuss the results.
• Are the children dropping most of the litter?
• Are they polluting their own school environment?
• What can be done within the school?
• What can be done about the litter which appears to be blowing into the school?

Further activity
The children could compare the types of litter found in the school grounds with that found in the street (see Chapter 6). They might also like to consider whether more litter bins should be provided outside the school and, if so, where they should be placed.

Safety
• Ensure that the children do not 'sniff' the marker pens.
• Ensure that the children wear plastic gloves when collecting litter and/or wash their hands thoroughly afterwards.
• Children should not pick up items which are likely to cut them e.g. broken bottles and fragments of tins etc.

Content
People drop litter deliberately because they have little consideration for the environment and are too lazy to find a bin or take it home, or inadvertently, perhaps by dislodging a sweet wrapper as they take a handkerchief from their pocket. Litter is a form of pollution and everybody has a responsibility to reduce it by not dropping tissues or sweet wrappers or over-filling the dustbin so that some of the rubbish blows away.

added, depending on the children's ability. A monthly chart could record the number of days a particular weather type was experienced, and totals could be added at the end of the month. Again, children could record more than one type of weather each day, such as wind and rain or sun and cloud.

Ask the children how the weather will or did affect:
- what they wear;
- what they do;
- how plants grow.

How does the weather differ in the summer compared to the winter? What happens to plants in the autumn and what happens to them in the spring? The last question will help to develop ideas that plants find it difficult to grow if it is very cold (compare to the polar regions) or if it is too hot and dry (compare to the desert areas).

Content
By taking weather records over a week, a month and a term children will be introduced to the idea of rigorous, systematic recording. They will also be able to compare the weather with previous weeks and months and realise that the weather is changeable but follows some sort of pattern. This will be particularly noticeable if temperature is recorded. There will also be opportunities to discuss the effect the weather, and possibly the climate, has on them, their surroundings and the growth of plants.

Subject links
NC science, geography
Scottish 5–14 science, social subjects

4. For better or for worse?

Theme
Environmental change; Pollution (depending on the activity).

Age range
Five to eleven.

Group size
Pairs or small groups.

What you need
Camera, paper, clipboards, pens and pencils, a visit to an area (or areas) near to the school which has undergone some form of change whether it be perceived as improving or damaging the environment.

What to do
Prior to the visit, talk to the children about changes in the environment with which they might be familiar. Have these changes been advantageous or detrimental? Would a new factory on an old, disused site which was full of wildlife but where rubbish was continually tipped be beneficial or harmful? Might it be beneficial to some people and some wildlife but detrimental to other people and to other wildlife species?

Take the children to an area where a significant environmental change is taking place or photograph such a change to use in future years. If the change is still taking place, get the children to record it through sketches, pictures, writing, photographs and poems. Discuss with the children the changes they are seeing taking place. How do they feel about them? Will the changes benefit them? Will they benefit their families or friends? Might they be detrimental or beneficial to the environment? Discuss with them such complex issues as whether it is better to have a modern development or derelict land. Why does 'waste' land always seem to be built on in time? Why isn't it left as 'waste' land?

If the change has already taken place, try to provide the children with photographs of the site prior to the development. The local history society, council or occupier of the site might well be able to help. If these are not available, build up a picture in the children's minds of the site prior to development or show them a similar site. Get the children to draw pictures of the site prior to change. Take the children to the site of the development and get them to sketch and comment on the changes. Do they like what they see? Are the changes for the better? For whom and what? Are the changes detrimental in some way? To whom or what? Why have these changes been brought about? Was there really a need for them?

Further activity
As a contrast it would be useful to visit an area where the environment has clearly been improved and an area where the environment has been harmed. These might include:
• a new playing field or playground;
• a pedestrian crossing on a dangerous road;
• a pedestrianised street in the town;
• a street where access is restricted and/or speed bumps have been installed;
• an area where trees are being/have been planted;
• an unsightly development;
• a new road system;
• destruction of woods or a wilderness area built upon;
• a waste dump or area where litter has been deposited;
• remnants of an industrial site or abandoned building.

Content
Just as 'one person's meat is another one's poison', so a detrimental change to the environment as perceived by one person may be beneficial to another. A derelict site might have been home to a rich variety of wildlife and might have made a wonderful place for a Sunday afternoon walk or somewhere to walk the dog. However, once a factory has been built in its place, some of the children's parents might have obtained a job there. Black smoke might be given off from the chimney sometimes, but at the same time the lake in the grounds might be home to many birds and might be the only substantial water body for miles.

The complex nature of environmental changes should be discussed with the children. Encourage them to articulate what they like, but make sure they are prepared to substantiate their views.

Subject links
NC science, geography
Scottish 5–14 social subjects

5. I spy with my little eye!

Theme
Environmental change.

Age range
Six to eleven.

Group size
Small groups collating their results for the whole class.

The school and home environment

What you need
Pens or pencils, clipboard, copies of photocopiable page 188, bird identification books, binoculars if available, drawing and display materials.

What to do
Talk to the children about British birds and ask them which birds they might see around the school grounds. Make a composite list and display it in the classroom. Ask the children to make a list of the birds they see in the school grounds, using photocopiable page 188 as an identification sheet, and to write where (the habitat) they saw them. This could start as a focused activity, possibly involving a walk around the school grounds, but could continue for a week or so involving individual identification, whether in or outside the classroom. The children could see if a particular bird is found in one type of habitat only (field, trees, hedge, concrete or tarmac) and show their results graphically in the most appropriate manner.

The activity could be repeated at different times throughout the year to see if there are any differences in the birds spotted.

Content
By carrying out this activity the children will acquire knowledge of ten or more common British birds which are seen around schools and homes. Individual species of birds frequent different habitats, although there is often substantial overlap. For example, a pied wagtail can often be found looking for insects on tarmac and concrete around school grounds, blackbirds will be found on the grass and in hedges and trees, while redwings and fieldfares will be found mainly on the grass.

Some birds will be present at different times of the year. For example, the redwing will only be found in the winter and the fieldfare is more likely to be seen in the winter as both are winter migrants. Other birds such as the blackbird and robin may be seen throughout the year, while swallows and swifts will only be present in the spring and summer.

Subject links
NC science
Scottish 5–14 science

6. Energy saver – 1

Theme
Conservation and pollution.

Age range
Eight to eleven.

Group size
Whole class and then pairs or individuals.

What you need
Copies of photocopiable page 189, pens or pencils.

What to do
Talk to the children about where energy is used in the school and the home. In the school, this would include the heating system, the lighting and other sources such as kettles, tape recorders etc. At home this would include the central heating system, gas, electric and solid fuel fires, cookers, electrical items such as cassette players and CDs, lights, and so on.

Ask the children how energy might be saved in the school. Hopefully, they will come up with ideas such as closing the windows and outside doors, reducing the temperature of the thermostat, turning off lights when the room is not in use, ensuring that the hot water taps are not dripping, etc. Discuss with the children the need to save energy, mentioning the high cost of energy and the relative shortage of some types of energy reserves in the world. Ask them what energy-saving features could be included in the design of new houses and other buildings.

Give the children copies of photocopiable page 189 and ask them to work either individually or in pairs and identify, by ringing items on the sheet, the opportunities to minimise energy loss and subsequently to save money. Ask them also to annotate the items they ring, saying how a reduction in energy loss might be brought about.

Further activity
Develop this activity by asking the children to design an energy-saving house of the future. Encourage them to talk to their parents and/or to visit a DIY shop, electricity/gas board or electricity shop to gain further information. Introduce ideas such as solar panels for heating, south facing windows to trap the sun's heat, draught proofing, insulation, use of electronic timers and so on. The children could make a display of their designs and make short presentations.

Content
Energy may be conserved in the home and other buildings by a number of means. The children might identify certain circumstances where energy may be saved, but may not be so familiar with lagging pipes and hot water tanks and the role of carpets to prevent heat loss. Energy loss in the form of heat is serious and expensive. For example, a door left open allows heat to escape, makes the room colder and means that the boiler has to burn more fuel to compensate which in turn causes pollution. The high cost of fuel bills should be emphasised, as should the shortage of fossil fuels such as gas, oil and coal. The individual level of responsibility should be stressed.

Photocopiable page 189 shows a picture of a house where energy savings could be made by:
• switching off the lights and other electrical items not being used;
• insulating the roof space;
• double-glazing the windows;
• draught-proofing the doors;
• lagging the hot water tank and pipes in the roof space;
• turning the central heating thermostat down by one or two degrees;
• supplying cavity wall insulation;
• switching off or mending dripping taps;
• using the shower rather than the bath;
• fitting thermostats on all radiators;
• fitting dimmer switches to lights;
• ensuring that light bulbs use no more electricity than required to illuminate a room adequately.

Subject links
NC science and technology
Scottish 5–14 science and technology

The school and home environment   133

7. Energy saver – 2

Theme
Conservation and pollution.

Age range
Eight to eleven.

Group size
Whole class and then pairs or individuals.

What you need
Copies of photocopiable pages 189 and 190, pens or pencils, display materials.

What to do
Remind the children about energy loss in houses and other buildings. Using a diagram of a house similar to the one above, ask them to predict how much heat, as a percentage, escapes through each part of the house indicated by the arrows. Ask the children to use photocopiable page 190 to carry out an energy-saving audit in their own home with the help of a parent or guardian. The children need to document, in the second column on the sheet, the type of energy saver in each area/part of the house, for example, PVC double-glazed windows. They also need to say how energy may be saved if there is no energy-saving device present, for example, draught excluders around doors and windows.

Discuss and collate the results. How many children have double glazing in their homes? How many of these have PVC, hardwood or aluminium double glazing? Get the children to draw bar charts or histograms to show their findings. What is the average temperature of the thermostat in the houses? How could money be saved? Using the diagram of a poorly insulated house on photocopiable page 189, ask them to consider where money would be best spent to reduce the heating bills. These and many more questions may be asked and issues raised using the children's data. For example, the children could suggest the next course of action in their home to reduce the energy bill further.

Safety
The energy-saving survey should be carried out with the help of an adult, particularly where access to a loft is involved.

Content
Heat loss from a house is expensive and subsequently involves using up more scarce energy resources. Burning fuels causes pollution. Heat loss from a house with no insulation occurs as follows:
• 35 per cent through the walls;
• 25 per cent through the roof;
• 15 per cent as draughts around doors and windows;
• 15 per cent to the ground;
• 10 per cent through windows.

Subject links
NC science and technology
Scottish 5–14 science and technology

8. The school pond – A whole investigation

Theme
Conservation; Environmental change; Plants, animals and their habitats.

Age range
Five to seven.

Group size
Whole class working in groups.

What you need
Magnifying glass or hand lens reference aids (for example, *Oxford Clue Books,* paper, pens, pencils, long-handled pond net, small net, plastic teaspoons, plastic containers, white tray, bucket, clean water, aquarium with gravel (optional), photocopiable page 191.

Planning and preparation
For the purpose of this investigation it is assumed that there is a pond in the school grounds or in the locality. If the latter is the case, permission may need to be sought from the council or land owner. Ensure that the pond is safe for the age of the children; steep-sided water bodies should, if possible, be avoided. Also ensure that you have sufficient equipment for the visit which should include for each group:
• A long-handled pond net for collecting animals from the surface, from the vegetation and the bottom of the pond;
• A small net for transferring animals from one container to another;
• Plastic teaspoons for older children in which to view and transfer animals from one container to another;
• A white tray containing water in which to place animals for observation;
• A magnifying glass or hand lens;
• Identification materials and paper and pens with which to record findings;
• A bucket containing water in which to store animals and in which to carry them into the classroom, if required.

If an aquarium is to be set up in the classroom, it needs to be set up in advance of the visit. The aquarium should be clean, preferably with some washed gravel and mud at the bottom. Gently pour some pond water from the bucket or buckets into the aquarium, preferably on to a plate or a shallow tray so that the force of the water disturbs the mud and gravel as little as possible. Remove the plate. Add some water plants from the pond. Let the tank stand for a few days to allow the contents time to settle before adding the pond animals. Do not place it too close to a radiator or in direct sunshine. An aerator should be added, if available, to ensure that an adequate supply of oxygen is provided.

A visit to the pond at different times of the year would be most beneficial.

Investigating

Map of the pond
Ask the children to draw a picture of the pond, showing its shape and the positions of any trees and plants. This should have enough room beneath for the children to stick pictures of the pond animals they find.

Observing the pond closely
What can the pupils hear? What can they see? Is the water moving? Is the water clear or muddy? Can they see any animals in the water? Can they see any bubbles in the water? Can they see the bottom of the pond? What does it look like? Can they see any reflections?

Pond-dipping
Show the children how to use the net by sweeping it around in the water (see Chapter 2, *Sampling and collecting techniques*). Explain that if they go too deep into the mud they will collect a great deal of heavy, smelly mud! Partly fill the trays with water. Allow each child to collect animals with the net and to deposit the contents into the buckets. The other children in the group may then transfer animals to the trays for further observation, drawing and identification. If buckets are not available, the contents of the net may be placed directly

The school and home environment 135

into the white trays as long as there is not too much mud to cloud the water.

The children should be allowed to enjoy their pond-dipping, but some structure will be needed for recording their findings. If required, older or more able children could be asked to investigate where most of the animals are found by sampling:
• the surface of the water;
• the open water;
• the water around plants;
• the mud at the bottom of the pond.

Encourage the children to observe the animals carefully noting such features as the size, shape, colour, number of legs, number of wings and the way they move. How are the animals different and how are they similar? Encourage them to draw large pictures but to indicate the real size of the animal by the side. This activity should preferably be carried out at the side of the pond, but weather conditions and other circumstances might make it a classroom activity.

Return the animals to the pond before leaving unless further observations are to be made in the classroom or an aquarium is set up. Explain the importance of conservation to children and tell them that the law prevents animals such as the great crested newt from being collected. Ask the children why it is good to have a pond in the school grounds or in the garden at home. Explain to them that they are giving a new home to wildlife, in particular frogs and newts which are declining in numbers because ponds and ditches are being drained.

Identifying the pond animals

Give the children copies of photocopiable page 191, which shows pictures of the animals the children should encounter. Ask them to cut out from photocopiable page 191 pictures of any animals they found in the pond and to stick them on the appropriate place on the picture they drew earlier in the activity. Ask them how many different plants and different animals the pond is home to.

Recording and communicating

Ask the children to produce a pond folder into which they place:
• a plan or map of the school pond;
• any observations of the pond that they made, for example, clear water;
• drawings of the animals which they found in the pond;
• their drawings and its stick-on additions from photocopiable page 191, showing the animals which make their home in the pond.

Subject links

NC science and geography
Scottish 5–14 science and social subjects

CHAPTER 11

Leisure

Children will look forward to the time when they can enjoy leisure away from work, engaging in sporting, artistic and other recreational activities. Leisure activities cover a wide range of activities from participating in sports to eating out, from playing in the school playground to walking in the countryside or relaxing on a sun-drenched beach.

In recent years more time has become available for leisure in developed countries through people having longer holidays and a shorter working week. Tourism and outdoor leisure pursuits in particular have increased through greater mobility due to car ownership and road building, cheaper air travel, increased use of land for leisure facilities rather than for farming, and better diet and health care. Greater access to the countryside means that more people now enjoy a day out in the countryside or go away for weekends, short breaks or longer holidays. Ready-made package tours and activity holidays encourage use of the countryside and aid tourist development. New holiday resorts are being created and such amenities as fast food outlets and car parks are springing up to support the tourist industry.

It is important that leisure activities and tourism are planned carefully so that we can enjoy a variety of environments without spoiling them. These include beaches, rivers, lakes, woodlands, forests, mountains and country parks. The activities in this chapter will encourage children to become aware of the impact of leisure on the environment and the importance of maintaining a balance between conservation of the environment and the freedom to enjoy the leisure facilities it has to offer.

BACKGROUND

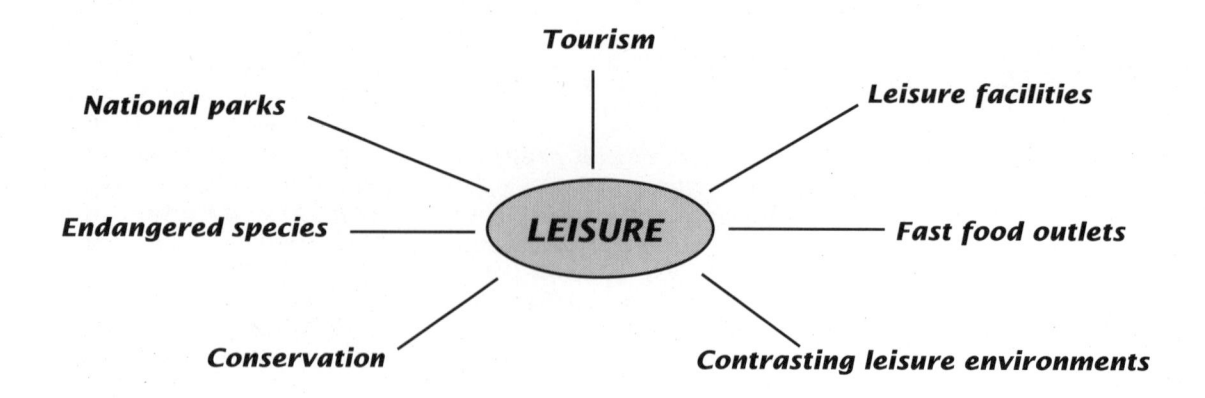

LEISURE connects to:
- Tourism
- National parks
- Leisure facilities
- Endangered species
- Fast food outlets
- Conservation
- Contrasting leisure environments

	Progression in teaching and learning	
Theme	Details of activity and activity number	
	Key Stage 1 (P1–3)	Key Stage 2 (P4–7)
Conservation	Leisure environments (1)	Endangered species (7) Conservation of habitats (8)
Environmental change	The playground as a leisure environment (2) Recreational use of land (3) Fast food outlets (4)	Leisure facilities – provision and location (5) Impact of tourism (6, 8)
Plants, animals and their habitats		Plants and animals in National parks (8)
Pollution	Recreation and pollution (3) Litter pollution (4)	Tourism and pollution (8)

ACTIVITIES

1. A sense of place

Theme
Conservation.

Age range
Five to seven.

Group size
Small groups.

What you need
Old magazines, coloured pencils, pencils, paper.

What to do
Using the old magazines, cut out pictures of people involved in various leisure activities, for example, sailing, ski-ing, walking, fishing, skateboarding, riding and so on. Then separate each person from the environment in which their activity occurs. There should be enough pictures to give each group an opportunity to look at a variety of leisure activities.

Discuss with the children various ways in which we use the environment to relax and enjoy outdoor leisure activities. Give each group pictures of people enjoying leisure activities and a range of environments where these activities occur. Explain to the children that they should match up the person with the appropriate environment, for example, the skier needs snow to ski (although not always!). Ask the children to think about other outdoor recreational activities. Ask them to draw their own pictures of people taking part in these activities.

Further activity
Initiate a discussion about how certain leisure activities can spoil or harm particular environments, for example, ski-tows and other machinery can mar the landscape for summer users. Speed boats and jet-skis can disturb peaceful lakes and have a detrimental effect on the natural wildlife. Ask the children to think of other examples and encourage them to suggest ways in which disturbance and damage to environments can be limited.

Content
This activity introduces children to the idea that we use the environment in different ways for leisure purposes, for example, physical recreation and peaceful relaxation. It also helps them to become aware of the range of environments used for recreation and realise that different recreational activities have different environmental requirements. The discussion in the further activity will expose the children to other issues involved, i.e. that sometimes there are detrimental consequences for environments when they are used for leisure activities. These can also be positive consequences for environments, for example, waste land can be cleared and landscaped and developed as a country park, golf course or for other recreational facilities.

Subject links
NC geography
Scottish 5–14 social subjects

Leisure 139

2. Design our playground

Theme
Environmental change.

Age range
Five to seven.

Group size
Whole class then small groups.

What you need
Clipboards, paper, pencils.

What to do
Discuss with the children how the school playground environment can be designed to meet their needs. Talk to them about school playtime. Where do they play and what games do they play at playtime? What are the activities they would enjoy at playtime but are unable to because of limiting factors such as lack of facilities or space? What do they think is needed in the playground?

They should then work in groups to carry out a small survey where they ask children in other classes what they would like in the playground. It is better to focus these questions by generating a list of ideas first and then asking for other ideas. The children could consider a range of facilities: swings, climbing frame, sand pit and so on. In addition they might wish to include (after discussion) other facilities such as litter bins, flowers and shrubs, seats and playground games marked out on the ground. Encourage the children to consider constraints such as safety, space and cost.

Ask each child to draw a picture of their ideal playground.

Further activity
This activity could be extended to consider other issues such as safety and the problem of litter.

Content
This activity helps children to think about their own leisure environment – the playground. They will consider factors which are important to them to help them to enjoy their recreational time and they will be introduced to the concept of environmental management. This entails assessing need and the planning and implementation of change. The playground is an environment with which the children will readily identify and they will be keen to discuss possible improvements.

Subject links
NC art and technology
Scottish 5–14 technology

3. A day out

Theme
Environmental change;
Pollution.

Age range
Five to eleven.

Group size
Whole class discussion, followed up by individuals.

What you need
Paper, pencils.

What to do
Talk to the children about holiday times and weekends when they might go out for the day. What sort of places do they visit and what do they do when they have reached their destination? A number of options may emerge, such as going out to the countryside – visiting a country park or a woodland area or a walk in the country. Other possibilities are a visit to the seaside or a trip to a theme park, a hands-on museum, or one of the many heritage centres which are springing up in large cities.

Make a class list of the day trips that are suggested and write next to each excursion the means of transport needed to reach the destination. What facilities did the children use at the destination, for example, walking on footpaths, use of a car, parking, use of litter bins, snack food outlets and so on? The younger children could draw a picture of their day out with facilities available on their day visit.

Focus attention on the amount of land that has been

used to support the main holiday (or visitor) destination, such as car parks, restaurants, cafés, roads, hotels, visitor centres, toilet blocks and so on. Encourage the children to consider what they and other visitors have brought into the area on the day of the visit. This would include litter, car fumes, human waste. How does the environment and the local community deal with this extra pollution? The older children could draw a simple flow chart to summarise the route taken by waste after it has been brought into the holiday/visitor destination, for example:
Waste from picnic lunch ➜ Litter bin ➜ Refuse collectors ➜ Rubbish tip.
This will provide the basis for discussion on the indirect effects of the visitor/tourist activities on an area.

Content
This activity is designed to help children understand the recreational use of different habitats and the environmental problems which are being caused by increased use of the land for leisure purposes.

The holiday industry has become more diversified but the growth of this industry has created environmental problems such as an increase in the amount of traffic on the roads and the overcrowding of some popular recreational facilities. This impact is not restricted solely to the actual site itself but has a knock-on effect on parts of the surrounding area, for example, waste generated by holiday makers has to be disposed of.

Subject links
NC geography
Scottish 5–14 social subjects

4. Fast food

Theme
Pollution; Environmental change.

Age range
Five to eleven.

Group size
Whole class, then small groups.

What you need
Clipboards, paper, pencils.

What to do
This activity could be stimulated through a class visit to a fast food outlet. Most, if not all children, will have eaten a meal in a fast food outlet. Talk to them about the type of food that is on offer there. What would a typical menu include? Encourage the children to consider such factors as how fresh the food is, are there fresh vegetables and fruit included in the menus, might the food contain colourings or additives, how is the food cooked and served? What are the children's favourite choices from the menu? Discuss with the children their idea of a healthy and balanced meal.

The children could work in groups to explore different aspects of the fast food outlet. How is the food packaged and what happens to the packaging once the food is consumed? Does the restaurant recycle any of the paper products that are used? Other areas to explore are facilities such as seating, litter bins, provision of toilets and no-smoking areas. Are there busy times of the day, and if so how does the restaurant cope? Do people from all age groups use the restaurant or is it mostly younger people? What implications might this have for noise pollution? The children should now draw up a table outlining the good and bad aspects of a fast food outlet.

Leisure

Content
The purpose of this activity is to identify the changes that have taken place in the environment since the introduction of fast food outlets. This will inevitably introduce issues such as healthy eating, recycling, litter production and use of resources, and help children to evaluate such a facility in the light of these issues.

Subject links
NC science
Scottish 5–14 social subjects, science and health

5. Sports facilities

Theme
Environmental change.

Age range
Seven to eleven.

Group size
Whole class, leading to work in small groups.

What you need
Map of the local environment, coloured pens and pencils, paper.

What to do
Discuss with the children the sort of sports activities which they enjoy. Sports activities will naturally divide into those activities which can be carried out at home and those which need more sophisticated facilities such as tennis courts, bowling alleys and so on.

Ask them to make a list of the sports activities in which they are involved and where locally they go to play these sports. As a class, generate a list of all the sports facilities in the area that the children can think of. Do they know how long the facilities have been located in a particular place? They could ask parents and grandparents if they remember when the facilities were provided in the locality. Which sports facilities would they like to see provided which do not exist in their locality at present?

The children could work in groups and mark on a local map the position of all the sports facilities which have been identified. These could be colour-coded, for example, all the tennis courts in red, the football pitches in blue, the golf courses in green and so on. The children could look for any patterns which emerge such as are all the football pitches in one area of the town? Have the facilities always been in this location? If not, where were they previously? Encourage them to think about why the sports facilities are sited in particular locations.

Further activity
The children could investigate whether there has been an increase in sports facility provision in recent years in a response to increased leisure time. This could be done by comparing sports facilities on a contemporary map with those of a map of ten years ago.

Content
The purpose of this activity is to identify the location and use of sports facilities and provision for such activities in the local environment. Planning is an important aspect of environment management. The children will be able to explore the provision of sports facilities in their locality and can form views as to why these facilities are provided and where they are located.

Subject links
NC geography
Scottish 5–14 social subjects

6. Holiday time

Theme
Environmental change.

Age range
Seven to eleven.

Group size
Whole class then small groups.

What you need
A selection of travel agents' holiday brochures (including a variety from large city holidays to rural, unspoilt island environments).

What to do
Introduce the activity by asking the children about their most recent holiday, or where they would have liked to go on holiday. Where did they go? Why did they go there? Who chose the holiday destination and how did they choose it? Talk about the holiday – where did the children stay – hotel, camp site, self-catering accommodation, flat, apartment, chalet, cottage or holiday camp? Were there any other hotels or other types of accommodation close by? What habitats did the resort rely on – beach, sand dunes, woodland, lakes, rivers and so on? Were there many other people using the beach and amenities or having the same sort of holiday in the area?

Ask the children to work in groups to look at the holiday brochures. They should list the countries which are advertised in the brochures. How many brochures advertise holidays to the same country or same resort in a country?

Ask the children to read the descriptions of the holiday destinations. How detailed are these? Are there photographs showing the location and accommodation and type of habitat such as beach, lake and so on?

Each group should discuss and choose a resort which they would like to visit. What factors influence their decision? Would they choose a hotel in a busy area with many amenities to choose from, or would they choose a quiet destination with fewer amenities in the area? How would they travel there – aeroplane, car, ferry, train, bus? Would there need to be an airport near to the resort? When they have made their choice each group should summarise their conclusions in the form of a short presentation to the rest of the class. Encourage the class to ask questions and to compare ideas.

Further activity
Ask a member of staff from a local travel agency to come into the classroom to talk to the children about the most popular holiday destinations and the reasons for people choosing a holiday destination.

Content
This activity will help children to understand the impact of tourism on an area in terms of building accommodation and other amenities, travel links such as airport, roads and rail networks, destination of habitats.

Subject links
NC geography
Scottish 5–14 social subjects

7. I'm going to the zoo

Theme
Conservation.

Age range
Seven to eleven.

Group size
Whole class, small groups.

What you need
Reference books on endangered species and the role zoos have in the conservation of these species.

What to do
Start off with a class discussion on why the children think people visit zoos. What are zoos for? Organise a class debate where children will first work in groups of 5 to 6 to discuss both the pros and cons of zoos. There are a number of issues which need careful thought and intervention may be needed within the groups in order to ensure the children's thinking is broadened. The children should use the reference books provided to brief themselves on the various

Leisure

issues involved such as conservation and the role zoos play in the breeding of endangered species of wild animals. They should use their research and discussions to prepare their points of view. A class debate can then take place. Groups could decide whether they will be in favour or against the existence of zoos and they should put their respective views forward as part of the debate.

Ask the children to make posters to present their various views on whether or not zoos have a role in the modern world. The posters might serve as publicity for the debate which could be presented to the school in an assembly.

If there is a zoo in the school area you could invite the education officer to talk to the children and discuss relevant issues with them.

Content

The purpose of the activity is to encourage the children to examine the role of zoos for education and conservation purposes. The activity could take place in the context of a class visit to a zoo or as part of research the children are carrying out into endangered species.

Until recently a zoo was a place to visit and admire animals in captivity. Zoos used to take many animals from the wild. Today, zoos aim to educate people about conservation of wild animals. Zoos also breed endangered species and in some cases return animals to the wild.

The positive aspects of zoos are their role in conservation and education and the service they offer to the public. They give people the opportunity to see animals they might never see in the wild. The animals in zoos are also used to research into the ecology and biology of various species. The negative aspects of zoos are the problems of enclosing animals in small spaces in captivity, the need to cull excess animals in zoos and the risks associated with removing animals from the wild, such as the likelihood of animals dying in transit.

Subject links
NC science
Scottish 5–14 science

8. National parks – A whole investigation

Theme
Conservation; Pollution; Plants, animals and their habitats.

Age range
Seven to eleven.

Group size
Whole class, then small groups.

What you need
Copies of photocopiable page 192, pens or pencils, paper, information provided by National Park authorities about the parks.

Planning and preparation

As more and more people take the opportunity to enjoy the countryside, the popular National Parks take much of the strain. There are eleven of these spread over some of the most beautiful land in England and Wales.

This activity is designed to help introduce children to National Parks and to help them understand the demands of people visiting the National Parks and the need for conservation of habitats. These demands exist in all the National Parks from the high mountains of Snowdonia to the low fens of the Norfolk Broads and the deep lakes of the Lake District. National Park Authorities must preserve and enhance the natural beauty of the Parks whilst promoting their enjoyment by the public.

It is important that the children understand that the National Parks are owned mainly by the people who live and work within them but there is extensive public access to the open countryside and many miles of public footpaths. The needs of the local community must be considered.

Talk to the children about the National Parks of England and Wales and the fact that they contain some of the most beautiful areas of countryside in Britain. These are areas of land which have been specially designated and protected by the Government to remain as they are, natural and unspoilt, and to be enjoyed now and in the future. Aspects such as quality of landscape and the wildlife they contain should be discussed. Other issues to identify in a general discussion are the importance of National Parks in providing opportunities for physical recreation and peaceful relaxation. National Parks in other countries could be identified such as Yellowstone, Grand Canyon (both USA), Serengeti, Masai Mara (both East Africa) and Mount Cook (New Zealand).

Each child should be provided with photocopiable page 192 showing the National Parks in England and Wales. They should study it, then identify each park on the map from the list provided. Discuss with the children the contrasting landscapes of these National Parks from open heather moorland to coastal cliffs, grasslands, lakes and woodland. (This information can be obtained from literature supplied by each National Park – addresses can be found in *Resources,* chapter 13.)

Tell the children that they are going to produce a holiday brochure (or booklet) in their groups on National Parks, showing how they provide for visitors and how they are used as a leisure facility by the public while still conserving the landscape. Ideally the focus of the investigation should be a visit to a National Park to give first-hand experience of the environment.

Investigating

Information gathering

The first stage is to collect as much information as possible on the eleven National Parks (or however many the teacher wishes to include). This can easily be done by writing off to the Education Officer of each National Park. If the class is divided into small groups of two or three, each group could take responsibility for collecting information about one National Park. Many National Parks provide free fact sheets, maps and other detailed literature which will give helpful information about the area. The children will need to be explicit about the investigation they are carrying out and should ask for specific information about such aspects as wildlife conservation, recreation, farming, forestry, landscape, mineral extraction, historic places and safety in the park. The children should then work in groups to examine different agreed aspects of the Parks or focus on the nearest National Park to their area. If this is the case, one or more of the following aspects could be addressed as part of the investigation. (Each group could explore one issue.)

Tourism and recreation

The children could investigate various aspects of tourism. Where do most visitors come from? Which parts of the Parks do the people visit – are some areas more popular than others? Often surveys have been carried out by the National Park Authorities which list the range of activities which people undertake on a visit. These could be examined by the children. They could first give their own view on which activities people may pursue and they could compare it with the list provided by the National Park and consider the ways the local population might benefit from visitors. The provision of car parks, picnic areas and information centres could all be investigated.

Questions to ask the children are:
• What problems does tourism bring? (Discuss here erosion of footpaths, trampling of vegetation, disturbance to wildlife, congestion of beauty spots, damage to farmland.)
• What are the benefits of tourism? (Discuss here factors such as employment, preservation of historic

building sites, income for local people through provision of accommodation for visitors, continuation of crafts such as well dressing in the Peak National Park.)

Safety
Discuss safety issues with the children such as changing weather conditions making the environment dangerous for visitors. Many people visiting the Parks in good weather cannot imagine how dangerous it can be when conditions change. Ask the children to make a poster providing safety guidelines such as: always carrying a map and compass; taking waterproofs and warm clothing, strong footwear, plenty of food and a small first aid kit; planning the route carefully is important as is telling someone else when and where you are going.

Farming
The children could investigate farming in the National Park. They could find out what type of farming is undertaken. What animals are kept, what size are the farms? Do they think it is difficult to make a living as a hill farmer? They could think about the problems visitors bring to the farmer by ignoring the country code. How might farmers supplement their income from visitors?

Wildlife conservation
Encourage the children to use the information provided by the National Parks to investigate some of the plant and animal species which abound. Particularly encourage the children to examine the range of habitats in the Park (such as woodland, moorland, grassland, cliffs) and to acknowledge that different species live in different habitats. There are information leaflets available from the National Parks on the plants to be found within the area. These leaflets could be requested when the children initially write off for information.

The country code
A group of children could devise a poster to advise visitors to the Parks about their behaviour in the Park, and how they can help to look after the environment. They could then add to their list (if necessary) by referring to the country code (see Chapter 3). They could illustrate their poster with cartoons or pictures to communicate their message more effectively.

The visit
The visit to the National Park should take place once some preliminary work has been done in analysing the information which has been gathered. It is important that the children understand that whichever National Park they visit much of the landscape and habitats will be the same regardless of the Park.

A small number of issues should be addressed on the visit as the children will probably only be able to go for a day visit. The following areas could be investigated during the visit: landscape, wildlife, recreation and tourism. Discuss the need for safety precautions during the visit and stress the need to follow the country code.

Recording and communicating
Ask the children in their groups to make information booklets or holiday brochures which explain what National Parks are and give helpful information to visitors to the Park. The children can divide up the tasks involved between themselves, for example research, writing, design and artwork. This could include some or all of the aspects studied. The booklets could be illustrated and guidance should be given to visitors as to their appropriate behaviour in the National Park environment. Photographs of the visit to the Park can be included. Recommendations could be made as to how visitors can enjoy the National Park environment without jeopardising wildlife or spoiling the landscape.

The children could also make posters advertising 'What to do in the National Park'. These could include activities such as walking, cycling, fishing, climbing, sailing, swimming.

Subject links
NC science, geography, English
Scottish 5–14 science, social subjects

CHAPTER 12

The churchyard

There are thousands of churchyards in Britain, many of which have become important areas for nature conservation. A wide variety of flowers, trees, birds and insects can be found in the churchyard and moss and lichen abound. Within the churchyard there are opportunities for children to explore aspects of our history which provide a wealth of information to research. There are records of family history inscribed on the headstones and gravestones and information can be collected from these about local people in the area.

There are likely to be other foci of interest in a churchyard such as churchyard monuments, church crosses, sundials and the church building itself.

Now that much of our environment is under threat from building developments, the churchyard contains a range of habitats which up to now have been relatively safe. It is important, therefore, that children come to understand the nature conservation and historical values of such a variety of habitats and learn to look after this environment in an informed way. The activities in this chapter will help them to reach such an understanding.

The visit to the churchyard

All of the activities in this chapter are based on or stimulated by a visit or visits to a churchyard by the children. It is important, however, for the children to understand that essentially, a churchyard is the area around a church and it belongs to the community represented by a parish. The church is a place of worship and should be respected as such. Guidelines for visits should be well established with the children in advance. There are also some essential preparations for teachers before they take children on such visits.

Guidelines for visits

For teachers:
The teacher should contact the vicar or priest to get permission for the visit. Arrange convenient times to visit, i.e. not when a church service is taking place.

For children:
• Treat the churchyard with respect.
• Be quiet and do not run or shout.
• Walk around graves, not over them.
• Try to keep to pathways as much as possible.
• Try not to disturb wildlife in the churchyard.
• Do not drop litter.
• Do not damage the lichens which are growing on the stones or walls.

The churchyard

BACKGROUND

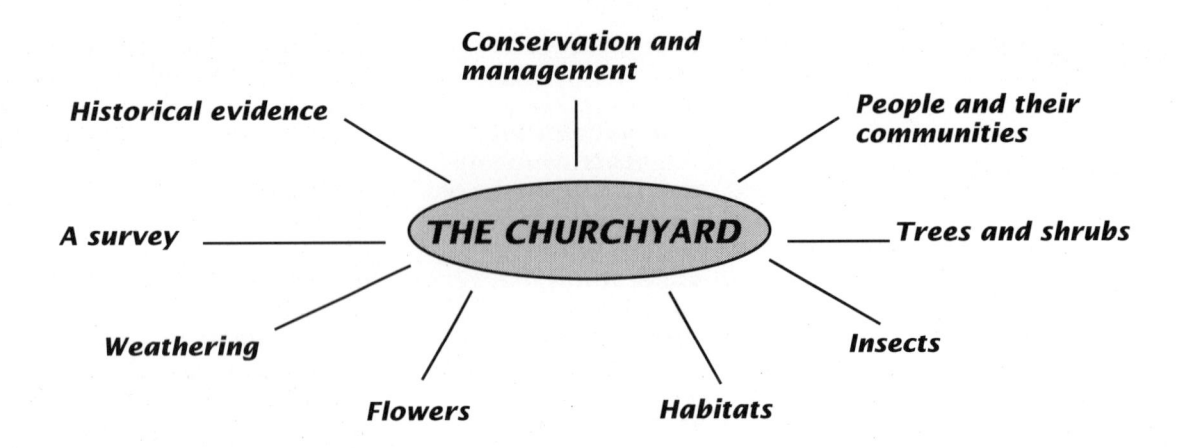

Concept map centred on **THE CHURCHYARD** with branches to:
- Historical evidence
- Conservation and management
- People and their communities
- A survey
- Trees and shrubs
- Weathering
- Insects
- Flowers
- Habitats

Theme	Progression in teaching and learning	
	Details of activity and activity number	
	Key Stage 1 (P1–3)	**Key Stage 2 (P4–7)**
Conservation	Cultural conservation of churchyard features (1)	Biodiversity (2) Investigation of habitat requirements of different butterflies (7)
	Conserving the churchyard – A whole investigation (8)	
Environmental change		Using historical evidence (6)
	Conserving the churchyard – A whole investigation (8)	
Plants, animals and their habitats	Identifying trees and shrubs (3)	Identification and location of trees and shrubs (4)
		Butterfly identification and survey (7)
	Conserving the churchyard – A whole investigation (8)	
Pollution	Atmospheric pollution – lichens as indicators of pollution (5)	
	Conserving the churchyard – A whole investigation (8)	

ACTIVITIES

1. A treasure hunt

Theme
Conservation.

Age range
Five to seven.

Group size
Small groups, supervised if possible.

What you need
Clipboards, pencils, paper.

What to do
Organise a treasure hunt with the children by providing them with a list of features which they will find in the churchyard. These could include: a sundial, a holly tree, a gargoyle on the exterior of the church, a church cross, a carved pillar, a weather vane, an arch-shaped window, lichens on gravestones and so on. The children could work in small groups, each with an adult to help. They should look for each feature and record where they found it in the churchyard. Stress the fact that they should not run or shout in the churchyard and they should try and stay on the paths as much as possible. They should not walk over graves but should walk around them.

On returning to the classroom talk to the children about what they found on their treasure hunt and what clues their discoveries gave them about how people lived in the past.

Content
The purpose of this activity is to use the churchyard environment to develop an understanding of people and their society by identifying items and features on the exterior of the church and in the churchyard. Talk to the children about such features.

Examining the different features in the churchyard can help the children to build up a picture of how people lived in the past. They will have used sources of historical evidence to develop this understanding.

Subject links
NC history, science and English
Scottish 5–14 social subjects and science

2. What's in the churchyard?

Theme
Conservation.

Age range
Seven to eleven.

Group size
Whole class, then small groups.

What you need
Clipboards, paper, pencils, reference books.

The churchyard 149

What to do

The purpose of this activity is to broaden the children's knowledge of features in a churchyard other than gravestones or headstones and to carry out a detailed survey. Much can be learned from examining such structures as monuments, crosses and other antiquities. During a visit to the churchyard ask the children to make a list of other features which they can see in the churchyard. Discuss with the children the value of these objects and whether it is worth conserving them for the future and if so, how. They could then divide up into groups to examine these features more closely. They could also look at the exterior of the church itself. Does it have a weather vane, sundial or gargoyles? Does it have any characteristic architectural features which relate it to a particular period?

If there is a churchyard cross does it have any figures or symbols carved on it? Are there any inscriptions on it? What material is it made of?

Some churchyards contain elaborately carved table tombs which bear inscriptions of historical interest. Often there is a sundial standing on a pedestal. The shadow cast by the metal gnomon indicates the time of day.

The entrance to many churches is through the lych-gate. The children could sketch the lych-gate and look on it for any carvings which would indicate when it was built.

Back in the classroom, ask the children to make a class book containing drawings and written information supplemented from reference book materials.

Content

Examining the different features in the churchyard can help the children to build up a picture of the history of the church, its parishioners and their lifestyle. This information is valuable in understanding the history of an area. The objects in the churchyard will have a value in their own right as part of the cultural heritage of the local community. This activity will give the children an insight into cultural conservation.

Subject links

NC history and English
Scottish 5–14 social subjects

3. Trees and shrubs – 1

Theme

Plants, animals and their habitats.

Age range

Five to seven.

Group size

Whole class, then small groups.

What you need

Clipboards, paper, pencils, wax crayons, large pieces of paper for bark rubbings, reference books.

What to do

The purpose of this activity is to introduce the children to common species of trees and shrubs found in a churchyard and to investigate the folklore associated with those species. Discuss with the children before the visit some of the types of trees and shrubs which they may see. The children should work in small groups on the field visit, each group accompanied by an adult. They should identify the more common trees and shrubs such as yew, laurel and holly and talk about parts of the tree such as the trunk, branch, leaves, bark and roots. Some of the older trees have extensive root systems spreading across a large area at the base of the trees. The children could visit the churchyard in summer and winter and be able to see that evergreen trees do not lose their leaves in winter. They could take some bark rubbings which could be displayed in class. Back in the classroom talk to the children about some of the stories associated with the trees and shrubs.

Content
Investigations into the names and symbolic meanings of species of trees and shrubs can give much information about beliefs and customs. Yew trees are often found in churchyards. They are evergreen trees and may have been planted hundreds of years ago. They are poisonous to animals. Holly trees are also evergreens and bear red berries. The prickles of the tree are a reminder of the crown of thorns worn by Jesus when he was crucified and the red berries are symbols of drops of blood shed by Christ. The laurel is an evergreen shrub, the leaves of which were worn as a crown of victory in ancient Roman athletic competitions.

Subject links
NC science, history and art
Scottish 5–14 science and social subjects

4. Trees and shrubs – 2

Theme
Plants, animals and their habitats.

Age range
Seven to eleven.

Group size
Small groups.

What you need
Clipboards, paper, pencils, reference books on trees and shrubs, recording sheets, cameras.

What to do
The purpose of this activity is to identify the trees and shrubs growing in the churchyard and to find out whether certain species or types of tree (such as evergreens) are commonly found in the churchyard. Discuss with the children the importance of trees in the churchyard in that they provide shelter from wind, shade from the summer sun and are important habitats for birds and other wildlife. They also create an attractive environment for people to visit.

Before the visit to the churchyard, discuss with the children the trees that they are likely to see. Evergreens commonly found in churchyards include yew, holly and laurel. Deciduous trees such as oak, beech, elm and lime were also planted in churchyards, often bordering pathways. Reference books can be used to help familiarise the children with these trees so that they will be able to identify them on the visit.

The children should work in small groups and record the species of trees and shrubs they find in the churchyard. They should record their location in the churchyard, for example, near a pathway or on the edge of the site, and if possible take photographs of the trees and shrubs. Can they tell if the trees have been planted – for example are they growing in a straight line – or have some grown naturally through seed dispersal? They should collect samples of fallen leaves to identify on returning to the classroom. A class display can be made of the photographs and leaves, with extra information taken from reference books about the trees and shrubs.

Content
This activity helps children to recognise and name common trees and shrubs in the local

environment. It also helps them to identify the factors that influence the location for the planting of trees and shrubs such as creation of a boundary, provision of shade and the aesthetic role trees have in the churchyard situation.

Subject links
NC science
Scottish 5–14 science

5. Stones – weathering well

Theme
Pollution.

Age range
Five to eleven.

Group size
Small groups.

What you need
Clipboards, paper, pencils, magnifiers.

What to do
Discuss with the children before their visit to the churchyard the effects of weathering on buildings and stones. They will need to understand that wind, rain, frost and temperature changes will affect the headstones and gravestones. Encourage them to look for stones that have worn away in places. The stones may have a crumbly appearance. The younger children can observe which sides of the stones are damaged by the weather – can the older children make a connection about the direction of the prevailing wind and the most worn side of the stones?

Ask the children to examine the stones carefully and make notes on appearance, colour, texture. Is there anything growing on the stones? They will almost certainly find many lichens growing. Do they find the lichens in sunny or shady parts of the churchyard? Are the lichens growing on different types of materials such as limestone, marble or sandstone? Close observations of the lichens can be made using magnifiers. Are there different sorts of lichens growing or are they all the same sort? What other plant-life is growing on the stones? Are there any mosses or ferns? Are these plants only growing on parts of the stone or are they evenly distributed across the stone? The children should record their observations and make sketches of any plants which they find growing.

On returning to the classroom older children could carry out research to find if they can identify the lichens into the broad categories of crusty, leafy or shrubby lichens. The children could then explore the relationship of lichens to atmospheric pollution from the information in the reference books.

Content
Weathering is the process by which the physical and chemical natures of materials are altered. Rain, wind and temperature changes are the major factors involved in this. Carbon dioxide in the atmosphere makes rainwater acidic and this breaks down the chemical calcium carbonate in limestone. Acid rain also erodes stonework. Different species of lichens tolerate different levels of atmospheric pollution. Consequently, they are good indicators of air pollution in a locality. Lichens are two plants, an alga and a fungus which live together for mutual benefit. Crusty lichens indicate a lot of pollution, leafy lichens indicate a little air pollution and shrubby lichens indicate no air pollution.

Subject links
NC science
Scottish 5–14 science

6. Stones – grave matters

Theme
Environmental change.

Age range
Seven to eleven.

Group size
Small groups.

What you need
Clipboards, paper, pencils, large pieces of paper and wax crayons for rubbings, a camera.

What to do
The purpose of this activity is to collect, record and discuss the wealth of historical and local information which can be collected from headstones and gravestones. These stones will often provide information about the people who lived in the parish or district going back several hundred years. The children could design their own sheet to record the information they collect from the stones, showing, for example, date of record, site, height, material, inscription, decoration, name, date of death and age. Each group could study one or two headstones/gravestones in detail, collecting written information, making a rubbing of the stone, taking a photograph of the stone. Inscriptions on the stones could be examined – what is the lettering like, do these inscriptions give any other information about the person who is buried, for example, occupation of the person, family relationships, cause of death? Are there any biblical quotations on the stone? A photograph should be taken of each stone that is studied and this can be attached to the record sheet. Other information that should be recorded is the measurements of the stone, the type of stone of which it is made, location of the stone in the churchyard. Churches often keep old records and documents such as parish registers which give details of births, deaths and marriages going back over many years. Permission may be asked to access these documents for relevant information.

On returning to the classroom, the children can display their record sheets and discuss the information they have collected about the local history of the parish. Can they identify any local families who lived in the area?

Content
This activity helps children to understand the amount of historical information which can be collected from a churchyard. Gravestones can give information about the history of the families who lived in a parish. Inscriptions often record names, details of relationships and occupations. Information on gravestones often reveals how healthy a community was – early deaths in the same year could indicate an epidemic.

Subject links
NC history and English
Scottish 5–14 social subjects

7. Butterfly sanctuary

Theme
Conservation; Plants, animals and their habitats.

Age range
Seven to eleven.

Group size
Small groups.

What you need
Clipboards, coloured pencils, pencils, paper, a field guide to

The churchyard 153

identification of British butterflies or *The Hamlyn guide to butterflies of the British Isles* by J. A. Thomas.

What to do

This activity could become part of a much larger study of common butterflies and comparison of habitats for butterflies and should be undertaken during late spring and in the summer term.

The children should work in small groups for this activity. They should design a sheet on which to record their observations. This could show location, weather, name of butterfly, colour, markings, vegetation of area and perhaps a drawing. It is very important that they are as quiet as possible and should avoid sudden movements in order to avoid disturbing the butterflies and other wildlife that they will see. Tell the children that they are going to make a record of the butterflies that visit the churchyard, in order to find out if it provides a good habitat for these insects.

Observations that they will make will include the type of butterfly they see, the type of plant on which the butterflies settle and feed, the areas of the churchyard where butterflies are most abundant (are they shady or sunny areas?), the weather conditions (is it cloudy or sunny?) for example. What colour flowers do the butterflies prefer? They should record colour of flowers and markings of butterflies.

On returning to the classroom the children should work together as a group to share their data. They can make more careful drawings of the butterflies they have seen and identify them. Which butterflies are the most frequent visitors to the churchyard and which plants and areas of the churchyard do the butterflies prefer? Which butterflies prefer sunny areas to shady areas?

A classroom display can be made which includes the children's drawings. It could also include a map of the churchyard showing areas the butterflies frequent. The children could present their results to another class or to the whole school at assembly.

Further activity

The butterfly survey can be linked with a survey which identifies common wild flowers in the churchyard. For example, by identifying which butterfly caterpillar species feeds on which particular plant species.

Content

The children should become familiar with the appearance of the most common species of butterflies before they embark on the field work in the churchyard. Many habitats for butterflies are gradually being lost because of changes in the environment. Churchyards, however, remain important places to find butterflies as there are often an abundance

Figure 1

Butterfly	Preferred habitat
Small copper	paths and grassy areas
Common blue	paths and grassy areas
Meadow brown	grasses, sunny, sheltered areas
Ringlet	edge of churchyard, shady areas
Gatekeeper	edge of churchyard, shrubs, sunny areas
Red admiral	hedgerows and nettles
Small tortoiseshell	stinging nettles
Wall	bare, sun-baked ground
Brimstone	woods, hedgerows
Peacock	bramble and stinging nettle
Large white	flowers
Small white	flowers
Orange tip	damp places
Holly blue	holly, ivy and yew trees
Speckled wood	shady areas

of flowers, trees and shrubs and there may be wild areas.

Common butterflies which are seen in churchyards are listed with the type of area they prefer in Figure 1 on the previous page.

The adult butterflies feed on the flowers but the caterpillar larvae use the leaves of specific plants such as nettles on which to feed. This is a good opportunity to discuss the life cycle of a butterfly with the children. There are four stages to the life cycle: egg, caterpillar, chrysalis and adult butterfly. Butterflies fly during the day and most are bright in colour.

Subject links
NC science, English and art
Scottish 5–14 science

8. Conserving the churchyard – A whole investigation

Theme
Conservation; Environmental change; Plants, animals and their habitats; Pollution.

Age range
Seven to eleven.

Group size
Whole class, small groups.

What you need
Pens, paper, clipboards, a camera, reference books on relevant wildlife and vegetation.

Planning and preparation
The children will be carrying out a whole survey of the churchyard to examine its importance for wildlife and cultural heritage. On completion they must then make recommendations as to the management and care of the churchyard environment. They could work in small groups, each group examining a different aspect of the environment. Discuss with the children which aspects of the churchyard each group will consider. You may wish to take the children on an initial visit in order to assess the range of habitats to be covered. Alternatively, you could provide the children with photographs of the churchyard in order to help them make their decisions. The churchyard could be divided up into habitats and wildlife types such as grass, flowers, trees and shrubs, gravestones, headstones and walls and pathways, birds, butterflies.

Investigating

Map of the churchyard
The children could draw up a map of the churchyard including position of the church, graves, pathways, trees and shrubs, any wild areas, grassed areas, flowers and the direction of north.

Trees and shrubs
The trees in the churchyard should be identified and their location recorded (see activity 4, Trees and Shrubs – 2). Where are the evergreen trees and where are the deciduous trees? The leaf litter lying under deciduous trees provides a habitat for minibeasts.

Graves
The position of the graves can be recorded. Each one can be given a number or letter in order to make sure no grave is counted twice. Presence or absence of lichens should be recorded. The headstone/gravestone recording sheet from activity 6 could be used to obtain more detailed information.

Pathways
The children should look closely to see what is growing on the pathways. They may find grasses, herbs, mosses, lichens and wild flowers. Ask them to see if there are any

The churchyard 155

more plants growing on the edges of the paths than down the centre of the paths where people have trodden. They could compare different paths for species type and also compare more heavily used paths with those less frequently used. Are there any plants growing in the cracks between paving stones?

Grassed areas
The children should compare mown areas of grass and longer grass. Are there any flowers growing amongst the grasses? Can they identify some of the more common grasses using reference books? Are there different flowers growing in the shade of the trees than in the sunny areas? Areas of long grass also provide cover for mammals such as voles and mice. Mown areas provide poor cover but can be attractive grazing for rabbits and squirrels.

Flowers
Flowers may be planted in borders or may be growing wild. Common wild flowers should be identified. The children will probably find bluebells, cowslips, primroses, red campion, buttercups, daisies, clover, dandelions, stinging nettles and groundsel. Pansies, crocuses, daffodils and tulips may be found in the borders. The children should record the flowers they find dividing them up into cultivated and wild flowers.

This information will be important in helping to describe the different types of habitat and wildlife value.

Birds
A survey of the birds using the churchyard should be undertaken. The children may see blackbirds, robins, song thrushes, wrens, house sparrows, wood pigeons, collared doves, great tits, blue tits, greenfinches, starlings, house martins and swallows. What are the birds feeding on? What parts of the churchyard do they use and for what activities, for example, roosting, nesting, feeding and so on. Do they cause any damage to the environment in any way?

Butterflies
Ask the children to observe the butterflies in the churchyard. They should make a note of any that they see and which flowers they settle on. (See activity 7 – Butterfly sanctuary).

Recording and communicating
The children should then draw up a list of recommendations for the future management of the churchyard. (See guidance notes at the end of this chapter.) The children should decide which habitat wildlife types merit conservation management and for what reason, for example, flowers could be planted to attract a greater variety of butterflies. A management plan should be produced for each of the chosen habitat types and presented to the vicar/priest and churchwarden who could be invited into the classroom for a presentation of the results of the survey, including the recommendations, which could be written into a report and given to the parishioners. The children should consider how they will record their results and it is recommended that they design a recording sheet of their own. A photographic record is also a good idea.

Subject links
NC science, geography and history
Scottish 5–14 science and social subjects

Guidance notes

Possible suggestions for conserving the churchyard
Future management of the churchyard – recommendations:
• Plant flowers to attract a greater variety of butterflies and other insects.
• Provide nesting boxes for birds.
• Maintain a wild area to encourage growth of wild flowers.
• Discourage use of herbicides and pesticides.
• Plan mowing times to allow wild plants to set seed.
• Create a compost heap for leaf litter and grass cuttings.
• Improve structure of hedges to fill gaps and improve diversity of shrubs.
• Discourage the cleaning of gravestones to remove lichens.
• Provide information to the public through church notice boards or purpose-built signs and information leaflets.

CHAPTER 13

Resources

This chapter provides a list of useful addresses of environmental groups and resource materials which will be helpful for the activities within this book.

Many of these organisations provide materials, often at no cost, and many produce resource catalogues. The range of resources available for primary schools is considerable and the following list summarises some of the more useful organisations teachers should find helpful.

RESOURCES

International organisations

Friends of the Earth
26–28 Underwood Street
London
N1 7JQ

Friends of the Earth is an international campaigning organisation which tries to protect the natural environment. They provide a subscription scheme for schools known as School Friends. Schools receive a starter pack including a poster and resources, and then subsequent packs follow. They also have a catalogue of other resources available.

Greenpeace
Canonbury Villas
London
N1 2PN

Greenpeace campaigns against environmental issues by non-violent protests which are backed by scientific research. Greenpeace sells products through Traidcraft plc and offers a range of factsheets.

World Wide Fund for Nature UK
Panda House
Weyside Park
Catteshall Lane
Godalming
Surrey GU7 1XR

The WWF raises money for the conservation of wildlife. It also offers a comprehensive educational programme for schools. It works with other conservation organisations, government, industry, media and the public to protect the natural environment, stem the decline in animal and plant species and reduce pollution.

Other organisations

Aluminium Can Recycling Association
Suite 308
I-Mex House
52 Blucher Street
Birmingham
B1 1QU

The Aluminium Can Recycling Association provides a schools' information pack on can recycling, which contains a magnet, posters and a project plan giving children ideas on how to set up their own recycling station. It can also give details of recycling schemes around the country and offers two other packs: one for individual children and another for adults wishing to take part.

Association for Science Education (ASE)
College Lane
Hatfield
Hertfordshire
AL10 9AA

The ASE is an organisation run by teachers for teachers. You can join as an individual teacher or as a school subscriber. ASE members receive *Primary Science Review*, *ASE Primary Science*, and the chance to order a multitude of other publications by the ASE in this subject area.

BBC Wildlife Subscriptions Department
PO Box 425
Woking
Surrey
GU21 1GP

BBC Enterprises publish this monthly journal containing useful reference material on the environment.

BP Educational Service
PO Box 934
Poole
Dorset
BH17 7BR

Contact this address to obtain a catalogue of resource materials and films on free loan. The hire address is: BP Video Library, Unit 2, Drywall Estate, Castle Road, Merston, Sittingbourne, Kent ME10 3RL.

The British Butterfly Conservation Society
PO Box 222
Dedham
Colchester
Essex
CO7 6EY

The society produces an education pack for children available for a small charge to cover postage and packing.

British Trust for Conservation Volunteers
36 St Mary's Street
Wallingford
Oxfordshire OX10 0EU

The BTCV involves people of all ages in practical conservation programmes, providing all necessary tools as well as training and advice.

**Centre for Alternative Technology
Llewyngwern Quarry
Machynlleth
Powys
SY20 9AZ**

**Centre for Global Education
University of York
Heslington
York
YO1 5DD**

This centre promotes a global perspective in schools through research, curriculum development, and teacher training in global education. They can give advice about other appropriate organisations to contact.

**Civic Trust
17 Carlton House Terrace
London
SW1Y 5AW**

The Civic Trust encourages the protection and improvement of the built environment through conferences, projects and reports. They produce two publications specifically for the 9–13 age group.

**Council for Environmental Education
University of Reading
London Road
Reading
RG1 5AQ**

The CEE provides a national focus in England, Wales and Northern Ireland, encouraging and promoting an environmental approach to education. It has a national resource centre and library which is the most comprehensive collection of environmental education materials in the UK, and produces a list (available by sending a stamped, addressed envelope) of the wide range of resources that it produces.

**Council for Protection of Rural England
Warwick House
25 Buckingham Palace Road
London
SW1W 0PP**

The CPRE publishes leaflets on coutryside topics which may be of interest to teachers, but nothing specifically for school children.

**Countryside Commission
John Dower House
Crescent Place
Cheltenham
Gloucestershire
GL50 3RA**

This organisation produces information to do with countryside matters, some of which is geared towards school children.

**Department of the Environment
PO Box 151
London
E15 2HF**

The DoE publishes leaflets including: *Global Atmosphere and Air Quality*, *Every Home Helps* (an energy saver pack) and *Wake up to what you can do for the Environment*.

**The Dustbin Pack
Waste Watch
Coca Cola and Scheppes Limited
Consumer Response Centre
Cray Road
Sidcup
Kent
DA14 5DF**

The Dustbin Pack is a free pack designed to help teachers raise awareness in schools of the possibilities of reuse and recycling of everyday materials.

**English Heritage Education Service
429 Oxford Street
London
W1R 2HD**

English Heritage is responsible for the protection and preservation of environmental heritage. A catalogue of information resources is provided, many of which are suitable for the primary school age group.

**English Nature
Northminster House
Northminster Road
Peterborough
PE1 1UA**

English Nature is the official group responsible for nature conservation in the UK. It manages nature reserves and gives leaflets and advice on all aspects of nature conservation.

**Farming and Wildlife Advisory Group
National Agricultural Centre
Stoneleigh
Kenilworth
Warwickshire
CV8 2RX**

The FWAG has local branches throughout the country and publishes advisory leaflets for farmers concerning environmentally aware farming practices. These leaflets are too technical for children, but the Group may be able to advise on individual queries.

**Forestry Commission
231 Corstorphine Road
Edinburgh
EH12 7AT**

The Forestry Commission promotes forestry in Britain and encourages wide use of its forests for educational purposes. They produce a schools pack which includes a teachers' handbook, posters and leaflets.

**Groundwork Foundation
85–87 Cornwall Street
Birmingham
B3 3BY**

The Groundwork Foundation promotes environmental improvement and offers practical support for projects. They also run their own educational projects for schools and have an educational officer to contact.

**Henry Doubleday Research Association
Ryton Organic Gardens
Ryton-on-Dunsmore
Coventry
CV8 3LG**

The HDRA promotes and gives advice on organic gardening, growing and food. It runs Ryton Organic Gardens which are demonstration organic gardens open to the public all year round. They produce information suited to the primary age group.

**Learning through Landscapes
Third Floor
Southside Offices
The Law Courts
Winchester
SO23 9DL**

Learning through Landscapes provides a free information pack for teachers as well as a file of photocopiable materials including a school grounds survey pack.

**Living Churchyard
Arthur Rank Centre
National Agricultural Centre
Stoneleigh Park
Kenilworth
Warwickshire
CV8 2LZ**

The Living Churchyard runs the Church and Conservation Project which is designed to help churches and others see the potential for enhancing wildlife interests in the management of the churchyards. It also runs the Natural Heritage of Cathedrals scheme which aims to make children aware of the precincts and outside area of the cathedral with its wildlife which has been established over centuries. The organisation can give details of schemes local to schools and acts as a resource and advice centre.

**National Council for the Conservation of Plants and Gardens
The Pines
Wisley Garden
Woking
Surrey
GU23 6QB**

The Council produces some posters of the plant life in different environments. They have regional branches, and the Isle of Wight branch is currently producing a project called *Conserving our Garden Plants* for teachers and school children.

**National Rivers Authority
Eastbury House
30–34 Albert Embankment
London SE1 7TL**

**National Society for Clean Air and Environmental Protection
136 North Street
Brighton BN1 1RG**

The NSCA seeks the improvement of the environment by promoting clean air through the reduction of air pollution, noise and other atmospheric contaminants. They publish books, reports and other educational leaflets.

**The National Trust
36 Queen Anne's Gate
London
SW1H 9AS**

The National Trust preserves places of specific historic interest or natural beauty. Members can enter properties free. *Nature Conservation, Trees* and *Coastal Areas* are examples of leaflets produced.

**Pictorial Charts Education Trust
27 Kirchen Road
West Ealing
London
W13 0UD**

The Pictorial Charts Educational Trust publishes a selection of environmental posters including *Air Pollution in Transport* and *The Wetlands of the World*.

**Plantlife
The Natural History Museum
Cromwell Road
London
SW7 5BD**

Plantlife is a plant conservation charity established to halt the loss of plants in Britain and Europe and put wild flowers back into the countryside. Plantlife achieves this through special management programmes, acquiring land, lobbying for changes in legislation, campaigning to save plant-rich places and informing and educating the public. A recent publication *The Acid Test for Plants* gives an overview of the damage to plant communities caused by acid rain. Information produced tends to be aimed at a higher age group, but could be adapted by a teacher of the primary age range.

The Ramblers' Association
1-5 Wandsworth Road
London
SW8 2XX

The Royal Horticultural Society
80 Vincent Square
London
SW1P 2PE

Staff can give advice about how to create a garden to attract birds or butterflies, as well as help with other gardening queries.

Royal Society for Nature Conservation
The Green
Witham Park
Waterside South
Lincoln
LN5 7JR

(See **WATCH**).

Royal Society for the Protection of Birds
The Lodge
Sandy
Bedfordshire
SG19 2DL

The RSPB is responsible for the protection and preservation of the British bird population. It has a junior wing, the Young Ornithologists' Club (YOC) which publishes the monthly *Birdlife* magazine for its members, as well as producing other information, films and leaflets. Membership allows free entry into RSPB Nature Reserves. (There are many of these to be found around the country – ask for details). School membership is available at a small fee per child, and includes a magazine per five children with one for the teacher, as well as a beginners' pack containing a mobile to make, competitions and information.

Scottish Environmental Education Council
Department of Environmental Science
University of Sterling
Stirling
FK9 4LA

The Council has set up the Stewardship Scheme, run for the 5-14 age group, which has attracted many Scottish schools. This gives the opportunity to develop a whole school environmental policy through project work in an environmental award scheme. Other help and information is available for teachers.

Shell Education Service
Shell-Mex House
Strand
London
WC2R 0DX

The Shell Education Service supplies much free education material on oil and related subjects. Two useful publications are *Farming in the UK* and *Chemicals on the Farm*.

Soil Association
86 Colston Street
Bristol
BS1 5BB

The Association publishes a journal and a range of leaflets and booklets. Two new publications for the Primary school age group are *Living Soil* (KS2) and *Food, Farming and Future* (KS2/3) on organic farming.

Tidy Britain Group
The Pier
Wigan
WN3 4EX

The Tidy Britain Group (originally the Keep Britain Tidy Group) encourages the removal of litter. It provides free factsheets and leaflets on litter, recycling and waste.

Understanding Electricity
The Electricity Council
30 Millbank
London
SW1P 4RD

Understanding Electricity is the educational service of the electricity supply industries. Its aim is to improve the knowledge of young people about basic electrical principles and their applications. A catalogue of resource materials is available, many of which are free. Videos and computer software can be bought from the catalogue.

Waste Watch
Hobart House
Grosvenor Place
London
SW1X 7AE

This is a national project promoting local recycling schemes.

WATCH
The Green
Witham Park
Waterside South
Lincoln
LN5 7JR

WATCH is the junior wing of the Royal Society for Nature Conservation. It has many projects all over the country which are undertaken by groups of children. For a modest annual fee the WATCH education service provide *WATCHword* which is a magazine for school children, and *Link,* which is an activity-based resource for teachers or youth group leaders to provide projects for children. This will also enable groups to be in touch with their local wildlife trust who can give advice on how to manage a wildlife area or give details of local wildlife areas. Other very interesting products are *Batpack* and *International Batpack* (fronted by 'Kevin the Fruit Bat'), and *Enviroscope.*

Educational suppliers

Berol Limited
Old Medow Road
King's Lynn
Norfolk
PE30 4JR

Invicta Plastics
Harborough Road
Oadby
Leicester
LE2 4LB

NES Arnold Limited
Ludlow Hill Road
West Bridgford
Nottingham
NG2 6HD

Philip Harris Education
Lynn Lane
Shenstone
Lichfield
Staffordshire
WS14 0EE

National Parks

England and Wales
Brecon Beacons National Park
7 Glamorgan Street
Brecon
Powys
LD3 7DP
Tel. 0874 624437

The Broads Authority
Thomas Harvey House
18 Colegate
Norwich
NR3 1BQ
Tel. 0603 610734

Dartmoor National Park
Parke
Haytor Road
Bovey Tracey
Newton Abbot
Devon
TQ13 9JQ
Tel. 0626 832093

Dyfed County Council
National Park Division
County Offices
St Thomas' Green
Haverfordwest
Dyfed
SA61 1QZ
Tel. 0437 764591

Exmoor National Park
Exmoor House
Dulveton
Somerset
TA22 9HL
Tel. 0398 23665

Lake District National Park
Murley House
Moss
Oxenholme Road
Kendal
Cumbria
LA9 7RL
Tel. 0539 724555

North York Moors National Park
North Vicarage
Bondgate
Helmsley
York
YO6 5BP
Tel. 0439 770657

Northumberland National Park
Eastburn
South Park
Hexham
Northumberland
NE46 1BS
Tel. 0434 605555

Peak Park Joint Planning Board
Aldern House
Baslow Road
Bakewell
Derbyshire
DE45 1AE
Tel. 0629 814321

Snowdonia National Park
Penrhyndeudraeth
Gwynedd
LL48 6LS
Tel. 0766 770274

Yorkshire Dales National Park
Information Services
Colvend
Hebden Road
Grassington
Skipton
North Yorkshire
BD23 5LB
Tel. 0756 752748

PHOTOCOPIABLES

The pages in this section can be photocopied and adapted to suit your own needs and those of your class; they do not need to be declared in respect of any photocopying licence. Each photocopiable page relates to a specific activity in the main body of the book, although some can be used for more than one activity. The appropriate activity and page references are given above each photocopiable sheet.

Assessment and Record Keeping   163

Is it polluted – how can I tell? page 15

All-in-one at Walkham – to build or not to build? page 17

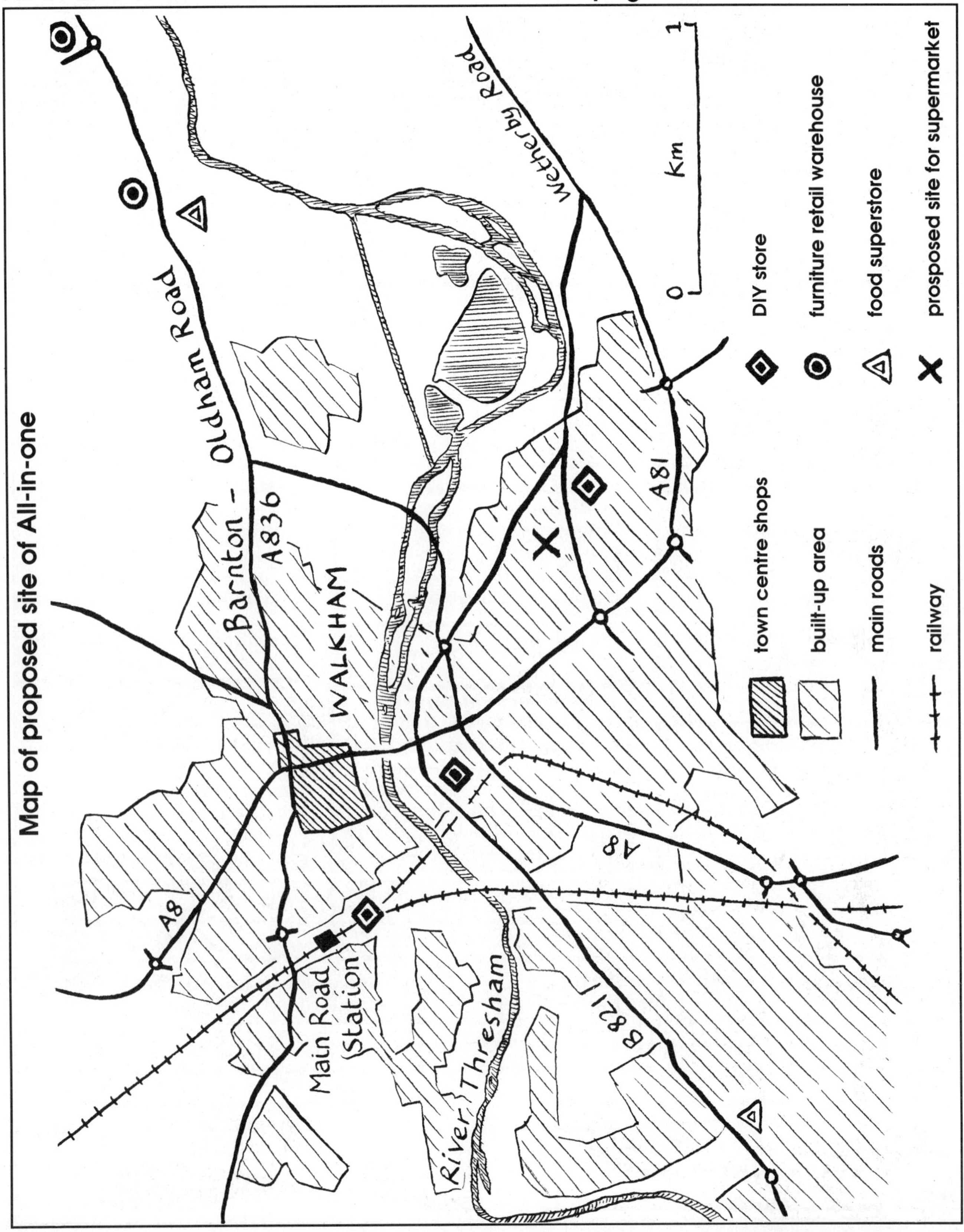
Map of proposed site of All-in-one
Oldham Road
Barnton – Oldham Road
A836
WALKHAM
Wetherby Road
A81
A8
A8
B821
Main Road Station
River Thresham
Km
0
1
town centre shops
built-up area
main roads
railway
DIY store
furniture retail warehouse
food superstore
prosposed site for supermarket

All-in-one at Walkham – to build or not to build? page 17

All-in-One – Roles and issues

I. N. Charge: the inspector
Presides over the meeting ensuring that everyone has a chance to give their views.

S. Tone: the architect
Will the building fit into the environment? The nature of the building materials, height of building, layout and design of car park need to be considered?

S. Hop: All-in-One
Promotes company credibility and its commitment to the local community and the environment?

C. Hart: the local authority planner
Where is the best place to site the supermarket considering the local plans and other factors such as traffic?

N. Gine: the local authority traffic expert
Will the presence of a supermarket cause traffic jams and an increase in occurrence of accidents? When are most people likely to use the supermarket? What is the largest number of cars predicted for any one time?

P. Dinn: the noise expert
Is there a problem for local residents associated with noise, for example, delivery vehicles coming in the middle of the night and using reversing sirens, slamming vehicle doors and so on?

B. Green: the ecologist
Will the store damage the existing wildlife value? Will pollution be caused by building the store? Will habitats be created?

M. O'Tor: the engineer
Are there any drainage problems – is it a wet area? Will it need to be drained first? Is there a need to remove soil and subsoil from the site? Can services such as water and electricity be provided?

C. Profit: the economist
Is there a need for another supermarket in Walkham? Will the shop make a sufficient profit to exist in future years?

T. Past: local historian
What would be the impact of the supermarket on local features, for example, buildings being demolished, the change in the architectural character of the locality, and the indirect effects such as the loss of local shops or changes to the town centre.

Urban Wildlife Trust How will the change in the local environment affect wildlife in the area? Is rough ground being destroyed that provided a habitat for butterflies, birds and wild flowers?

G. Arden: the landscape architect
What views would be spoiled by building the supermarket? What landscape is planned for the supermarket?

C. Ream: local dairy milkman
The milk-round could not compete with the supermarket and so community contact would be lost.

Local residents action group
Adding up all the effects, building the supermarket is not acceptable to local residents.

Local shopkeepers
What will be the impact on business?

What can we recycle? page 22

Investigating habitats, page 26

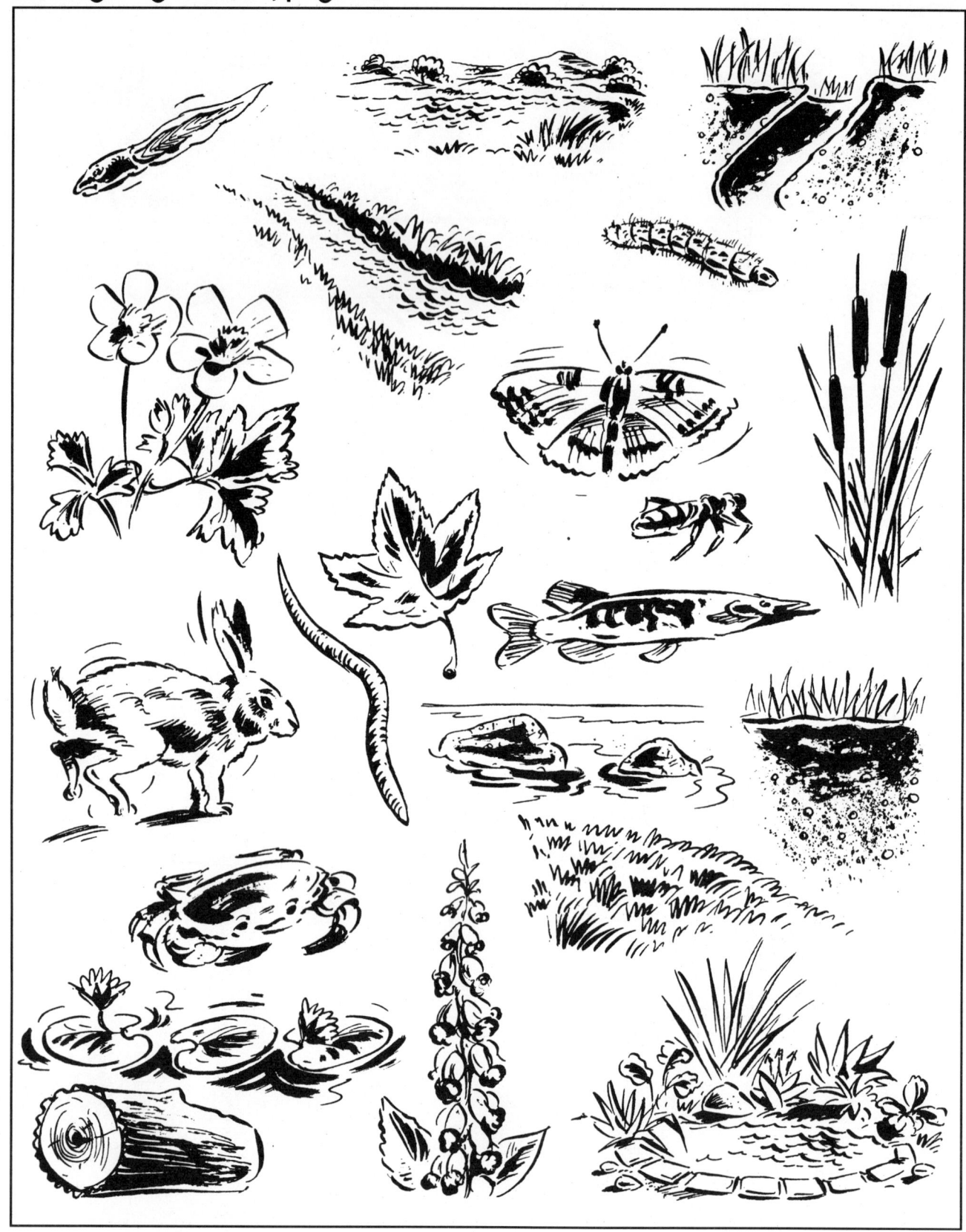

168 Photocopiable pages

Animals in danger, page 26

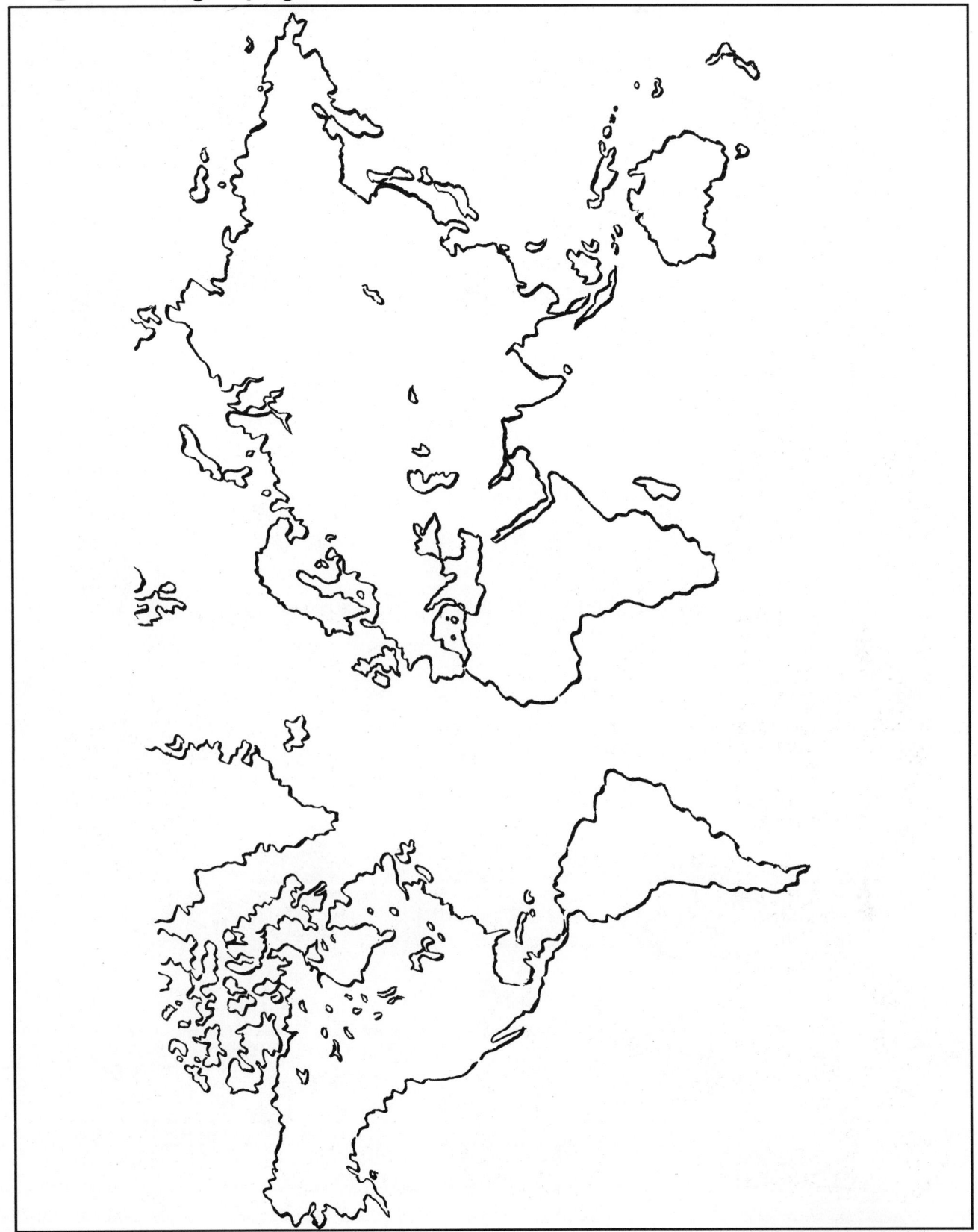

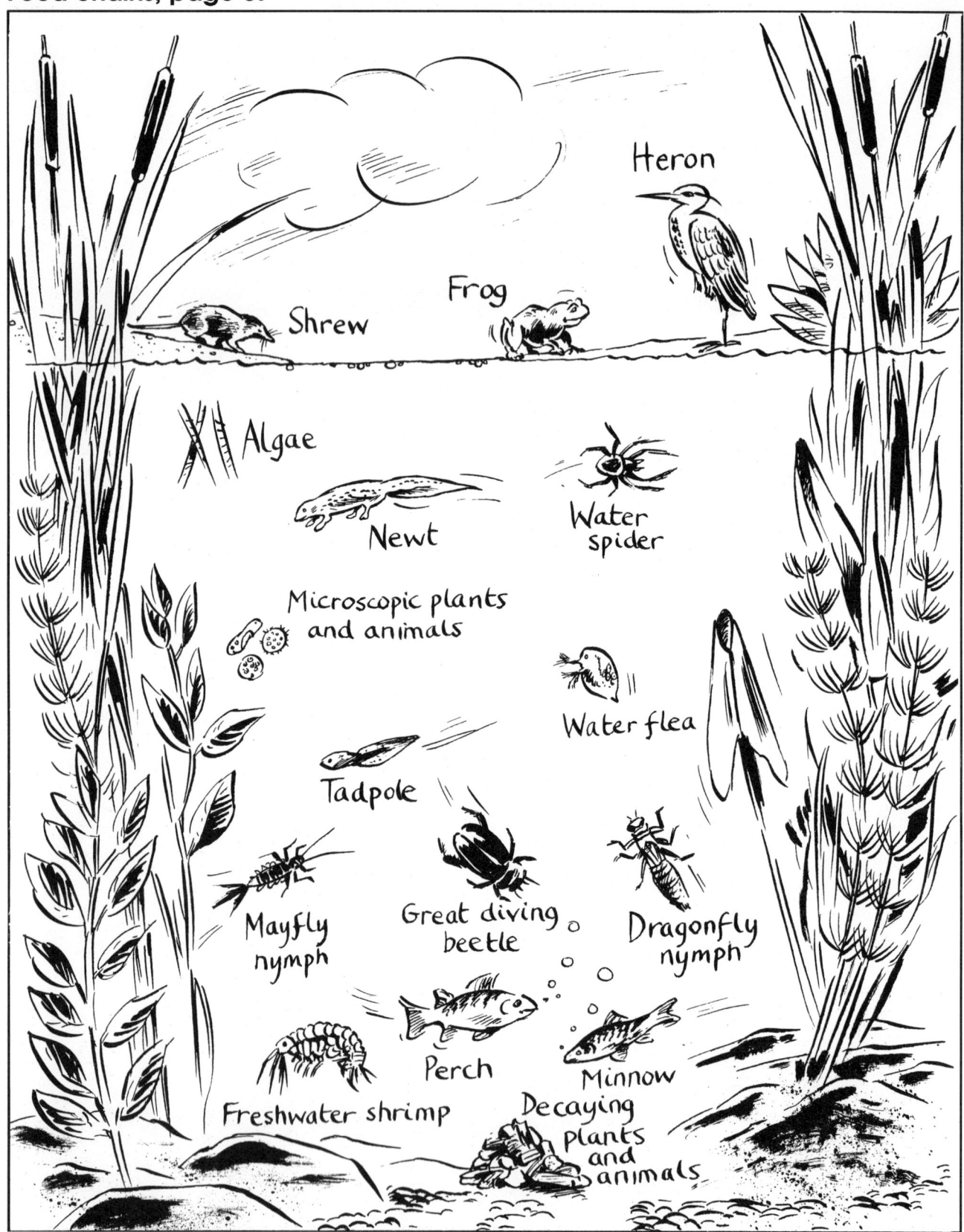

Food chains, page 37

Heron

Shrew Frog

Algae

Newt Water spider

Microscopic plants and animals

Water flea

Tadpole

Mayfly nymph Great diving beetle Dragonfly nymph

Freshwater shrimp Perch Minnow

Decaying plants and animals

Food chains, page 37

Pond food chains and food webs

Look carefully at the food chains below which show the feeding habits and relationships of animals which live in fresh water:

SUN → Algae → Tadpole → Dragonfly nymph → Perch → Heron

SUN → Microscopic plants → Microscopic animals → Water flea → Newt → Great diving beetle → Water shrew

SUN → Microscopic plants → Microscopic animals → Mayfly nymph → Dragonfly nymph

SUN → Microscopic plants → Microscopic animals → Mayfly nymph → Water spider → Frog → Heron

SUN → Decaying leaves → Freshwater shrimp → Water spider → Newt

SUN → Water plants → Tadpole → Great diving beetle → Heron

SUN → Water plants → Minnow → Water beetle

Now build up a food web using the plants and animals in these food chains by cutting out the pictures of them which appear on photocopiable page 171. Take a piece of paper and place the plants at the bottom of the page, then the animals which eat the plants, then higher up the animals which eat these animals and finishing up with the larger animals at the top.

Remember, you only have one picture of each animal. When your teacher has checked your food web stick down the pictures. Leave space to draw arrows between the animals to show what eats what. Finally fill in the arrows and draw a pond outline around your web.

Where can we buy it? page 59

Item name	Picture of item	Supermarket	Baker	Newsagent	Butcher	Greengrocer	Wine merchant
Sausages							
Apples							
Crisps							
Flour							
Loaf of bread							
Potatoes							
Shampoo							
Sugar							
Sweets							
Newspaper							
Bottle of wine							
Toothpaste							
Washing powder							
Biscuits							
Comic							
Butter							
Pork chop							

Adding it in, page 61

COLOURS are in the 100 series

E101	riboflavin (the same as vitamin B_2)
E102	tartrazine
E110	sunset yellow FCF
E140	chlorophyll (occurs naturally in green plants)
E150	caramel
E160(a)	various carotenes (occur naturally in plants)
E160(d)	lycopene (occurs naturally in tomatoes)

PRESERVATIVES are in the 200 series

E200	sorbic acid
E210	benzoic acid
E211–E219	derivatives of benzoic acid
E220	sulphur dioxide
E221–E227	sodium sulphite and derivatives
E249–E250	nitrites
E251–E252	nitrates

ANTIOXIDANTS are in the 300 series

E300	L-ascorbic acid (the same as vitamin C)
E301–E304	derivatives of ascorbic acid
E306	naturally-occurring tocopherols (similar to vitamin E)
E307–309	synthetic tocopherols (similar to vitamin E)
E320	BHA – butylated hydroxyanisole
E321	BHT – butylated hydroxytoluene
E322	lecithin (NB also acts as an emulsifier)

EMULSIFIERS AND STABILISERS are in the 400 series

E400–E404	alginic acid and derivatives (found in seaweeds)
E407	carrageenan (found in seaweeds)
E410	locust bean gum (extracted from carob seeds)
E440(a)	pectin (found in apples and other fruits and vegetables)
E460	cellulose (found in fruits and vegetables)
E461–E466	derivatives of cellulose

FLAVOURINGS do not yet have any serial numbers

Other groups of additives include acids, anti-caking agents, anti-foaming agents, flavour modifiers, glazing agents, packaging gases and solvents. Some are in the 200s, some in the 300s, 400s, 500, 600s or 900s. Perhaps the best known is the flavour enhancer MSG (monosodium glutamate) 621.

Taken from *Living Today: Facts about Food Additives* (leaflet produced by J. Sainsbury)

Lots of energy, page 75

174 *Photocopiable pages*

What was the farm like long ago? page 86

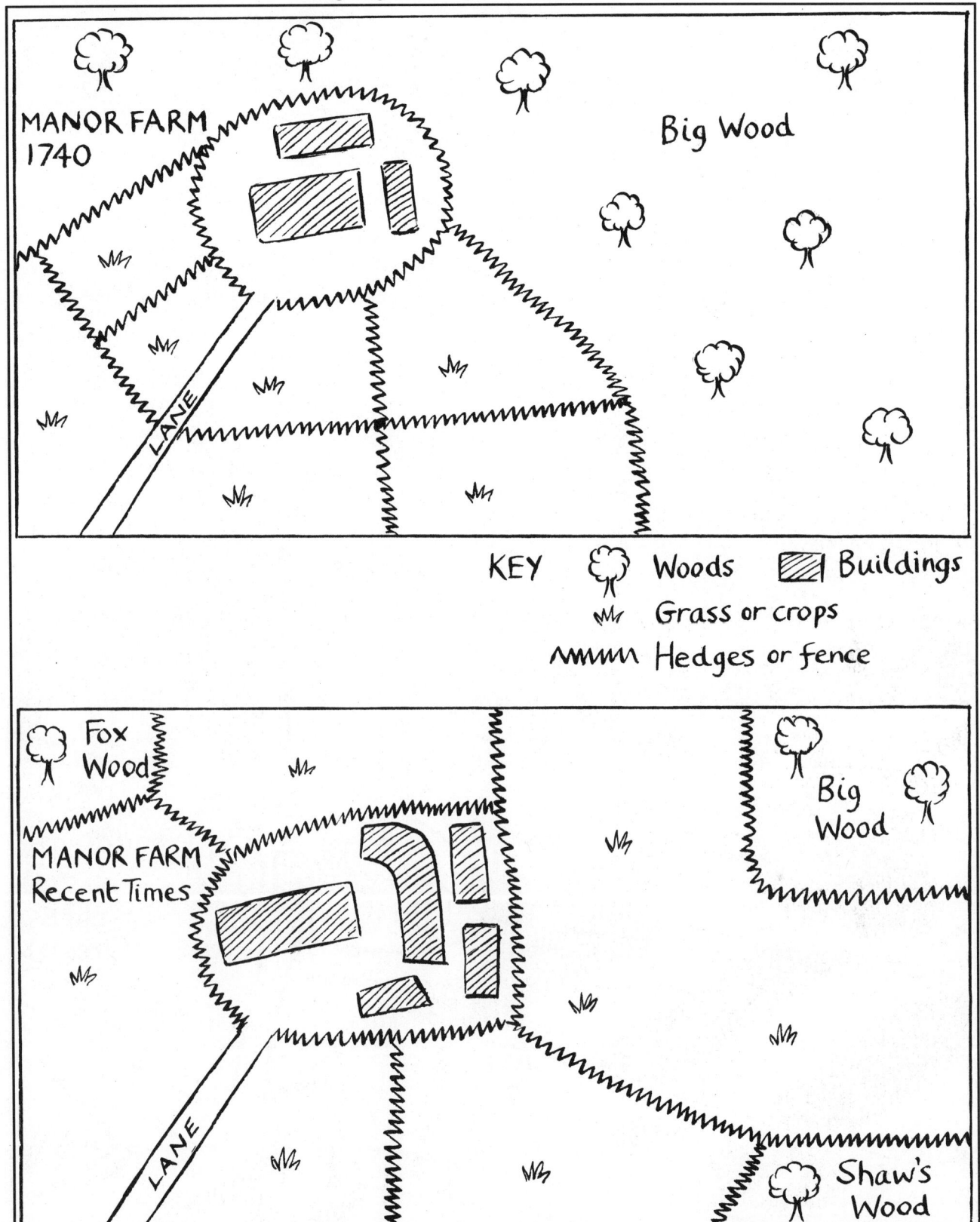

MANOR FARM 1740

Big Wood

LANE

KEY
- Woods
- Buildings
- Grass or crops
- Hedges or fence

Fox Wood

MANOR FARM Recent Times

Big Wood

LANE

Shaw's Wood

Photocopiable pages 175

Production or wildlife; is it a choice? page 92

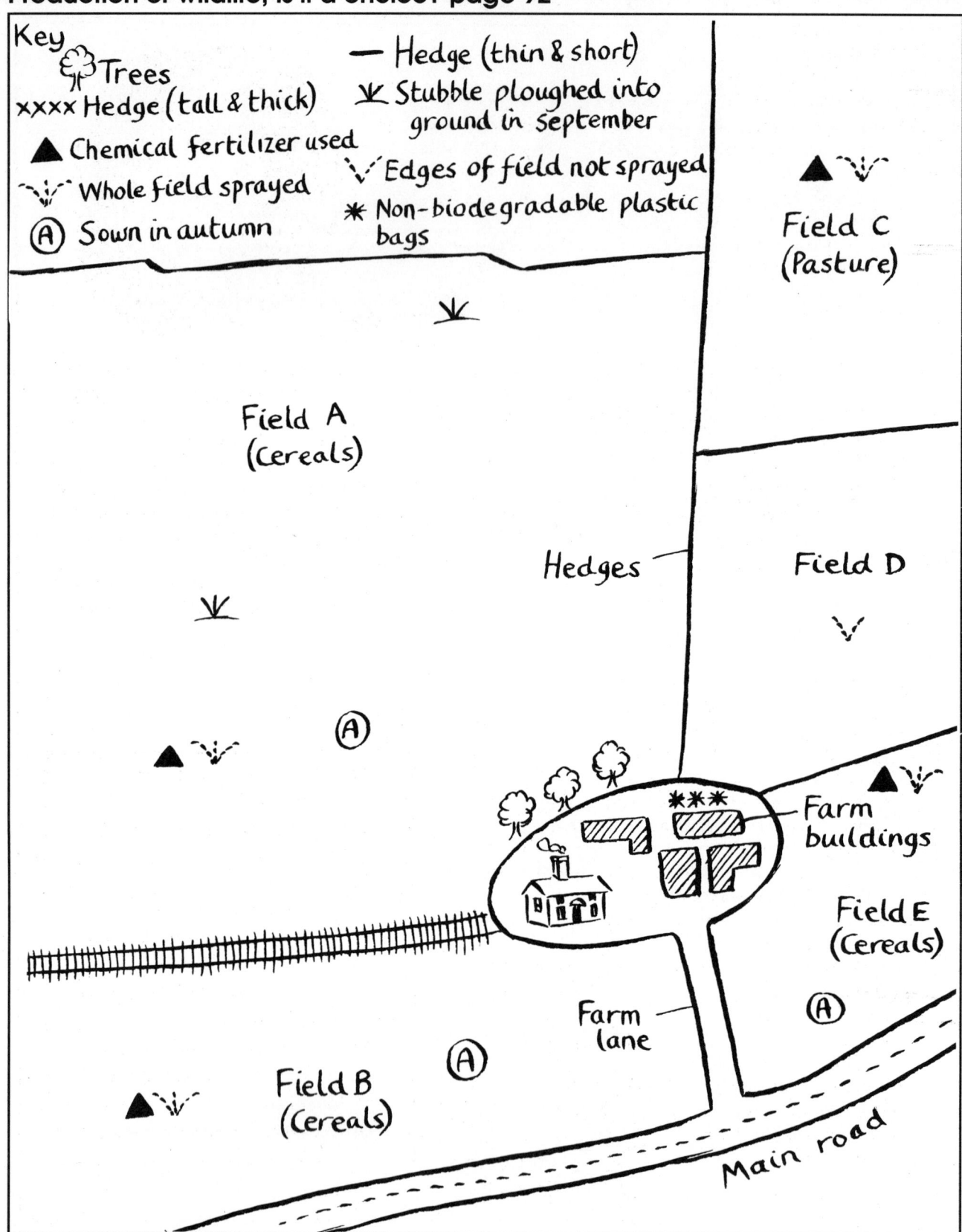

Key
- 🌳 Trees
- xxxx Hedge (tall & thick)
- ▲ Chemical fertilizer used
- ⋎ Whole field sprayed
- Ⓐ Sown in autumn
- — Hedge (thin & short)
- ⋎ Stubble ploughed into ground in September
- ⋎ Edges of field not sprayed
- ✱ Non-biodegradable plastic bags

Field A (Cereals)

Field B (Cereals)

Field C (Pasture)

Field D

Field E (Cereals)

Farm buildings

Farm lane

Hedges

Main road

176 *Photocopiable pages*

Production or wildlife; is it a choice? page 92

Barn owl

Barn owls used to be common on farms because they caught rats and mice in barns that stored grain, nested in hollow trees in the hedgerows and hunted voles and mice in the grassy fields.

However, in modern times access to barns is more difficult, more and more hedges have been cut down and there are fewer old meadows and patches of rough ground on farms.

If the number of barn owls is to increase, there will need to be an increase in rough grasslands on farms and elsewhere.

Grey partridge

Grey partridges used to be common on farms because their lifestyle is suited to living around the edges of fields. They nest at the base of hedges and eat weeds and seeds. Their young eat insects which feed on the weeds.

In recent years farmers have removed hedges and left less rough areas on the edges of their fields. They have also used insecticides and weed killers to improve the yields of their crops. These changes have reduced the homes for partridges and killed their food source.

If the number of grey partridges is to increase, there will need to be an increase in weedy field edges on farms and elsewhere.

Cirl bunting

Cirl buntings used to be common on farms which had thick hedges and trees surrounding fields. Today, they are only found in the west of England.

They feed on weed seeds found around fields and cereal grains found in the stubble after harvesting.

The environment is now not so suited to their life style. Hedges have been removed, the rough edges to fields have few weeds as they have been reduced in size and are often sprayed with weed killers. In addition, the stubble is often removed by ploughing soon after harvesting. These changes in farming lead to less food and shelter.

If the number of cirl buntings is to increase, there will need to be a return to more traditional farming methods. Hedges should be allowed to grow, rough edges to fields would need to increase and stubble would need to remain in the fields until early spring.

Management improvements

1. Planting a hedge.
2. Allow hedges to grow higher/thicker.
3. Sow cereals in spring not autumn.
4. Build a pond on the farm.
5. Plough stubble into the ground in early spring not the autumn.
6. Allow the edges of a field to grow into rough grass.
7. Stop using chemical fertilisers.
8. Stop spraying the edges of the fields
9. Plant more trees.
10. Use biodegradeable plastic bags.

How environmentally is the farm? page 93

What the farmer has done to the environment	Points given	Points taken away
0 Farmed the land	10	
1a. Planted a hedge recently	1	
1b. Removed a hedge recently		1
2a. Allows hedges to grow tall and thick	1	
2b. Allows hedges to be cut regularly		1
3a. Sows cereals in spring not autumn	1	
3b. Sows cereals in autumn not spring		1
4a. Built a pond on the farm recently	1	
4b. Filled in a pond on the farm recently		1
5a. Ploughs stubble into the ground in early spring not autumn	1	
5b. Ploughs stubble into the ground in autumn not early spring		1
6a. Allows the edges of a field to grow into rough grass	1	
6b. Has removed rough grass from the edge of the field		1
7a. Stopped spraying the edges of the fields	1	
7b. Uses chemical fertilisers		1
8a. Stopped spraying the edges of the fields	1	
8b. Sprays the edges of the fields		1
9a. Has planted trees recently	1	
9b. Has cut down trees recently to plant crops		1
10a. Uses biodegradeable plastic bags	1	
10b. Does not use biodegradeable plastic bags		1
Total points given = **Total points taken away =**		

Total Environmentally Friendly score is found by subtracting the total points taken away from the total points given: _____ minus _____ = _____

Which tree? page 109

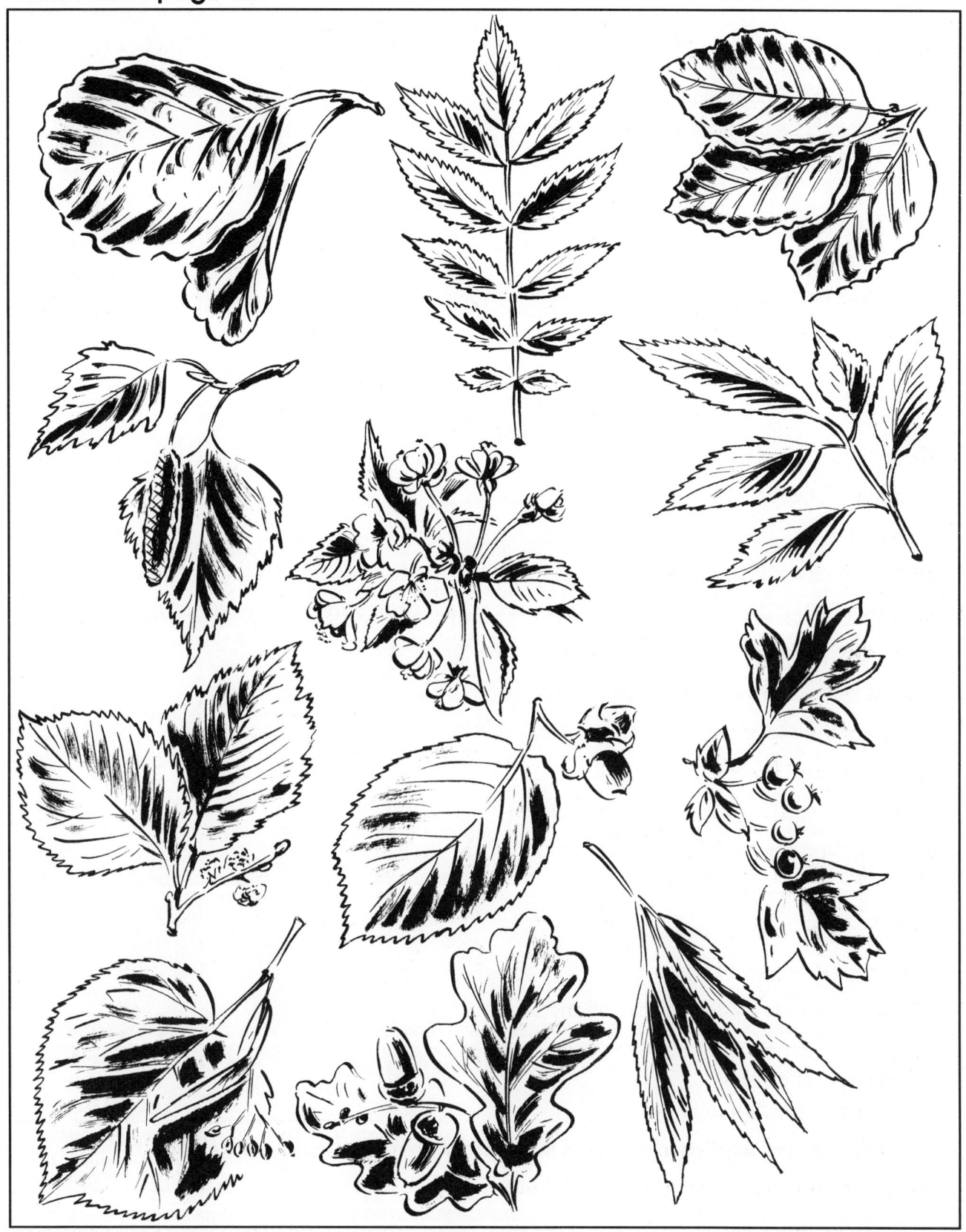

Photocopiable pages 179

Key to winter twigs page, 110

ALDER
Twig – Brown
Buds – purple on short stalks

ASH
Twig – Grey
Buds – Black

BEECH
Twig – Brown
Buds – Brown, 2cm long and cigar-shaped

BIRCH
Twig – Brown and bendy
Buds – purple/green

ELM
Twig – Brown, zig-zags between buds
Buds – Brown and may have white hairs

HAZEL
Twig – Brown
Buds – Pale brown or greenish

OAK
Twig – Brown
Buds – Pale brown in groups at end of twig

HORSE-CHESTNUT
Twig – Thick and brown with distinct scars
Buds – Large sticky end bud

LIME
Twig – Brown/red, zig-zags between buds
Buds – Red/green

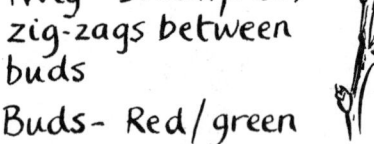

OAK
Twig – Brown
Buds – Pale brown in groups at end of twig

SYCAMORE
Twig – Green/brown
Buds – Green

WILLOW
Twig – Brown, orange or green, bendy
Buds – small and close to twig

ELDER
Twig – Brown, white where cut

CHERRY
Twig – Reddish brown
Buds – Reddish in clusters at end of twig

Tracks and signs, page 113

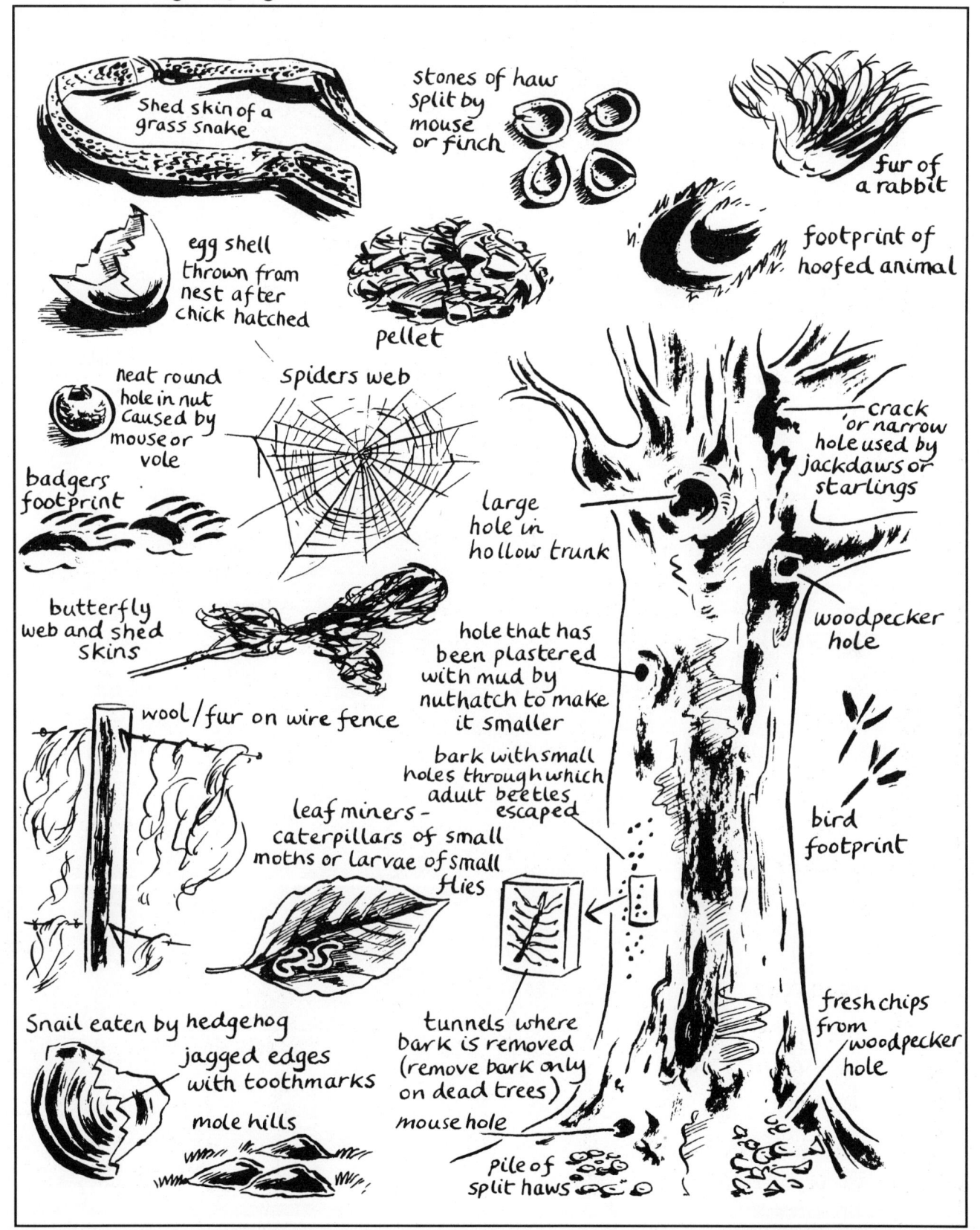

- Shed skin of a grass snake
- stones of haw split by mouse or finch
- fur of a rabbit
- egg shell thrown from nest after chick hatched
- pellet
- footprint of hoofed animal
- neat round hole in nut caused by mouse or vole
- spiders web
- crack or narrow hole used by jackdaws or starlings
- badgers footprint
- large hole in hollow trunk
- woodpecker hole
- butterfly web and shed skins
- hole that has been plastered with mud by nuthatch to make it smaller
- wool/fur on wire fence
- bark with small holes through which adult beetles escaped
- bird footprint
- leaf miners – caterpillars of small moths or larvae of small flies
- Snail eaten by hedgehog – jagged edges with toothmarks
- tunnels where bark is removed (remove bark only on dead trees)
- mouse hole
- pile of split haws
- fresh chips from woodpecker hole
- mole hills

Photocopiable pages 181

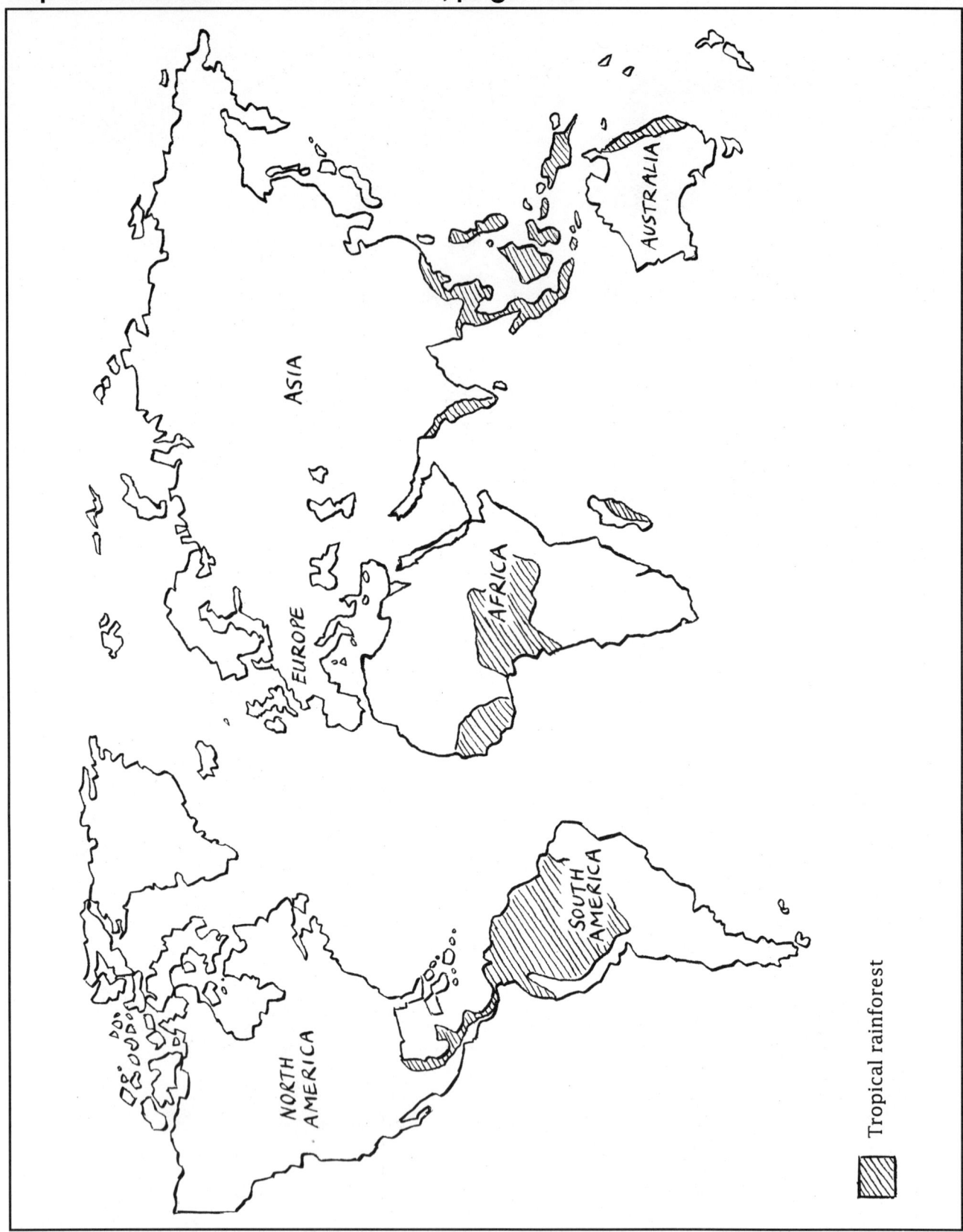

Tropical rainforest and deforestation, page 117

Tropical rainforest

182 Photocopiable pages

The sustainable forest game, page 120

Number of years →

Photocopiable pages **183**

The sustainable forest game, page 120

Teachers' note: In order to have enough discs and tokens to play, please photocopy this page twice.

5 years	10 years	15 years	20 years	25 years
30 years	35 years	40 years	45 years	50 years

£1,000	£1,000	£1,000	£1,000	£1,000
£1,000	£1,000	£1,000	£1,000	£1,000

£100	£100	£100	£100	£100	£100	£100	£100	£100	£100

5 YEARS	10 YEARS	15 YEARS	20 YEARS	25 YEARS
30 YEARS	35 YEARS	40 YEARS	45 YEARS	50 YEARS
55 YEARS	60 YEARS	65 YEARS	70 YEARS	75 YEARS

The sustainable forest game, page 120

The game:
1. Collect photocopiable page 183. This is a game board showing a forest with hexagonal areas of mature trees ready to be cut down, to provide wood for matches for a small community.
2. It takes FIFTY years from the time a tree is planted to the time it is mature and ready to be chopped down to supply wood for matches.
3. One or two hexagonal areas of forest can be cut down every FIVE years.
4. One hexagonal area of forest takes FIVE years to plant with young trees.
5. Therefore, every five years, one or two hexagonal areas may be cut down and only one area may be replanted with young trees.

How to play:
1. To begin the game, place the '5 years' token in the 'number of years' box at the bottom of the board and decide what you are going to do to the forest in this first period. This is your first five-year management plan.
2. Place axe symbols over the one or two hexagonal areas of forest on the board that you have chosen to cut down. Collect £1000 for each hexagonal area you have cut down.
3. You may now replant one hexagonal area by placing a '5 years growth' disc on top of the axe symbol. It costs £100 to plant each area.
4. Next place the '10 years token in the 'number of years' box at the bottom of the board and decide what you are going to do to the forest now. This is your management plan for the following five years.
5. Choose one or two more hexagonal areas to cut down and place axe symbols over these hexagonal areas on the board. Replant one area as above by placing a '5 years growth' disc on top of the axe symbol.
   Ten years have now passed so the trees in the first replanted hexagonal areas are now ten years old. Therefore you must replace the 'five years growth' disc with a '10 years growth' disc on this hexagonal area.
6. Continue the game for 75 YEARS or more, on each turn remembering to:
   - Show the time passing by adding the following 5 year interval token to the pile on the 'number of years' box at the bottom of the board;
   - Collect £1,000 each time you cut down an hexagonal area of trees, £2,000 if you cut down two areas;
   - Pay £100 to plant each hexagonal area with trees;
   - Add an extra 5 years growth to the trees you have planted to indicate how they are maturing.

Switch off, turn off, close, page 127

Open doors	where found	
Dripping taps	where found	
Open windows	where found	
Lights left on	where found	

Where does litter come from? page 128

Type of litter	Number found – Tick each item (✓)
Chocolate bar wrappers	
Crisp packets	
Tissues	
Drinks boxes and cans	
Polythene or paper bags	
Other paper items	

I spy with my little eye, page 131

Blackbird (Female) (Male)
Robin
Starling
Carrion crow
Rook
Wren
Jackdaw
Pheasant
Greenfinch (Male)
Kestrel
(Male) House sparrow (female)
Great tit
Blue tit
Chaffinch (Male)
Skylark
Bullfinch (Male)
Magpie
Wood pigeon
Dunnock
Pied wagtail
Song thrush
Mistle thrush
Swallow
House martin

188 Photocopiable pages

Energy saver – 1, page 132

Energy saver – 2, page 134

Area/part of house	Description/type of energy saver present	If not present, describe how energy may be saved
Loft space		
Windows		
Walls		
Floors		
Radiators (thermostats fitted)		
Light (size of bulb)		
Bath/shower		
Draft excluders around doors and windows		
Dripping taps		
Windows left open		

The temperature of the house thermstat is _____°C

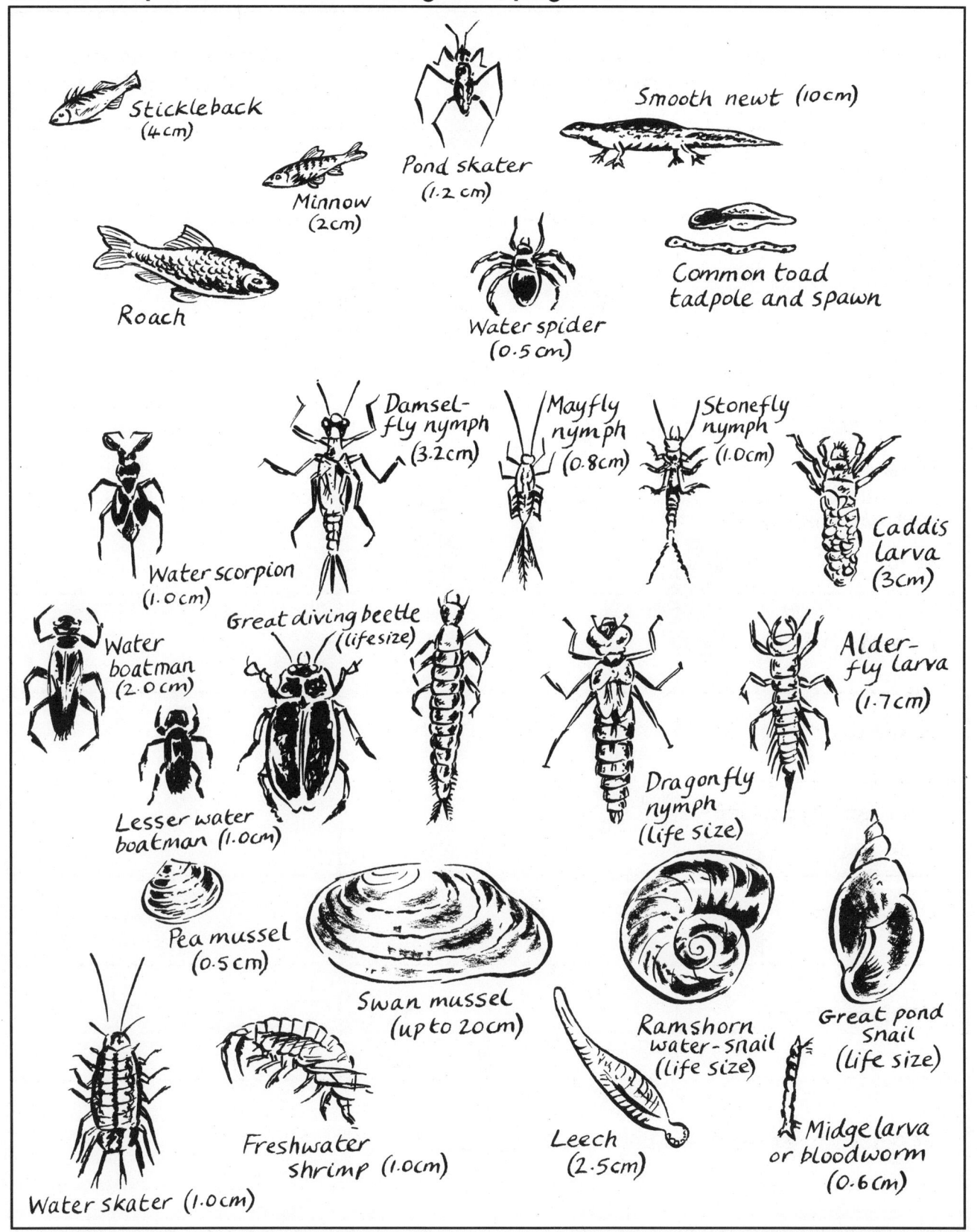

The school pond – A whole investigation, page 134

Stickleback (4cm)

Minnow (2cm)

Pond skater (1.2 cm)

Smooth newt (10cm)

Roach

Water spider (0.5 cm)

Common toad tadpole and spawn

Water scorpion (1.0cm)

Damselfly nymph (3.2cm)

Mayfly nymph (0.8cm)

Stonefly nymph (1.0cm)

Caddis larva (3cm)

Water boatman (2.0cm)

Great diving beetle (life size)

Lesser water boatman (1.0cm)

Dragonfly nymph (life size)

Alderfly larva (1.7cm)

Pea mussel (0.5cm)

Swan mussel (up to 20cm)

Ramshorn water-snail (life size)

Great pond snail (life size)

Water skater (1.0cm)

Freshwater shrimp (1.0cm)

Leech (2.5cm)

Midge larva or bloodworm (0.6cm)

Photocopiable pages 191

National parks – A whole investigation, page 144

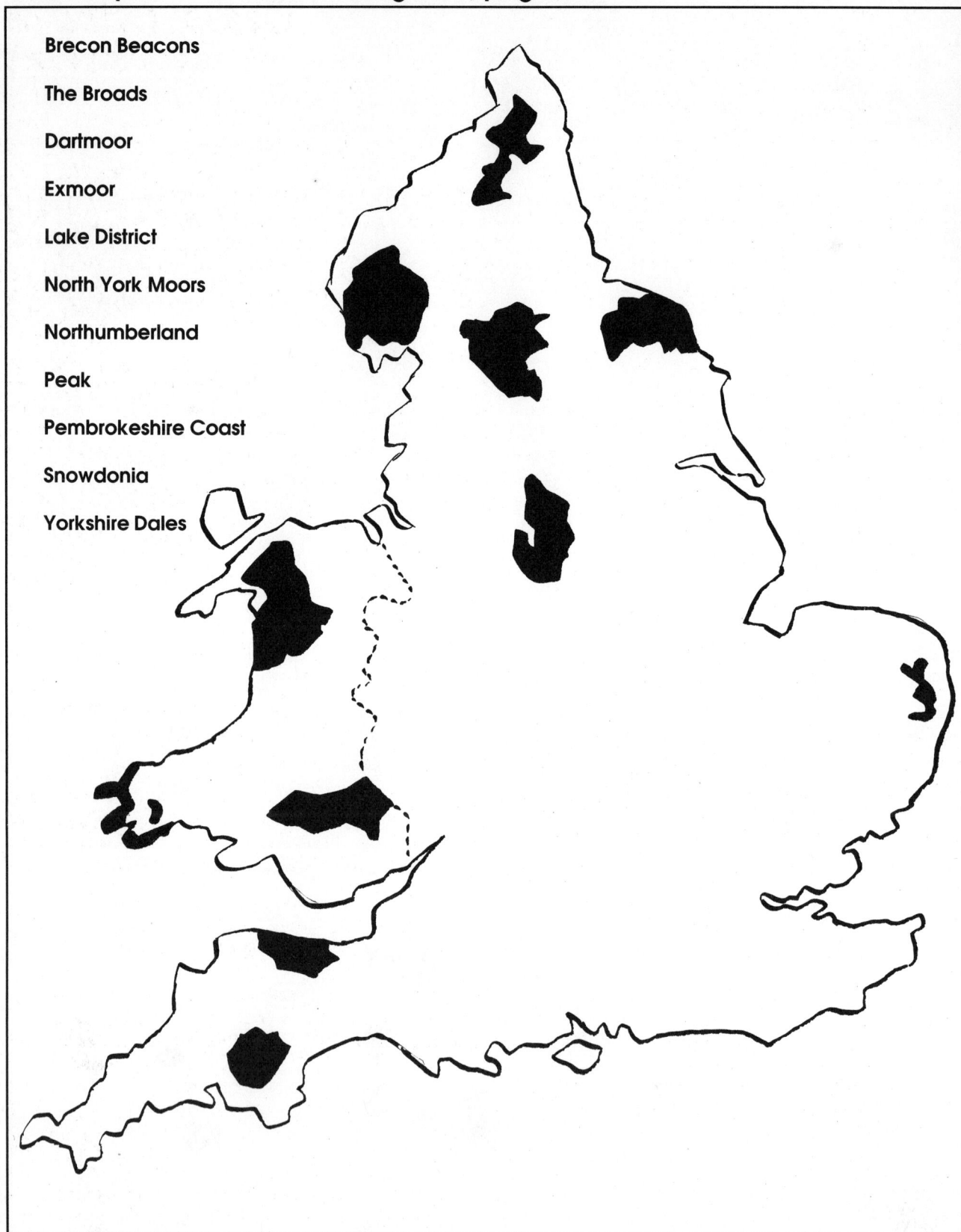

- Brecon Beacons
- The Broads
- Dartmoor
- Exmoor
- Lake District
- North York Moors
- Northumberland
- Peak
- Pembrokeshire Coast
- Snowdonia
- Yorkshire Dales